SOCIOLOGICAL THEORY

ICE

DATE DUE			
Mar 1 '77			

SOCIOLOGICAL THEORY
IN RESEARCH PRACTICE

ELIZABETH A. FREIDHEIM

SCHENKMAN PUBLISHING COMPANY

Cambridge, Massachusetts

Schenkman Publishing Company, Inc.
3 Mt. Auburn Place
Cambridge, Massachusetts 02138

30 1. 0 1 8
F 8 8 s
9 9 6 0 0
Jan. 1977

Library of Congress Cataloging in Publication Data

Freidheim, Elizabeth A.
   Sociological theory in research practice.

   1. Sociology — History.   2. Sociological research — History.
I. Title.
HM19.F76   301'.01'8   76-27837
ISBN 0-87073-015-0 paperback.

Printed in the United States of America

Table of Contents

v

Preface

The complex enterprise of science requires constant attention to both theory building and data gathering. Some, however, view this enterprise as an exercise in magic: a procedure for combining the proper liquids to produce a bad smell in the laboratory. Others mistake science for a listing of facts, a summary of information about the structure of crystals or the classification of hominoids. In their efforts to memorize formulae and collect typologies, they can miss the exciting aspects of science, the reasoning that distinguishes alchemy from chemistry, the theory that transforms biology from an exercise in classification to a study of evolutionary development. In other words, they fail to notice that no matter how atheoretical a particular scientist may be, he makes some assumptions that give direction to his work. Without a theory of genetics, for example, there would be no reason to search for Pithecanthropus and no explanation for his remains should they be discovered by chance.

Sociologists are less likely than most to think of science as alchemy. To date we have discovered no magic formula. Sociologists do collect colorful (and boring) facts about campus radicals, homosexuality in prisons, the racial attitudes of blue-collar workers, and unnumbered other social topics. But, like any other scientific "facts," these sociological data are no more valuable than the thought and observation behind them. When we read that 85 per cent of the respondents in a survey believe free education should extend through four years of college, we may wonder if they are a cross-section of the entire population, a group of philanthropists-for-higher-education, or students in Professor Survey's freshman class. When we are told that slum areas inevitably suffer disorganization, we may wonder if "disorganization" means high-crime rates, low employment, or just "slum" life styles. In the first example, improper sampling could transform the representative survey into a forum for some special-interest group. In the second, a poorly con-

vii

ceptualized definition could force the poor reader to travel the circle from slums that are disorganized to disorganization which signals the existence of a slum. Since similar problems can occur at every stage of the research process, we must learn to evaluate the methodology behind substantive findings if we hope to read sociological reports intelligently.

One way to acquire skill in research evaluation is by observing the masters, by reviewing both their successes and their failures. Karl Marx, to name one, made many important statements about social class, working life, historical change, power, and other major sociological variables. Still his predictions about social change — a major emphasis in his work — proved wrong: for England he foresaw a working man's society created through a revolution of the proletariat; but instead England actually experienced social reform legislated by the middle class. Why were his predictions off target? If his research design was faulty, then surely we should analyze it for clues about how we could do better. Or how we could do as well?

We cannot, of course, simply consider one small piece of Marx's work. Often enough a thinker like Marx evolves a major thesis and documents the evidence for it in a series of related projects. *Manifesto of the Communist Party* suggests the broad outlines of his theory of historical change, change ultimately powered by a rising economic group that revolts against its old exploiters. *Capital* documents the pressures for change within the society of his day, misery in the mine and factory, to show that, once again, an exploited class was being pushed to revolt. Together all of his works argue that objective-economic conditions directly or indirectly influence the rest of social life. To study these conditions and their effects, Marx observed concrete historical situations and overt reactions to them. He did not probe the moral ideals we share with our families; he did not depict how religion reinforces these ideals both for the individual and for the society sharing a common form of worship. Problems such as these and the methods necessary to explore them lay outside of his research concerns. In other words, to understand the research of Marx, or any other thinker who builds on a consistent theme, we must consider his major interests and determine how these interests influenced both his methodology and his choice of specific substantive topics.

To promote such understanding, this book introduces the theoretical orientations and empirical work of seventeen eminent sociologists by reviewing how these men defined sociology and its subject matter, how they defined science and its procedures, and finally, how they practiced these ideas in empirical research. In terms of this framework, Marx defined social science as the study of man's objective behavior occurring within specific historical-economic situations. With this conceptualization Marx naturally posited economic conditions as *the* causal variables of social life. Then he researched this variable by studying the economic correlates of historical revolutionary change, and documenting the economic conditions of present "pre-revolutionary" society. Finally, given the conditions of his time, he had to predict that economic miseries would cause a massive societal upheaval — especially since his theory did not weigh the causal impact of nationalism and other non-economic loyalties that might prove as important as class in affecting the course of social change. In other words, a theorist's basic assumptions about the nature of sociology and society (including the tradition he either adopted or fought) determine what situations he chooses to observe, what hypotheses he formulates, what data-gathering strategies the utilizes, and the types of conclusions he presents. Although some theorists are not as consistent as Marx in following their own prescriptions, this framework does assess the very real relationship between a sociologist's theoretical orientation to social science and the ways he actually practices his craft.

However, the book's format has deficiencies that may disappoint readers who are looking for Talcott Parsons-in-a-capsule or an analysis of Charles Horton Cooley's primary group. In the process of discussing the empirical work of these sociologists, I refer to many important ideas developed by each man, but I do not analyze their ideas unless they are part of my discussion of the relationship between theory and research. Further, I do not classify either the men or their ideas according to "schools" of sociological thought. Although it can be satisfying to know where a theorist belongs on some concept field, to distinguish the "social actionists" from the "formalists," this knowledge often provides more security than information. Unless we are considering a one-man school, we must recognize these labels as handy guides to intellectual orientations, not descriptions of any man's thought. So, I have chosen to concentrate on the individual thought systems. Once we understand these, it is much easier to comprehend the real meaning of a school.

Even though each sociologist developed a distinctive orientation, all shared the scientific concerns of their day. First, they had to consider the practical impact of their studies. Whether they hoped to provide the ideology for revolution or information about surviving with the *status quo,* all early sociologists addressed the social problems of the nineteenth century. Nineteenth-century theorists also defended sociology as a legitimate discipline against contemporaries who, for various reasons, denied the very possibility of a "human" science. Some claimed sociology, like biology and physics, was a study of observable phenomena; others sought ways to explore subjective "human" material scientifically. No matter which side they argued, sociologists designed a methodology to meet the needs of social science as they defined it. Consequently, in the chapter on "Sociology: Research for Reform," I have reviewed these nineteenth-century concerns as they affected sociology: first, the combination of social disorder and scientific progress that encouraged men to hope for social order engineered through science; then, the debates over whether a "human" study like sociology could be a science, the discussions about methodological choices that occur in both "human" and "non-human" science, and the directions for "human" science suggested by the disciplines already in the field when sociology began.

The problems defined in the nineteenth century continue to this day. Of course modern sociologists do not argue the possibility of a social science, but they still debate whether social science is primarily objective or primarily subjective. Instead of looking to physics and biology for guidance, twentieth-century sociologists have developed theories and research strategies from the tradition of their own discipline: the extremely objective tradition has produced sophisticated technicians who search for ever more elegant ways to measure and describe the observable world; the subjective tradition has encouraged sociologists to explore the symbolic communication between members of a social group and to probe the view of social life that a single man constructs in his own head. Because these trends have become important features of sociology in the 1970s, I will review them in the concluding chapter on "Some Contemporary

Viewpoints." In that chapter I will also reconsider the social impact of sociology because, once again, sociologists are questioning the practical purpose of their science.

The chapters between describe how seventeen outstanding sociologists met the problems of studying society scientifically. No one has developed the great master plan, but each has suggested solutions — occasionally contradictory ones — to important methodological problems. Some sociologists like August Comte, Herbert Spencer, and Albion Woodbury Small defined basic issues that sociology must address; although none of these men were exemplary researchers, they pioneered areas that others have worked more carefully. Karl Marx and William Graham Sumner both devoted more time to researching a topic of interest than to articulating a methodology; however, Marx's analysis of power and Sumner's ideas about norms remain among the key contributions that sociological research has made to general knowledge. George Homans, Gabriel Tarde, and Vilfredo Pareto have responded to the subjective nature of social life by explaining it in terms of individual motives; using different methods, all three have reduced the social whole to the sum of its component human parts. Three other theorists, Charles Horton Cooley, Talcott Parsons, and Max Weber, explored subjective meanings as they occur socially; these men concentrated on interpreting meanings that arise only because man is a member of a group. Many sociologists have centered attention on the correlates of external behavior: Emile Durkheim and Robert King Merton traced the wide-ranging repercussions of various social patterns; Georg Simmel and Robert Park detailed how external conditions can limit the possible sequences of social activity in a situation. Finally, Hubert Blalock and George Lundberg have explicitly examined the assumptions behind various research methodologies and techniques.

Before proceeding to these theorists, I must thank those who have suggested plausible solutions for the problems of writing this book. First, the unnamed members of one graduate class and five undergraduate classes in sociological theory taught at Loyola University of Chicago between 1971 and 1974. These students struggled through several drafts of the manuscript telling me when my exposition was unclear and my prose boring. Two students, Anne O'Gorman and Anne Keffer, reviewed the penultimate draft to discover all the pages where an intelligent reader who did not already know the field would have trouble understanding my point. Jai Ryu of Loyola University and John V. Hickey of Leeds University (Yorkshire) both used the manuscript to teach a course and made useful comments about content and clarity. Finally, Thomas M. Gannon, Robert J. McNamara, and S. Kirson Weinberg (all of Loyola) criticized various chapters and Hubert M. Blalock suggested improvements for Chapter 18. If I have managed to untangle the confusing exposition originally written into this manuscript, I owe a debt to all of them.

But my earliest debt is to William M. Bates (of Loyola). Originally a collaborator, he suggested the basic theme, the format for the main chapters and the list of theorists to be included. Other commitments drew him away from this project but he remained a helpful critic long after he ceased to be a collaborator.

SOCIOLOGICAL THEORY IN RESEACH PRACTICE

Sociology: Research for Reform

What is sociology? The scientific study of men in society . . . of human interaction . . . of social institutions . . . of men's subjective orientations toward each other. Social theorists answering that question have provided dozens of different versions with two areas of agreement: all claim that sociology is "scientific" and all agree that it studies the behavior — particularly the symbolic or "meaningful" behavior — of men in groups. But how? In the following chapters we will review the answers provided by seventeen important sociologists, their scientific precepts and their research practices, the ways they defined social science and the ways they performed empirical work in the field. Our concern will focus on the basic orientation of these men, the underlying logic of their analysis, not the sophisticated scales they constructed to measure the religious attitudes of Hottentots. Thus, we will consider scientific methodology in the broad sense — for example, the way Max Weber defined "subjective orientations," why he considered them important, and his strategies for understanding the subjective states of men who were long dead, safe from the probing of a researcher with questionnaires and interview schedules.

We must realize, however, that the sociological enterprise did not appear full-blown on the writing desk of our Founding Father, Auguste Comte. Rather it was the response to key nineteenth-century concerns, a human effort to understand and control social phenomena by applying the powers of physical science which had increased enormously during the previous two centuries. To understand why there is a sociology, we must consider both the intellectual-scientific revolution that stirred seventeenth-century thinkers and the social upheavals that appalled nineteenth-century reformers. To comprehend the conceptual problems that challenged early sociologists, we must discuss the nature of science, the scientific presuppositions

1

common during the nineteenth-century, and the effects these have had on sociology.

HISTORICAL BACKGROUND

In their more retrospective moments, sociologists may trace their roots back to ancient Greek thought. Although it can give us a sense of permanence to know that Aristotle said it first, we must admit that the science of sociology could not have developed in ancient Athens, medieval Arabia, or many other settings that nonetheless produced thoughtful men concerned about society. The emergence of sociology as a distinctive discipline needed a special combination of circumstances. First, it required a particular orientation toward science, namely, a culture that highly valued scientific thought, believed in progress, and hoped science could somehow effect that progress in social areas. Just as critical, it required a *raison d'etre,* a motive for men to produce scientific social analysis, a constellation of social problems significant enough to command attention.

The first necessary condition, a cultural milieu that encouraged men to think scientifically about social life, had its roots in the physics and astronomy of the seventeenth century. That had been an era of spectacular advance in physical science, culminating in Isaac Newton's publication of the *Principia* in 1687. Building on the science of his day, Newton demonstrated how motion in the physical world could be described and predicted in a few elegant mathematical propositions. It was a mind-expanding achievement — to formulate laws summarizing the revolutions of planets around the sun and the flight of cannon balls on the battlefield. More than that, Newton offered not just a simple well-reasoned description of the world, but a description could be verified by man's observations. Indeed, he had begun with observation and then sought general trends, summarized these trends in "laws," and used his laws to predict the outcome of future observations.

It is not Newton's scientific achievement (important though that was) which interests us, however, but its broader intellectual consequences — namely, belief in progress and belief that man could use observation and reason to effect progress in social areas. Medieval thinkers had not hoped for widespread social progress and reform. Looking back to Greek models in art, philosophy, literature, mathematics, and science, they could not think of Western Europe as an advanced society, at least not in secular terms. But by the end of the seventeenth century Europeans could point to scientific achievements — indeed revolutions — in physics, medicine, astronomy, in man's ability to observe and control his world. This was clear evidence of the progress that could be wrought by scientific reasoning. If men could improve their physical conditions through scientific planning, why could they not apply the same reasoning to the problems of industrial society? Eighteenth-century Enlightenment thinkers advanced this faith by applying scientific techniques (or at least their variations of these techniques) to social life. For example, the most influential *philosophé*, Jean-Jacques Rousseau, observed the inequities spawned by social inequality and concluded that society imposed unnatural constraints on man's freedom. Reasoning further, he decided men should ignore artificial constraints of tradition; decide through consensus what they wanted from society; and charge the state with enforcing the provisions of this general will. Thus all men would be free of unnatural social constraints, free to obey their own will embodied in the general will. But what is the general will? And what happens to the freedom of those who do not subscribe to this consensus? In the end, Rousseau's "general will" became a plan for those strong enough to enforce their ideas. Consequently some of the "enlightened despots" of the era translated these doctrines into a secular, eighteenth-century version of the divine right of kings. For these rulers, their way (formerly known as God's way) became the reasonable way. However, the ultimate triumph of "reasonable" thinking occurred in the French Revolution. In their efforts to restore natural human freedom, the revolutionists attacked the authority of the family, religion, the university, and other traditional groups that stood between the individual and the state. Among other things, they liberalized divorce and required civil marriages in addition to (or better in place of) religious ones. The result: the Reign of Terror and, later, the Napoleonic wars.

As the nineteenth century progressed, observers found other evidence of social ills: a wave of revolutions in 1830 and again in 1848, social protest literature like Dickens' *Hard Times* published in 1854, newspaper exposes of factory conditions in England. Many men continued to believe in progress, but they no longer deluded themselves that anyone could engineer this advance as neatly as one could design a new telescope. Seduced by the tranquil appearance of eras when all people cherished the same basic social values (or so it seemed from a life-time's distance), many even wondered if "progress" might mean recapturing earlier social patterns.

Because of these problems, nineteenth-century social thinkers were using science to ask new questions. They no longer searched for "natural man," the basis on which to construct a reasonable society. Instead they asked either "What holds society together?" or conversely, "What drives men apart?" In each instance, they examined groups — class groups, religious groups, family groups — to determine the influence of these traditional structures. Doing this they created sociology.

SUBJECT FOCUS

Although they all agreed that sociology studied groups in society, nineteenth-century theorists disagreed, often bitterly, about the exact subject area of the new science, sometimes quarrelling with all the grace of rival gang members eyeing two blocks of disputed "turf." These debates were not merely verbal squabbles. First, these disputes weighed the differences between natural sciences and cultural (unnatural?) ones. Second, they delineated sociology in its relationships with other social or cultural sciences. In both instances, they reflected the desire of sociologists to create a "real" science, a science that somehow adhered to the ideal standards used by Newton two centuries before.

The cultural-science debate highlighted the peculiar differences between humans and other objects of scientific scrutiny. Some social scientists, entranced by the elegance of Newton's summaries, hoped to develop a similar framework to describe social life. Others, more impressed by the differences between people who communicate with each other and planets that revolve in concert but without sending messages, argued that the study of society requires very different techniques and would produce very different results. Scientists who accepted the first viewpoint stressed *positivism,* objective observation: they said, "Watch events to delineate causal sequences." Society, they argued, could be studied by a detached observer, an outsider who examined human behavior in the village just as he would examine animal behavior in an anthill or the mechanical movement in a clock. Scientists who advocated the other approach stressed *Verstehen,* interpretative understanding: "Watch events to discern their human meanings, to discover the goals or purposes of the people involved." The scientist is not an outsider in society, they maintained; he should use his special insider's power to explain society in terms of human motives, to account for the goals that stir people to action.

Another, deeper issue lies beneath this debate over subject matter. When they doubted the possibility of scientific study of subjective cultural phenomena, scientists were really probing the very nature of science. Is science a set of techniques designed to record and measure only those objects we can reach directly through our senses? Or is it an approach to knowledge based on the interpretation of data? If science is such a set of techniques, then we are confined to studies that record and measure very concrete objects like the composition of water and the frequency of church attendance. If it is an approach to knowledge, we are challenged by the difficulty of applying this approach to intangibles like the nature and meaning of religious beliefs. There is a third resolution to this controversy, however. If science must be objective and if social behavior is incomprehensible without subjective interpretations, then there can be no science of society. Naturally, sociologists fought this view — either by making their research as objective or "scientific" as possible or by reconceptualizing scientific techniques to fit the special data of social science. Comte, for example, did stress *positivism*: observation without preconceptions, strict objectivity. However, he admitted that society included some extra, nonlogical facets and that such intangible items as human thought would prove enormously important. For him, the research problem would be finding an objective index of human thought. Other sociologists, like Max Weber, more fully accepted the challenge of cultural science and developed special research approaches to tease out the unspoken, half-understood meanings inherent in human behavior.

Once theorists accepted sociology as a legitimate science, they faced a second problem, delimiting the boundaries of subject matter. What areas of social life should sociology encompass? Comte answered: "Everything — sociology synthesizes all knowledge of society!" Most sociologists, however, entertained more modest visions. They concentrated on human interaction, wherever it occurred. For example, certain types of behavior occur when some members of a society own more than others. Economists may consider the market flow that produced this monetary distribution. Sociologists may analyze why and when the have-nots will revolt against those who have.

The border area between psychology and sociology raises a special scientific problem. If sociology studies the interaction of people in groups, can we explain this behavior by looking at the motives of individuals? Can we, in other words, explain social life by reducing the group to its component units, the individual members? Some sociologists, like Emile Durkheim, have argued that society is a reality *sui generis,* a reality in itself that can only be interpreted as a whole. For these theorists, explaining interaction in terms of individual motives would be as absurd as explaining human emotionality by tracing neuron distributions and brain contours. Instead of divining individual motives, they account for group activity by examining group properties. Groups behave in certain ways because their members obey group norms, belong to certain classes, believe in cultural values. In its extreme version, this thinking reifies social groups; in moderation, it points to the tremendous influence such groups exert over individual members. In the opposite camp, sociologists Gabriel Tarde and George Homans hold that we cannot account for a group except by detailing the activities of its members. Without people, they tell us, there would be no group; without individual human motives there would be no group activity; without angry men, for example, there would be no lynching. In sum, part of the debate over sociology's legitimacy as a science centers on the problem of choosing a level of analysis, of deciding whether to explain social life in terms of group properties or in terms of individual properties. Put more abstractly, the issue is to decide whether to analyze a social whole or its component parts.

Now that sociology has acquired journals, university chairs, associations, and all the other accouterments of an academic industry, theorists no longer argue about whether a science of society is even possible or whether such a science is simply duplicating the work of political science, economics, and other social studies. However, the scientific problems raised by these nineteenth-century controversies — the concern about the use of science to study intangible human affairs and the choice of levels of analysis — recur to this day.

METHODOLOGY

Simply deciding on a topic to study is not enough. Scientists must impose the order of reason on the chaotic appearance of data. This is the task of methodology — approaching and organizing the data on a given topic in a way that, somehow, makes sense. As scientists our goal is to construct a theory, to formulate a set of interrelated propositions that explain the types of events occurring in social life: an ambitious goal. To do this we need, at the very least, a general orientation suggesting some concepts or abstract ideas about important aspects of social life and some propositions detailing how these various aspects relate to each other.

Naturally the early sociologists looked to physical science for guidelines and examples showing how to engage in this process of theory building. In some ways, these borrowed tools proved helpful: a creative social scientist could translate the physical experiment and the biological analysis into a cross-cultural comparative study for testing theoretical ideas. On the other hand, given the differences between physical and social subject matter, we should not be surprised to find that conceptualizing society as if it were a huge machine or a giant animal encouraged some confusing nonsense among some confused social scientists.

But, for good and ill, the nineteenth-century physical science ideas about the nature of concepts and models about the relationships between variables entered the social-science repertoire and continue to influence sociology to this day. Particularly important are the ideas about how to define or describe the basic facets of social life and how to predict or explain the relationships between these facets. We will review some of the problems associated with both, first the concept and then the explanation.

Concepts   The concept is a mental construct, an abstract idea about the key properties of a type or category of objects, a selection of idealized traits that we consider important. We do not have a concept of the overstuffed maroon chair that stands in a neighbor's living room and squeaks whenever someone sits on it. But we do have a concept of "chair:" a piece of furniture, shaped for sitting, large enough for one person. . . . No one could describe all possible chairs, but most of us recognize one on sight because we have the general notion — the concept — of what a "chair" must be. A simple concept, but nonetheless it contains a series of related ideas about "sitting," "furniture," and so on. Imagine the ideas one must tie together in a complex concept like "society" or "human nature" or "social interaction."

While trying to choose from their overabundance of ideas and marshall them into proper scientific concepts, sociologists have, once again, confronted specific differences between sociology and the physical sciences. First, the social scientist has an "insider's" view of his subject matter. The problem, of course, is whether he may take advantage of his insight or whether science precludes all subjective judgment and rests only on the objective "outsider's" view. Second, the observer may try to record the whole social setting at once or select some aspect to examine — much as a biologist can study the entire dog or only its circulatory system. Finally, once a concept has been developed, the sociologist may subdivide it into types, that is, types of society, types of interaction, and the like. In the next few paragraphs we will review each of these concerns briefly, mentioning the problems as seen by nineteenth-century sociologists, some solutions suggested by them, and the related problems that still plague us.

The first concern, about objectivity, grew from comparisons between social life and physical activity. We observe the rotation of planets and the structure of cells from the outside. We do not interpret what rotation must mean to the planet or how growth changes the thoughts of a cell. As far as we know, such speculations will always be fruitless. However, in social life these interior meanings often explain behavior patterns that would appear peculiar if we simply observed them. For example, every so often about half the adults in the United States rush to buildings in their neighborhoods and put "X" marks on pieces of paper. This in itself is absurd — unless we are willing to consider "democracy," "civic responsibility," "clout," and a host of other ideas held by these voters. As I have already mentioned, some nineteenth-century theorists denied the possibility that such cultural matter could ever be examined scientifically.

Since no sociologist could hold that view, they were forced to choose one of the two other courses: the use of strictly objective techniques in the hope these would tap some truly human characteristics or the development of new techniques to handle the peculiar subject matter of sociology. Some theorists, like Comte, recommended *positive* methods, observation without preconception and without introspection. Although he failed to provide examples of this ideal, he urged us to observe and record social data without imposing our ideas on the interpretation. Following Comte's example (far beyond anything the Founding Father had intended), George Lundberg suggested that for scientific purposes only measurements were real. If we could not observe something directly, then we could not study it at all. Hence, for him, sociology became the study of verbal responses (on questionnaires) and other overt behavior.

But, we may argue, it is our ideas that impose order on any impressions we get from the observable world. We recognize a new chair in the house because we have a concept of "chair" in mind, not because someone has described the texture, color, and shape of the slipcover in exact detail. In the much more complex social world, we recognize the mad rushing about to put "X's" on paper because we have a concept about voting and its cultural meanings to people in certain political systems. In other words, sociologists who insist on strictly "objective" data can easily collect masses of accurate information about trivial items (how many people use the church basement to mark their "X's") without ever learning the significance or importance of the activity. On the other hand, the sociologists like Max Weber and Charles Horton Cooley, who used their own insight for interpretative understanding of society's cultural values, created new scientific problems. Using this understanding, they could build several different plausible explanations of the same phenomenon. For example, people may vote because they value democratic ideology, but they may or may not have any real understanding of what this ideology entails. Hence, the "meaning" of the vote could be one, or several, or a dozen meanings.

This objective-subjective dilemma persists in modern sociology as a tension between *reliability* and *validity*. If we define our concepts strictly in terms of what we can observe, we develop very accurate (reliable) measures of very trivial objects. If, for example, we define cultural values as "the responses recorded on a cultural value questionnaire," why do we care to study them? If, on the other hand, we define these values as "cultural meanings that define what is good and thus shape our ability to judge the world," how can we be sure that value scales created by middle-class university professors capture the meanings envisioned by migrant farm workers? How can we be sure we have validly tapped the real object of our concern? The questionnaire, properly administered, can prove very reliable: forty different researchers using the questions on the same group of workers might get the same answers. But accuracy does not guarantee validity. These workers might all reply "yes, I believe in democracy," and still not begin to imagine the concept of "democracy" assumed by the researcher. In contrast, if forty sociologists observed the behavior of farm workers — their voting patterns, their tavern discussions, their response to local governments — and tried to interpret what democracy must mean to these people, the research might yield forty different concepts of democracy.

The sociologists who modeled social science after the physical sciences, usually sought objective, accurate measures for human behavior. They sought reliability and assumed validity — a facile assumption, since we can never prove the validity of a tie between our concept and the data. Those who placed their primary focus on the subject matter and worked out a scientific technique specifically to use on human interaction, usually sought valid new ways to measure the essentially human qualities of social life; they could not simply assume reliability because it is quite easy to check on the accuracy of a measure. However, they hoped to support their points through the logic of their analysis.

The second major issue in concept construction is part of that perennial scientific question: How do we sort through a confusing overabundance of data and decide what selection of it will illuminate our scientific concerns? Even if we avoid the reduction to psychological explanation and focus exclusively on social data, we will find a bewilderingly complicated mass of information. Early sociologists solved this problem in two ways. Some declared that the whole is greater than and different from the sum of its parts and so chose to view an entire social situation. Others focused on the parts of the situation they considered most important: human interaction, its causes, forms, and effects. Two different views, each with its own distortion — roughly analogous to flying over Manhattan and then walking along 111th street.

For the first view, the city-map approach, sociologists borrowed a framework from nineteenth-century biology and history. This is not surprising, since all three disciplines studied evolutionary growth. Society, they argued, is like a growing animal or a developing species, best understood when viewed as a whole. Combining this framework with historical data, they explained the development of society as a whole. For example, Comte (once again the imitator of nineteenth-century science) hypothesized that society had progressed through three growth stages. Thus, to explain daily life in a fourteenth-century French village in his system, we should first recognize that Western Europe was progressing through the advanced theological stage. Proper understanding of this evolutionary stage, Comte would tell us, will illuminate most of the problems of fourteenth-century rural life.

That may be. Whole-to-part analysis, however, breaks down in several related areas. To begin, the *Weltansicht* of an entire continent probably does not explain the values that inform daily practice in some local region, unless we can assume that the same ideals exist everywhere regardless of the local economy, regardless of the vicissitudes of local history, the local political customs in the area, and all those other forces that may encourage regional differences. Comte understood this, of course, but like most of the whole-animal theorists, he hoped, eventually, we would know the whole so thoroughly that we could understand the parts. We understand heart action, for example, as a process that helps support animal life; so we can learn to understand rural life as a vital part of Western civilization. Time, technique, and the accumulation of data would bring us this knowledge.

Others, less enamored by holistic analysis, have denoted methodological problems that would plague us no matter how detailed our knowledge, namely fuzzy definitions of the whole with its components, inability to delimit the boundaries of some wholes, and a limited sample of important wholes like societies. First, we cannot avoid circular reasoning if we insist on understanding the parts solely in terms of the whole. If, for example, we use Cooley's definition of the primary groups as a collection of people who engage in intimate face-to-face contact, and then hypothesize that intimate contact creates the primary group, we are really taking two parts of a definition and analyzing them as if they were separate entities. Since, by definition, we have declared that everything within the whole belongs with everything else and that we can only understand it as a whole, we have no way of comparing the relative importance of variables or conditions limiting variables within this whole. We cannot judge, for instance, whether intimate emotional feelings depend more on how often people see each other or how many interests they have in common. A second problem occurs when we try to define the whole well enough to delimit its boundaries. What is a society? Is it the group living between the mountains and the sea? The people sharing a common language and living area? A nation-state? If we cannot define the boundaries of a society, we cannot assess the limits of societal change. When a government is defeated in war, does this mean a society has, in some sense, died? Finally, when we observe social wholes like society, we must select from a limited number of cases. The biologist can look at thousands of primates, but Comte could only observe one Western Europe, or for that matter, one advanced industrial culture. How could he judge which societal traits were important, which merely accidental?

In order to avoid these problems many sociologists analyzed part of a social situation (much as an astronomer would isolate planetary motion from all the other facets of the universe that he could study). They realized that groups had a recognizable coherence, a cohesive force. So, instead of examining the entire situation at once, these sociologists looked at the patterns of cohesion, that is, at social interaction. Durkheim noticed how this behavior creates social norms to circumscribe future action. Weber analyzed action as it is perceived by the actor. Robert Park described the external circumstances limiting action. And, of course, Karl Marx argued that one powerful institution, the economy, defined man's place in the power structure and, therefore, delimited the other areas of his social life. These men, and others, generally viewed interaction as the cause, the process, or the result of other features in the social setting. However, this analysis can focus on action far removed from a specific situation. When Park studied patterns of neighborhood change, he was actually observing neighborhood change in Chicago during the 1920's. Later research on population shifts in other cities and other eras revealed time and place affected this pattern far more than Park had originally thought.

For the third concept problem — the location of different types within a concept — sociologists could borrow tools developed in biology and techniques long current in social thought. By 1800 biologists had constructed taxonomies and demonstrated their use in comparative studies. These types marked important distinctions within various phenomena — types of diseases, types of species, types of bone structure — telling what collection of features one might expect to find together. To build the types, biologists would isolate the few important features that could be used to separate an overwhelming diversity of objects into a few comprehensible categories. For example, among the thousands and thousands of animal species, those with back bones seem significantly different from those without. Social thinkers had also recognized this device for imposing mental order on empirical chaos. Aristotle had categorized all governments (or more precisely, all governments known to him) as monarchies, aristocracies, or democracies depending on how many people held sovereign power. For his types, Montesquieu added the ways in which sovereignty is exercised and the particular sentiments and cultural values that inspire rulers. Considering all these factors he divided governments into republics, monarchies, and despotisms. In each typology, these men highlighted one or more key features, which, in turn, were related to a large number of others. Thus the types summarize a number of variables that tend to appear together. Later Ferdinand Toennies, Georg Simmel, Max Weber, and others developed the *ideal type,* a hypothetical construct describing the variables that could appear together if we play the social game to extremes. In Simmel's ideal-type flirtation, for example, a couple interacts with ritualized patterns of mutual flattery, coy shyness, and other amorous tricks best played by those who do not have serious intentions.

Such types continue to prove useful. First by providing handy labels — saying "vertabrate" is easier than saying "a member of the group of animals with segmented spinal columns or with a more primitive form of backbone"; discussing "bureaucracy" is easier than listing the hierarchy of control, written rules, and other variables associated with this type of authority. Beyond that, types become the variables in hypotheses. For example, we may analyze the importance of bureaucracy in contemporary life without separating each feature and considering it individually.

In sum, our concept definitions affect the rest of methodology in a variety of ways, three of which interest us here. First, we can pretend to be social outsiders and observe only the overt behavior of human beings or we can take advantage of our insiders' knowledge to fashion concepts that grasp the subjective meaning of this behavior. If we choose option one, we can develop accurate measures of surface behavior. With option two, we may measure something closer to the truly human side of social life, but we are less apt to measure it reliably. So, our choice between the insider's and the outsider's view often implies a priority on the value of reliability or validity.

A second set of choices, between studying a social whole or a group of parts, also affects the results of research. At one extreme, we may study a unique event (like the growth of civilization in Western Europe). But science does not explain unique events. It analyzes recurrent patterns. On the other hand, if we focus on small recurrent patterns in a society and fail to consider the total setting, we may analyze an event that does not exist at all. No flirtation process, for example, exists independent of cultural norms and interaction settings. A party game in one society is a serious invitation somewhere else.

The third concept problem, the development of types, also creates dilemmas. If we recognize types of social phenomenon we can anticipate how certain patterns of relationships will go together. This information can be useful in itself. But as scientists, we should be identifying types for further use. We do not want a type collection, however well labelled. Rather, we want to know what kinds of family structures, religious orientations, or forms of authority are associated with particular historical stages or attitudes toward the world or political ideologies. Concepts in other words, are part of the methodological process, not the end result of it. The goal of methodology is explanation.

Explanation.   An explanation is a law, a theory, or other statement suggesting why or how some phenomena occur as they do. More than a simple generalization, the explanation attempts to pinpoint the mechanism producing this effect, to identify the purpose of some occurrence, or, in general, to tell us more than we could know by observing raw data about the empirical world. If we generalize that low-income neighborhoods tend to produce a high number of juvenile delinquents per capita, we might explain this by referring to lower-class culture, anomie, learning processes, and other features of the social environment. Because we anticipate certain forms of explanation, we choose to examine certain variables by using the appropriate concepts. To research the relationship between lower-class culture and delinquency, we need to define the terms "culture," "social class," "delinquency," and several related concepts. Then we must delineate the hypothesized relationships between these items and observe the empirical world to see if our ideas correspond to empirical reality. Finally, with the research completed, we must explicate how we have fleshed out some details of our explanation or how we have destroyed some of its tenets. Either way, our initial ideas have affected the course and outcome of research.

So, the explanation is both part of the research process and its ultimate goal, something we may anticipate at the beginning and achieve at the end — although, of course, the explanation may charge *en route* if the original version did not account for empirical data. Explanation is, quite clearly, a complex business. Both *inductive* and *deductive* at the same time. Without assuming that any scientist works in one direction only, we may nevertheless wonder about some inductive and deductive possibilities. When mulling over a computer print-out, a collection of sermons, or a description of some historical event, what kind of patterns does a sociologist expect to find? What inductive path must be travelled from data to theory? Conversely, what sort of expectations, however vague, however well-defined, does the scientist bring to the interview or the field study?

Beginning with the inductive process, we can imagine the problems occuring to anyone who faces a mass of data, that is the problems of describing the relationships between phenomena.

To the uninitiated, solving this problem seems simple enough. Does murder occur most frequently during hot weather? Then hot weather causes murder. But, as we all know, people also commit homicide in the winter, although perhaps not as often. Does this mean there is no relationship between murder and weather? That does not seem right either, at least not to the police, court officials, reporters, and others familiar with homicide patterns. Apparently, weather is one of many factors affecting homicide. Or, perhaps, weather is related to something else that influences crime rates. So it goes in sociology; the phenomena we observe are terribly complex, related to numerous causes, conditions, restrictions, motives. We look for a limited number of important variables and try to assess their contribution to the total complex of relationships. More technically, we observe simple correlations and explain them in terms of causality, function, or some other abstract idea. And always, we deal with a small percentage of the possible relevant variables. Consequently, we never find a perfect relationship between any two variables, or any constellation of them. If there are four hundred twenty-seven "causes" of murder ranging from paranoid delusions to hot weather, we can never hope to account for more than a portion of them in any one study.

Working inductively, however, we can identify patterns of relationships. If we observe that wife-beating and divorce rise during summer months, and if murders between friends and relatives increase at the same time, we may conclude that these murders are part of a larger pattern of domestic disturbance. Perhaps family life and friendship deteriorate when social intimates are too hot and uncomfortable to enjoy close emotional contact. If other forms of interpersonal conflict also rise at the same time, we may hypothesize that there exists some more general relationship between weather and conflict. Looking at the climate variable, we may ask if summer weather represents more than just heat. Perhaps vacations encourage mischief, or too much togetherness encourages family violence, as it does at other holiday seasons. The possibilites are numerous — and need to be verified with more data.

In sum, induction involves more than simple observation followed by our straight-forward description of whatever we have seen. It is a creative non-logical leap between data and explanation. The most creative scientists are people who notice patterns no one else has seen. For them, familiar data requires fresh explanation. Following Newton, Darwin, and other physical scientists, nineteenth-century sociologists stressed inductive method. If sociology was to be a science, they said, it must build its theories from data instead of spinning new ideas from philosophical principles as social philosophy had done.

Induction, however, is not a leap from data into the unknown. The scientist has some preconceptions about his planned research, ranging from a general preference for some subject material to a tight-knit deductive system with very explicit predictions about what the empirical world will reveal. And, if the nineteenth-century heritage prescribed scientific induction, it also provided several overarching frameworks for analysis. Some frameworks specified the outline of the empirical world: "Society is like a large organism...." Others stressed the form of scientific statements: "Scientific generalizations should define the probability that an event will occur under certain conditions...." With either approach, the framework encompassed both subject focus and methodology because a choice in one area limited options in the other.

The search for an explanatory framework was critical for nineteenth-century sociology. Society as a subject matter has never been the exclusive province of sociologists. Before the official appearance of sociology, historians and anthropologists had been outlining the reasons for the French Revolution and listing the details of economic exchange among the Kwakiutl. If sociologists pretended to contribute new knowledge, they would have to do so by organizing the old material in a new way — a scientific way. The most obvious examples, as you may guess, were those set in physics and biology. To understand this we should consider some of these important explanatory frameworks available to nineteenth-century sociologists: first those based on ideas about the nature of society and then those based on ideas about the nature of scientific statements.

Newton's *Principia* has shown how motion in the physical world could be described in reasonable, mathematical statements. With a few physical laws, he explained the motion of an apple falling from a tree and the revolutions of the earth circling its sun. The world was a great machine. If one experimented to learn the antecedents and the consequences of different motions, one could predict the behavior of the machine. Experiments, laws, predictions — these were the *sine qua non* of science. Applying this principle to explanations of society, sociologists searched for causes (usually defined as immediate antecedents) in order to make predictions. "Prevision," as Herbert Spencer called it, "is the essence of science." Properly researched society could eventually become as predictable as the solar system.

The physics model has not dominated sociology, however. Although many early sociologists borrowed ideas from this model about "prevision," experiments, and other scientific apparatus, they also used a biological analogy. Like a living being, they argued, society can grow. Indeed, change is inherent in society as is in every other natural system. Others went further and argued that the social system develops toward some end state, perhaps dissolution, but more likely toward the technical-industrial complex already apparent in Western Europe. This growth is "caused" by mental development, an inherent dialectic, or some other force. Spencer, for example, conceptualized social change in this fashion when he searched for cosmic laws that could summarize the growth of an oak tree, the growth of society, and the growth of the universe. Many more analytical sociologists have also shared this model, viewing society as a total entity with inseparable parts, with healthy and unhealthy states, with proper rates of growth. In using a pure organic analogy (or even a modified version of it) sociologists also borrowed some biological techniques: taxonomy construction and comparative studies (which we have already considered) and the technique of analyzing how various parts of the organism function to support the whole. Durkheim compared institutions in different types of society to show how they function to hold society together. Among other things, he studied how religion reinforces solidarity feelings within primitive tribes and then searched for the institutions that perform analogous functions in modern societies.

Following Vilfredo Pareto's lead, many twentieth-century sociologists use the broader analogy of the system: society is a social system. . . . This conceptualization leaves us with many options — to analyze whole groups or focus on simple parts; to search for causes or define functions or examine subjective purposes; to build mathematical explanations or construct typologies or describe extreme cases; to conduct experiments or observe natural settings. Talcott Parsons, the most eminent systems analyst, developed a typology of functional prerequisites for system survival and analyzed how institutions perform these functions. Moving further from the organic-system analogy, Robert Merton looked at social beliefs and practices to predict the consequences or functions that would follow. Bureaucratic red tape, he suggested, produces the bureaucratic personality, a ritualistic corporation legalist who follows the rules and forgets the goals they are designed to serve. In sum, this general systems model provided a broader vision for sociology than its physical and organic predecessors had done.

Each of the system analogies implied a special content for explanation. Other kinds of models specified its form. These began with the obvious injunction that scientific theory should generate deductive hypotheses about the empirical world. But the end products of "deduction" could range from illustrative examples of concepts to conclusions drawn from a logical syllogism to statistical inferences.

Useful though it may be in organizing thought, all such deduction has limits. It specifies the form of our statements but not the shape of the empirical world. When we say:

> All men are mortal
> Socrates is a man
> Therefore Socrates is mortal.

we have made a true, if trivial, statement. But what if we change the second line to "God is a man?" This raises many, many issues about the existence and nature of something called "God." And also in society, the "real world" is more complex than the logical syllogism or the concept or the probability statement. When we research aspects of society, the problems of validly measuring variables in a complex world return to confound us. For example, when deducing propositions from his theory about how social life affects individual behavior, Durkheim hypothesized that changing social-cohesion levels affect the suicide rate. Therefore, urban (and less cohesive) areas should have higher rates than rural ones. In the empirical world, however, urban areas may develop new forms of social cohesion, perhaps becoming more cohesive than rural areas and thus destroying the use of urban location as a measure of social cohesion. Or a particular rural area may house a tight-knit suicidal cult, thus raising both the levels of cohesion and suicide at the same time. Durkheim could have explained these possibilities, of course, but the main point remains: here the empirical world exhibits tendencies that confound our deductive predictions even though our basic theoretical ideas may be quite sound. A coherent thought system is not enough.

Sociologists have, of course, employed the tools of logic, mathematics, and other deductive methods with success. Durkheim's use of mortality statistics enabled him to compare one area with another, something he could never have accomplished by detailing the despair behind each death. Our problem is simply to avoid becoming so beguiled by these tools that we mistake the structure of thought for the structure of data. When we flip a coin the frequency of "heads" and "tails" falls into a Bernoulli distribution with a fifty percent probability for either event. Thus, the chances of any given number of tosses can be calculated from a normal distribution. When a person dies, however, the choice between suicide and other causes of death is firmly skewed in favor of the latter.

In conclusion, explanation is both the end of science and part of the process. More than data description, explanation tells us "why" the data appears as it does. An explanation does not necessarily enable us to predict the future. We may learn to understand the spread of religious cults without being able to predict the rise and strength of future movements. Further, an explanation does not necessarily describe the "real" empirical world. If science studies typical patterns, general trends, the interplay of variables under ideal, specified conditions, then our explanations can never describe the complex empirical world in true detail. When we hypothesize that lower-class milieux encourage delinquency, we are assuming the existence of a dominant middle-class culture, relative isolation of the lower classes, and, as they say in natural science, "all other factors being constant. . . . " Consequently, our explanation can never be complete. We do not find the ideal where all other factors are constant, where religious cults are fully understandable, where all changes can be predicted a week ahead. Explanation must always remain in process. Inductive or deductive (whichever the direction) neat, abstract interpretations must adjust to a cluttered, detailed, changing empirical world.

RESEARCH

Regardless of how intangible or obvious the subject matter, whatever the types or categories of objects, no matter how elegant or cumbersome the explanation, in some way the scientific enterprise must tell us about the empirical world. Whatever else they borrowed from their nineteenth-century heritage, all sociologists have matched their scientific ideas against empirical social reality. For this activity, they have used two basic research strategies: finding the social patterns that do occur and looking for those that do not.

The first strategy — *verifying* that a given social activity does indeed display particular patterns — may involve the examination of a single variable, a type of social activity, or a combination of variables and types. In each instance, of course, we must define research operations carefully, paying special attention to the validity and reliability problems mentioned earlier. Further, we must look for observable empirical relationships that could reflect our hypothetical, theoretical ideas about causality, functional consequences, and other relationships that we will never be able to demonstrate conclusively.

Establishing the existence of a single phenomenon or of an empirical type can mean discovering if a phenomenon occurs anywhere. For example, William Graham Sumner claimed that almost any behavior, no matter how bizarre, will be sanctioned by some society, somewhere. Because the discovery of approved wife-swapping in eastern Utopia proves the existence of this practice as accepted behavior, Sumner could support his claim about bizarre norms by describing the sexual customs, dietary habits, kinship patterns, and other types of behavior routinely practiced in various societies. Thus one illustrative example of any approved custom or type of customs sufficed to prove its existence and verify Sumner's hypothesis.

Locating the empirical counterpart to an ideal type presents additional challenges because, as we know, an ideal type is not a description of some group of empirical phenomena, but an abstract conception of the possible characteristics of those phenomena. When he used such types in his empirical research, Weber would first define the type and then compare it with the "real" social world. He defined bureaucracy as that type of organization characterized by a hierarchy of control, well-defined regulations, specialized roles, and other organizational structures designed for administrative efficiency. Although he never located *the* bureaucracy (which completely incorporates all the traits he had outlined), he could discuss different empirical administrations as being more or less "bureaucratic" by measuring them against his ideal type.

Assessing the relationship between two or more variables is often an extension of this verification process. Having first established the existence of both variables we can then hypothesize that one variable encourages, inhibits or otherwise affects the existence of the other. For example, Merton hypothesized that a stress on originality in scientific work encouraged scientists to rush every new thought into print — even if the idea was not properly developed and, sometimes, even if the idea did not originate with the person who published first. To verify this hypothesis, Merton documented the simultaneous existence of both this cultural-scientific ideal and these publishing practices. (He further assumed, of course, that the co-existence of these two variables indicates a functional relationship). We may suspect, however, that plagiarism and hasty writing exist regardless of cultural ideas about scientific originality. To discover whether these scientific peccadilloes result from certain cultural values of a society or are simply an example of universal human venality, we would have to examine publishing practices in societies with and without that particular ideal. Then, if we discovered that the rush to print is noticeably higher in the societies stressing scientific originality, we might conclude — tentatively — that Merton's hypothesis is true.

Such a conclusion, however, could only be tentative because we cannot prove that any situation exists everywhere or that any two variables always go together. To provide a demonstration of universality we would need to perform an impossible research task. We might claim that stratification exists in all enduring human groups. Besides the problems of defining "enduring human groups" and "stratification," we then would be faced with the task of locating *all* such existing and historical groups and checking each for signs of a social hierarchy — an impossible task. Merton, of course, would face the same overwhelming problem of trying to examine every society (past and present) for scientific ideals and publishing practices.

The opposite strategy often proves easier. Thus if we claim that there are no enduring groups without strata, we need to produce only one strataless group to *falsify* our statement (that is, if we can find such a group). Sociologists continually use variations of this falsification strategy in their research — making a statement, proving that the statement is untrue and thus providing indirect support for some alternative hypotheses. Describing the relationship between weather and murder, we might state "murder occurs at a constant rate throughout the year." When (or if) data show seasonal fluctuations with a rise in June, July, and August, we have both falsified our original statement and indirectly supported the opposite idea that summertime encourages murder. Extending this falsification process further, we can support an hypothesis by eliminating a series of plausible alternatives. For example, Durkheim suggested that strong feelings of social cohesion or solidarity in a group would cause low suicide rates, assuming the group norms discouraged suicide. In his research on the topic, Durkheim observed mortality rates in several countries to eliminate nationality as an explanation for group differences. As he discounted this and several other explanations, his own hypotheses about the effects of group cohesion became more plausible. More recently, Herbert Blalock has elaborated ways to use inferential statistics in this basic strategy when we do not have numerous groups to study as Durkheim did.

Experimental research simply extends the falsification process by the addition of control groups. In experiments we hypothesize that all of the groups we are researching are alike in some respect and then we discover that they differ. The difference, however, is the relationship we really expected from the outset. Durkheim used this strategy in his study of suicide. He noticed that educated people living in urban areas had lower social cohesion and higher suicide rates than uneducated groups located in rural areas. However, he also observed that tight-knit religious groups like nineteenth-century French Jews had low suicide rates. If region and education are the critical variables, he reasoned, we might expect that urban, educated Jews would have high suicide rates. If, on the other hand, social cohesion is the really critical variable, the cohesive Jewish groups would have low suicide rates regardless of their location or the educational status of their members. Using the terminology of falsification, Durkheim could have hypothesized; "There is no difference between urban, educated Jews and any other urban, educated group." Actually, he constructed the experiment without using those terms. Nonetheless, he discovered that there was, indeed, a difference between Jewish and non-Jewish groups, thus falsifying the no-difference hypothesis and supporting his alternative explanation about social cohesion.

Our ability to conduct research relevant to theory rests on the two other stages in the theory-research process, specifically, on concept formation and explanation. Concepts must be defined unambiguously both in the theoretical constructs and in the research operations. When Durkheim studied the relationship between social cohesion and deviance, he used suicide rates (in a group that prohibited suicide) as his measure of deviation from social norms, and he used Jewish affiliation as part of his operational definition of social solidarity. Then assuming that suicide is a valid measure of deviance and that nineteenth-century Jews formed a cohesive group, Durkheim could conclude that any relationship between Jewish affiliation and suicide was also a relationship between cohesion and deviance. This particular relationship, however, was just one illustration of a broader issue, the relationship of deviance to society which, in turn, reflected Durkheim's ideas about normative regulation or very generally, the ways a society affects the behavior of its members. By demonstrating the relationship between life style and suicide, Durkheim also reinforced his general explanation. Just as a group situation seemed to encourage or impede suicide (regardless of individual motives) so, he explained, the group milieu defined broad areas of behavior for its members.

What if suicide rates remained constant despite variations in religious affiliations, educational level, residence location, and other "cohesion" indices? In that event we would need to examine the measured concepts and theoretical explanations. We might ask: Is suicide really a measure of deviance? Or, looking at Durkheim's explanation: Does cohesion affect deviance? We could not destroy Durkheim's entire theoretical edifice with a single study. However, an empirical study that does not confirm theoretical predictions certainly indicates the need to re-examine concepts, operations, and explantions.

The two basic research strategies reviewed here — verification and falsification — underlie all sociological research from the cross-cultural comparison to the small-group experiment. In order to transform our explanations of social life from the abstract speculations approprite for social philosophy to the more concrete verifiable statements appropriate for science, we must define out ideas in such a way that we can observe if a given proposition does or does not correspond to empirical reality.

CONCLUSION

Sociology — a discipline conceived by the union of science and social concern — reflects both aspects of its heritage. Whether sociologists hoped to affect social problems directly or wished simply to achieve a better understanding of the realities producing those problems, nineteenth-century theorists were initially inspired by reformist ideals to conduct social science research. These reformist ideals took one of two directions. Conservative ideology encouraged some sociologists to focus on mechanisms of social cohesion; radical ideologies encouraged many to examine social situations dividing groups within a society. Whichever ideology they used, however, sociologists turned to physical science and other social sciences for guidance in over-all methodology and research strategies. Stressing the scientific aspects of social science, many sociologists began inquiry about the relationship between sociology and other sciences. Some examined physical science first and then applied its principles to social life. For example, noticing that physical science examined repetitious phenomena, Tarde looked for repeating patterns in social life. Some other sociologists considered the peculiar subjective nature of sociological data and tried to adapt traditional scientific techniques and develop new ones to use on their data. If sociology is the study of interaction in human groups, they reasoned, it must explicitly take into account what subjective meanings this activity has for the participants. So, they concluded, we must employ whatever techniques we need to uncover these meanings — regardless of what researchers may be doing in chemistry or physics.

In the following chapters we will review the work of seventeen important sociologists, all of whom — from the nineteenth-century figures to those who are still alive — have considered the problem of researching social life in a scientific fashion. Although individually they have not answered all the questions or resolved all the dilemmas introduced in this chapter, collectively they have provided considerable elaboration of these issues and, doing so, have developed the science of sociology as we know it today.

Bibliography

Here and at the end of each succeeding chapter I have included a bibliography of secondary sources that I found particularly helpful when preparing the chapter. All of them, ranging from the elementary texts to the more complex analyses, handle some aspect of the chapter in considerably more detail than I did. I would urge readers to begin their additional studies here.

General history of intellectual and scientific developments
Becker, Carl L.
  1932 *The Heavenly City of the Eighteenth-Century Philosophers.*
       New Haven, Conn.: Yale University Press (1970).
Brinton, C. Crane
  1963 *Ideas and Men: The Story of Western Thought.* 2d ed.
       Englewood Cliffs, N.J.: Prentice-Hall.
Brinton, C. Crane, Christopher, John B., and Wolff, Robert Lee
  1960 *A History of Civilization.* Vol. 2. 2d ed. Englewood Cliffs, N.J.:
       Prentice-Hall.
Bryson, Gladys
  1945 *Man and Society: The Scottish Inquiry of the Eighteenth Century.*
       New York: A. M. Kelley (1968).
Butterfield, Herbert
  1957 *The Origins of Modern Science.* 1300-1800. Rev. ed.
       New York: Macmillan Company.
Hayek, F. A.
  1952 *The Counter-Revolution of Science: Studies on the Abuse of Reason.*
       Glencoe, Ill.: Free Press.
Kearney, Hugh F.
  1971 *Science and Change,* 1500-1700. New York: McGraw-Hill.
Mason, Stephen
  1962 *A History of the Sciences.* Rev. ed. New York: Collier (1968).
Whitehead, Alfred North
  1925 *Science and the Modern World.* New York: Free Press (1967).
History of Sociology
Aron, Raymond
  1965 "Montesquieu." Pp. 13-72 in *Main Currents in Sociological Thought:
       Volume I.* Garden City, N.Y.: Doubleday (1968).
Bottomore, T. B.
  1971 *Sociology: A Guide to Problems and Literature.*
       New York: Vintage (1972).
Bramson, Leon
  1961 "The uses of sociology." Pp. 11-26 in *The Political Context of
       Sociology.* Princeton, N.J.: Princeton University Press.
Buckley, Walter
  1967 *Sociology and Modern Systems Theory.* Englewood Cliffs, N.J.:
       Prentice-Hall.
Davis, Kingsley
  1959 "The myth of functional analysis as a special method in sociology
       and anthropology." Pp. 379-402 in N.J. Demerath III and Richard

A. Peterson (eds.), *System, Change, and Conflict: A Reader on Contemporary Sociological Theory and the Debate Over Functionalism.* New York: Free Press, 1967.

Douglas, Jack O.

1971 "The rhetoric of science and the origins of statistical social thought: the case of Durkheim's *Suicide.*" Pp. 44-57 in Edward A. Tiryakian (ed.), *The Phenomenon of Sociology.* New York: Appleton-Century-Croffs, 1971.

Durkheim, Emile

1890 "The principles of 1789 and sociology." Pp. 37-43 in Tiryakian *The Phenomenon.* . . .

Nisbet, Robert A.

1943 "The French Revolution and the rise of sociology in France." Pp. 27-37 in Tiryakian *The Phenomenon.* . . .

1966 "The two revolutions." Pp. 21-44 in *The Sociological Tradition.* New York: Basic Books.

Zeitlin, Irving M.

1968 *Ideology and the Development of Sociological Theory.* Englewood Cliffs, N.J.: Prentice-Hall.

Science and social science

Brown, Robert R.

1963 *Explanation in Social Science.* Chicago: Aldine.

Hansen, Norwood Russell

1958 "Theories." Pp. 70-92 in *Patterns of Discovery.* Cambridge: University Press (1972).

Kaplan, Abraham

1964 *The Conduct of Inquiry: Methodology for Behavioral Science.* San Francisco: Chandler.

Kuhn, Thomas S.

1970 *The Structure of Scientific Revolutions.* 2d ed. enlarged. Chicago: University of Chicago Press.

Popper, Karl R.

1959 *The Logic of Scientific Discovery.* New York: Harper Torchbooks (1968).

Reynolds, Paul Davidson

1971 *A Primer in Theory Construction.* Indianapolis: Bobbs-Merrill.

Shearing, Clifford D.

1973 "How to make theories untestable: a guide to theorists." *American Sociologists* 8 (February): 33-37.

Stinchcomb, Arthur L.

1968 *Constructing Social Theories.* New York: Harcourt, Brace and World.

Auguste Comte

Auguste Comte (1798-1857) ranks as the official founding father of sociology — he coined the word. He was not, of course, the first person to act like a sociologist; however, he did urge people to study society empirically in an era when many social thinkers still dabbled in social philosophy and thought of that as science. Furthermore, he pioneered research into a number of important sociological concerns: culture, social change, societal structures, group cohesion, and others. In spite of this, Comte had little immediate influence on sociology. Both his involved, wandering style and his irascible personality militated against a large personal following. Moreover, his strictures against theological thinking horrified many would-be followers, especially in the United States where sociology became very popular a generation after Comte had died. Finally, Comte dissipated his impact by promoting a substitute for Christianity, his scientific *religion of humanity*. Later sociologists have not ignored him entirely, however. A few — most notably Durkheim — have used his ideas and preserved them as a still-vital part of sociology.

Although Durkheim sharpened Comte's scientific vision while ignoring some of its religious facets, Comte himself built his science and his religion together. First he stressed the need for scientific observation uncolored by metaphysical and theological preconceptions. But, at the same time, he conceptualized society and, ultimately, humanity as a large, unified entity similar to a biological organism. Thus his biological framework replaced other preconceptions. To study the social organism, he looked for mechanisms encouraging stability and change — and translated these into sources of *order* and *progress*. Proper scientific thinking coupled with unbiased empirical observation would, he predicted, lead mankind to social unity, to an orderly and progressive social world, to a truly humane world-view embodied in the religion of humanity.

29

INTELLECTUAL BACKGROUND

Comte was the protégé of Henri Saint-Simon, a creative, imaginative, but disorganized social critic who dreamt of harnessing science in the service of social reform. Together these men wrote "Plan of the scientific operations necessary for reorganizing society" (1822) containing three basic ideas: a "law" of social-mental evolution (which ends with the development of social science), a plan for empirical research in social science, and a vision of how such science could effect social reform. Clearly they were building on the nineteenth-century tradition in these matters. Their unique contribution lies in their combination of these intellectual currents, and in their use of positive science as a vehicle for social-mental progress, a use that Comte continued to promote for the rest of his life.

Comte's scientific keystone — positivism — attacked the Enlightenment hope for reform engineered by the pure power of human reason and substituted the promise of reform built on observation of existing social forms coupled with true human feeling about social concerns. Negative Enlightenment thinkers criticized reality, juxtaposing their personal theological or metaphysical ideas of freedom, dignity, and other human goods against reality. For Comte this practice was absurd. Human good lay in reality, not in men's minds. Moreover, that good might vary with the era; it was not some god-given or reasonable ultimate (1844: 1-77). By observing society without theological and metaphysical preconceptions, scientists could discern the true empirical trends of an era instead of a philosopher's biased view of them. Eventually the single, positive analysis of social life would replace the numerous, competing, polemical interpretations. It was these competing ideals, a chaotic mental disunity in society, that had spawned the civil disorders of the nineteenth-century — with so many competing moralities, men were destined to live in disunity. A mental synthesis or *consensus* could destroy the rationale for such quarrels and thus restore social order. But, since none of the competing religious or philosophical doctrines could demonstrate its clear superiority over the rest, Comte did not expect modern societies to follow a single theological or metaphyical faith. Therefore, if men were to achieve mental unity and the resultant social cohesion, they would have to seek it through *positivism* — objective, empirical science — the basis of a truthful mental unity and therefore, the source of order in modern society (1858:36).

Comte also attacked another aspect of negative thinking. In addition to imposing their preconceptions of reality, the negative thinkers had exalted Reason by claiming that man, the reasonable creature, could use his intellect to shape his social destiny. Borrowing from Maistre, Bonald and other conservative thinkers, Comte opposed this doctrine and stressed traditional groups as the source of social unity. To unravel the secrets of social progress, he maintained, we should not construct a social contract. Rather we should use positive science to observe the family, the church, and other long-lasting consensual groups. It is only by examining these groups that he felt we would discover the traditional order undergirding social progress.

DEFINITION OF SOCIOLOGY

Comte expected his sociology to occupy a most important position in mankind's thought. Sociology, he said, is the ultimate end of human intellectual history, the zenith of the positive sciences. To understand this conception we must consider its three key facets: positivism, the law of three stages, and, the position of sociology within the field of positive science.

For Comte, the scientific or *positive* spirit is marked by "the steady subordination of the imagination to observation. . . . this habit of subjecting scientific conceptions to the facts. . . . " (1858: 452). Unlike theology and metaphysics, positive science ignores speculations about unknowable first and final causes and searches, instead, for empirically based laws, or "the invariable relations of succession and resemblance." Within the positivistic framework, in other words, a cause is the immediate precedent of some phenomenon. By examining a linked series of law-like relationships between an immediate precedent and its result, positive science can explain the known universe as part of some general law-fact such as gravitation. Theology and metaphysics, on the other hand, search for original causes, like a god or an entity called nature (1858:26).

These three mental outlooks — theological, metaphysical, positivistic — form a hierarchy. Theology is the most primitive type, positivism the most advanced. Throughout most of history mankind has used theological and metaphysical frameworks to think in terms of ultimate causes: God is a cause; nature is a cause. Positive science embodies a new intellectual trend, the search for immediate laws instead of remote causes. Gradually, man has applied the positive approach to various natural phenomena, first simple things then complex ones. According to Comte, this intellectual sequence (termed the *law of three stages*) occurs throughout human history. All individuals and all societies start with theological thinking. Some people and some groups eventually move through metaphysical thought to the more advanced positive stage (and even study the more complex positive sciences) (1858:25-30).

How does sociology fit within this scheme? Sociology is the most advanced positive science. After a society produces positive thinkers, and after these thinkers study relatively uncomplicated things like physics and biology — then scientists are ready to create a positive science of society:

> In mentioning just now the four principle categories of phenomena, — astronomical, physical, chemical, and physiological, — there was an omission which will have been noticed. Nothing was said of Social phenomena. Though involved with the physiological, Social phenomena demand a district classification, both on account of their importance and of their difficulty. . . . Now that the human mind has grasped celestial and terrestrial physics, — mechanical and chemical; organic physics, both vegetable and animal, — there remains one science, to fill up the series of sciences of observation, — Social Physics. (1858:30)

In sum, Social Physics — Comte later renamed it sociology — is the empirical study of "social phenomena." To understand this better, we should consider just what social features Comte preferred to study.

SUBJECT FOCUS

Reading through Come's work on "social phenomena," we can see that he intended to create a science of society. Actually, he was a little more specific: he wanted sociology to emphasize mental aspects of society. He used different words, of course, but in modern terms he stressed cultural values, a social Gestalt, or some similar set of mental constructs. Naturally enough, he drew his ideas for his subject matter from the law of three stages. Man's mental or intellectual progress dominates these evolutionary stages, and this progress occurs in the entire race, not just in an individual mind. For this reason sociology is really a study of group "mental science" (1853:38-40). In other words, sociology studies the peculiar mental influences that a group exerts over the person.

> In all Social phenomena we perceive the working of the physiological laws of the individual; and moreover something which modifies their effects, and which belongs to the influence of individuals over each other — singularly complicated in the case of the human race by the influence of generations on their successors. (1858:45-46)

What is "the influence of generations on their successors?" In our terms: culture — laws, religions, family patterns, and innumerable other practices and beliefs we have inherited from our parents.

This cultural system (the civilization of a society) exhibits a cohesive natural order based on human *consensus* (or mental unity). Indeed, the unity of society is so essential to its nature that we cannot study parts of society and we cannot work to improve society unless we first understand it as an ordered whole (1858:258-63). Comte further underscored this idea with his classification of scientific objects into unorganized and organized bodies. Astronomy, physics, and chemistry study unorganized bodies. Biology (or physiology) and sociology study organized ones (1858:45-46). Moreover, since all organized bodies — both individuals and social groups -- have a life as a whole, they must be observed and studied from a holistic point of view.

In other words, Comte's sociology examines the total cultural milieu in a society — a broad vision of a rather large, detailed subject. In the next section, we shall consider how Comte proposed to research this complex whole.

SCIENCE — THE PLAN

Comte wrote at length about the facets of positivism. He distinguished art from science, speculated about the future of positivistic society, and preached the religion of humanity — based, of course, on positive science. We will ignore these sidelines and concentrate, instead, on a few of Comte's ideas that affected research: his distinction between abstract and concrete science, his approach to organic studies, and his special recommendations for abstract, organic studies of society. But first, we must reconsider the nature of positive science.

As we have already noted, positivism requires men to concentrate on facts rather than speculate about possibilities. According to Comte, this positive emphasis marks the mature mind:

> In short the fundamental revolution which marks the passage of the human mind from its adolescence to its manhood consists in this — it abandons the inquiry after *causes*, properly so called, in every department of knowledge, as beyond its reach, and devotes itself instead to the simple search for *laws*, that is to say for constant relations existing between the phenomena observed. (1844:21)

Thus the mature person (and the positive scientist) rely on observation, not dreams, not speculations. Comte would tell us that we should not simply imagine a Utopia and then use it as our model for the good society. Rather we should observe good societies as they exist in nature and use them as our models for planning. The important object of study is not our idea about the causes of good social life but such life as it actually exists.

However, Comte did not recommend that scientists observe all the facts in an unorganized fashion. First, data stockpiling is a "desultory and fruitless" occupation; for scientific use, we must order data by describing it in laws (1858:26-27). Second, the overwhelming complexity of detail in a special situation usually precludes such organization. So, instead of doing *concrete* studies on a special situation, we should conduct *abstract* examinations of classes or types of situations (1851:30-32, 343-49). For example, we should outline the typical activities in a planned community instead of attempting an exhaustive — impossible — scientific summary of a commune near Flagstaff, Arizona. In theory, a concrete science is possible. In practice, we shall never be able to handle all the variables affecting John Jones's delinquent behavior, the growth of the Flagstaff commune, and any other particular situation. Comte did not carry his exposition further; he did not recommend practical guides for those of us who must decide what variables to include in our studies. However, although he offered no solution, he did highlight a conceptual problem that plagues sociological researchers to this day.

Comte's stress on abstract studies of social laws probably explains his distaste for statistical research as advocated by Quételet and other contemporaries. At first he objected to statistics because organic life is too complex, too varied for summary in elegant mathematical statements (1822:571-80). Later, he derided the "Calculus of Chances; a conception which presupposes that the phenomena considered are not subject to law" (1851:20). He apparently did not see the use of statistics for determining the likelihood that a general law might work in a special situation. What, for example, are the chances that the Flagstaff Commune will survive for five years? Perhaps Comte hoped to formulate laws completely predicting human activity. But his discussion of concrete and abstract science indicates that he never expected scientific "prevision" to work so well. More likely, he did not understand this mathematical tool and therefore dismissed it without real consideration if its possibilities.

Comte's judgement of statistics was also colored by his conception of organic studies. In organic matters, he wrote, the whole is real, easily seen, better known than its parts. When studying animals or societies, we should recognize this fact and examine the entire living being before considering small dependent sections of it. In an inorganic field like chemistry, by contrast, there are no living wholes. Hence in chemistry we would first study individual elements and then observe their combinations (1851: 517-18). As chemists, we might experiment to produce the possible combinations of oxygen: H_2O, CO_2, etc. But as biologists, we would be more likely to compare types of country robins with city ones or examine the wing action of a bird. In other words, as organic scientists we would examine the relationship of an organization to its environments and the function of parts within the whole. For the more complex organic studies of society, we would employ similar strategies — for example, comparing the world view Western Europe in 800 with Western Europe in 1800 or examining how common belief unites a society. Focusing on the organic whole, Comte did not compare different rates of heart-beats in robins and bluejays or the patterns of church attendance among Catholics and Protestants in Bavaria. Statistics simply did not complement his holistic studies.

Working with qualitative data, Comte recommended four strategies — observation, experiment, comparison, and historical comparison — designed to focus on society-as-a-unit and to detect the important activities of that unit. Theoretically, he wanted to de-

lineate routine social activity — he called this *statical* activity —
and to trace the course of social development — in *dynamical* studies.
For empirical research on the statics and dynamics of society, he
suggested a combination of his four strategies, each informed by his
holistic theoretical point of view. For proper *observation,* he noted,
must examine both *order* and *progress* in social groups. Specifically
we should look at related patterns of activity that co-exist within a
single society and at successive changes in these coherent patterns.
Experiments can highlight the ways in which normal activities go
together by showing what happens when some unusual activity
destroys the normal unity. However, since we cannot control or
manipulate the important patterns of society, we must rely on indirect experiment, a study of pathological cases and their effects,
for example, the effects of revolution (pathological disruption) in
society. Of course, our selection of "pathological cases" presupposes
that we already have some definition of normalcy. Comte's third
method, *comparison,* requires us to find similarities and differences
between our society and animal groups or other human ones. Since,
we may suppose, these societies are in different stages of development, comparison of different groups illustrates evolutionary phases
— without however, telling us the proper sequences. To determine
these sequences of development we need the *historical* method, a
logical extension of the comparative one to examine the same society in different eras (1858: 474-85).

In other words, Comte sought research strategies that would capture the sweep of history, the societal progression from theological
to metaphysical to positivistic stages. In his statical studies he wanted
to describe normal activity that would reflect the cultural milieu of
each stage. In his dynamical studies he wanted to trace the change
between stages. By observing the order and progress in society as a
whole, he hoped to establish his law of three stages as indisputable
fact and to show how the last stage would lead to a better life for
mankind.

RESEARCH — THE PRACTICE

Comte employed his methodological strategies in his research,
observing the regularities and changes in social patterns, comparing
different societies and different eras, examining pathological exceptions. In *Positive Philosophy,* he built an encyclopedia of empirical

science. Writing in an era before the footnote became fashionable, he ignored that research nicety. However, he obviously consulted many sources in history, science, and philosophy for his detailed information on mathematics, astronomy, physics, chemistry, biology, and social life. And with the sources, he described evolution — more important, he detailed the evolution of positivism, the growth of a scientific world view that could support social consensus in a modern world. However, he tried to do more. He tried to document — really to prove — the law of three stages. Toward this end, he outlined two key ideal types, placed them in an evolutionary schema, and accounted for deviations from this sequence.

The ideal types described societies with opposite definitions of truth. In one type (the *theological stage* and its modified form, the *metaphysical stage*) people search for absolute knowledge by attempting to uncover the origin and purpose of all phenomena. In the other type (the *positive stage*) people simply observe relationships between phenomena and note regularities in these relations (1858: 26-28). Historically these types do not appear in pure form. Even the most theocentric backwater, Comte explained, has produced people who use observation in some areas of life, most often for devising a solution to technical problems. (A fire either lights or it does not, regardless of our theories about the original cause of fire.) And to date even the most foreward thinking, scientifically-minded societies revert to theological and metaphysical preconceptions for ideas of human good, social reform, and other abstract-moral ideals. In such mixed situations, we should categorize a society according to its most advanced social-moral ideas. Thus religion-ridden nineteenth-century Europe with all its technical sophistication was, in Comte's judgment, just entering the positive stage (1858:544-45).

Comte did not simply label societies. In his law of three stages, he attempted to explain social change. Certainly he highlighted one of the major differences between industrial cultures and primitive-tribal ones. But did he delineate a law of social change? Comte defined laws as "the constant relations existing between the phenomena observed" (1844:21) or the "invariant relations of succession and resemblance" (1858:26). What invariant or constant relations did he observe in social change? Mankind's ever unfolding, ever changing intellectual capacity presents continuous sequence of new facets, not a constant relationship between regular features. Even when he examined the conditions for this mental change, Comte recorded growth instead of delineating law. Among other things, he noticed that an increasing division of labor allows some men to pursue scientific knowledge while others rule or conduct public worship. This separation of functions frees the knowledge experts to pursue truth as they personally envision it instead of proclaiming a politically expedient truth or religiously orthodox truth. Thus the increase of occupational specialists produces an increase in positive thought (1825:607-17). But does a law define this? Here again, Comte has discussed this phenomenon as a unique, evolving sequence, not a constant relationship. Perhaps an inevitable relationship does exist between increasing division of labor and increasing positivism. However, instead of analyzing these two variables to delineate their relationship in various societies, Comte simply suggested that one factor preceded and encouraged the other in the development of Western civilzation.

It was Comte's holistic conceptualization that precluded systematic examination of social laws (as he defined them). He examined the total situation as a totality and, since there was only one developed industrial civilization, he could only observe one sequence. Comte's difficulty unraveling the relationship between institutions within the total society became even more acute when he specified an historical situation. For example, he noted that certain types of spiritual rule undergirded certain types of temporal power. Papal-theological ideology, to name one, supported the feudal-military establishment. Furthermore, such combinations occurred as a package. Thus if one feature changed, the other must too — in step with the evolving sequence (1820). Using such a framework, Comte could avoid all serious analysis of the relationship between the church and state. Whatever relationship existed, he simply labelled as part of the evolutionary stage, just as a biologist might define the appropriate nervous system for different species of primates. Occasionally, however, a sickness strikes the social organism — war, civil disorder, backward thinking. Comte dismissed the violent rebellions of the nineteenth-century as a temporary aberration — a necessary, unpleasant symptom of decay in the old system (1858: 637-38). Examining nineteenth-century thought, he attributed the continuing power of Catholicism (backward theological thinking) to the pernicious influence of the Jesuits (a social black plague, perhaps?) (1858:652-53). In other words, Comte divided social events into two categories: first, progressive events that illustrated the evolutionary sequence toward social consensus under positivism and second, social pathologies that temporarily disrupted healthy growth. With such categories, Comte could explain any social pattern without ever being wrong. No one could test his theory because — by definition — every event fit the three-stage pattern as either normal development or pathological disruption.

In sum, Comte used his data to illustrate his theory. It is true that he made empirical observations. He did study society as a positive scientist. However, he allowed his theoretical model, the evolutionary law of three stages, to limit his vision instead of guiding it. He explained away facts that would not fit his theory. And since Comte insisted that he must observe the whole society rather than the parts, he did not feel compelled to account for the mechanisms — the institutional changes and other social forces — behind civil disorder and other evolutionary setbacks.

CONCLUSION

When we consider Comte as a social scientist, we must rank him as a prophet, a man who pointed to interesting research problems he could not solve himself. Although Comte wrote about a series of important scientific issues (integrating theory with research, building simple models of reality, using historical experiments to research complex situations), he often ignored these principles in his research practice. Instead, he simply defined a total situation as part of an evolutionary stage and gathered facts to illustrate the stage milieu.

The holistic framework that marred Comte's analysis grew from his conceptualization of science and his hope for social reform. Using a biological analogy he preferred to focus on the totality of society rather than examine the relationship between parts. And, hoping to promote a humanistic religion of social betterment, he preferred to stress mankind's essential mental unity rather than highlight its colorful subcultural peculiarities. However, even though we may fault Comte for circular reasoning — for explanation by definition — we must admire the breadth of his vision. He created a science of order and progress in society.

Bibliography

Comte, Auguste
  1820 "A brief estimate of modern history." Pp. 499-526 in Comte *System of Positive Polity*. Vol. 4. London: 1877; reprinted, New York: Burt Franklin (1966).
Comte, Auguste, and Saint Simon, Henri
  1822 "Plan of the scientific operations necessary for reorganizing society." Pp. 527-89 in *Polity*. Vol. 4.
Comte, Auguste
  1825 "Philosophical consideration on the sciences and savants." Pp. 590-617 in *Polity*. Vol. 4.
  1844 *A Discourse on the Positive Spirit*. London: William Reeves (1903).
  1851 *System of Positive Polity*. Vol. 1. London: 1875; reprinted, New York: Burt Franklin (1966).
  1853 *System of Positive Polity*. Vol. 3. London: 1876; reprinted, New York: Burt Franklin (1966).
  1858 *The Positive Philosophy of Auguste Comte*. Freely translated and condensed by Harriet Martineau. New York: Calvin Blanchard. (Original, larger edition in French, written from 1830-1842.)
Secondary sources
Aron, Raymond
  1965 "Auguste Comte." Pp. 73-143 in *Main Currents in Sociological Thought: Volume I*. Garden City, N.Y.: Doubleday (1968).
Barnes, Harry Elmer
  1948 "The social and political philosophy of Auguste Comte: positivist utopia and the religion of humanity." Pp. 81-109 in Barnes (ed.), *An Introduction to the History of Sociology*. Chicago: University of Chicago Press (1965).
Coser, Lewis A.
  1971 "Auguste Comte, 1798-1857." Pp. 3-41 in *Masters of Sociological Thought*. New York: Harcourt Brace Jovanovich.
Hayek, F. A.
  1952 *The Counter Revolution of Science: Studies on the Abuse of Reason*. New York: Free Press of Glencoe (1955).
Marcuse, Herbert
  1954 *Reason and Revolution: Hegel and the Rise of Social Theory*. 2d ed. Boston: Beacon Press (1960).
Martindale, Don
  1960 *The Nature and Types of Sociological Theory*. Boston: Houghton Mifflin.
Simpson, George
  1969 "Introduction." Pp. 1-23 in Simpson (ed.), *Auguste Comte, Sire of Sociology*. New York: Thomas Y. Crowell.

Karl Marx

Karl Marx (1818-1883) never claimed to be a sociologist; he disapproved of Comte's positive philosophy and, no doubt, would have avoided someone else's intellectual camp in any event. Therefore, we may ask: Why study Marx here? Because he developed concepts, chose variables, and worked on methodological problems that still appear in sociological literature. Social class, ideology, alienation, bureaucracy, and institutional analysis are still important subject areas in sociology. Modern writers still use economic situations as independent variables. And Marx's research ideas — including his mistakes — point up problems that are still critical in the analysis of total societies. In the generation following his death, many major works (for example, *The Division of Labor in Society* by Durkheim and *The Protestant Ethic and the Spirit of Capitalism* by Weber) were written to examine some of the issues he raised. The debate with Marx continues to this day. We cannot ignore him.

We have some other compelling reasons to continue the dialogue with Marx. Like many nineteenth-century social thinkers, he tried to delineate the future of society and our place within it. Facing the malaise of social unrest, these men suggested rather different cures. If they considered revolution to be the social disease, they sought ways to calm unruly elements in society. If they considered unrest to be a mere symptom, they wrote about eliminating the causes of the disorder. As we have seen, Comte belonged to the former group: he pleaded for education so that all people could learn positive principles and thus achieve the mental unity (or consensus) necessary for a smooth-running, trouble-free social system. Marx saw things differently and predicted revolution. Individual lives, he told us, are shaped by the prevailing economic system of a society. Furthermore, capitalism is an economic system that forces many to live in misery while a few enjoy luxury. We should not adjust to such a system — we should revolt againt it! Since the revolution succeeded (although not on Marx's terms), we may wonder about the brand of social science that could predict such results.

Because Marx-the-Revolutionary did not write a systematic methodological treatise, we must reconstruct his sociology piecemeal. Hence, this chapter includes the results of a little exercise in imagination, a definition of sociology that Marx might accepted if he had considered the matter. More important, it outlines the precepts and the practices of a sophisticated empirical researcher, a scientist who actually executed the research program Comte could only recommend, a scientist who conducted experimental-comparative studies instead of just suggesting them. And, this chapter shows how even a good scientist could interpret evidence through the distorting haze of preconception.

INTELLECTUAL BACKGROUND

Marx drew inspiration from many sources. French Utopian writers (especially Saint-Simon) taught him the value of rational planning for social change. But, in Marx's view, they were a shade too rational, trying to impose a bold ideal plan instead of working within the historical context of a situation (1865:198). Classical English economists (like Adam Smith, John Locke, and David Ricardo) provided a much more earth-bound view, as the English usually do. Marx acquired many of his economic concepts from them along with a feel for the immediate situation, an ability to look at the existing facts. German idealists (among whom Hegel is the most conspicuous in Marx's thinking) provided him with a theory for explaining idealized categories of social change. According to Hegel, social change occurs through a dialectic of spiritual forces: a dominant spirit, a challenge, and a synthesis of ideals, which becomes, in its turn, the dominant spirit in a later dialectic. Marx's own methodology — part reaction, part extension — criticized the excesses inherent in these positions, "If the Englishman transforms men into hats, the German transforms hats into ideas" (1847: 103). He examined the interaction of living humans, observed these people acting within an economic context, analyzed ideas formed by these actors. Marx translated the Hegelian dialectic into three-step theory of change beginning first with an historical-economic situation, then with the growth of another situation negating the inherent problems of the first, and finally a new synthesis.

But, however interesting these theoretical refinements might be, they were not sufficient ends in themselves. Even more important to Marx was the *raison d'etre* of science: to plan for revolution, to shape its course. Considering the waves of lower-class rebellions beginning in the French Revolution and the human misery that had appeared with the Industrial Revolution, conservative thinkers had tried to reunify society by uncovering the secrets of social harmony or, at least, the secrets of social control. Marx took another position: he did not fear the rebellion of a social class, rather he deplored the misery in which members of that class were compelled to live. As a scholar, he would document this problem, analyze its causes, and suggest a cure. This is the mission of social science: "The philosophers have only *interpreted* the world, in various ways; the point, however, is to *change* it" (1845:30).

DEFINITION OF SOCIOLOGY

What changes did Marx have in mind? He wanted to free the masses from exploitation by their economic masters. We all need to eat, shelter our families, and satisfy other basic needs, he argued. In an industrial society, workers sell their time to earn money for these needs. As long as a handful of men control factories and other tools of production, they can also control the workers who desire the use of these tools for their livelihood (1848:46-53). As a theorist, Marx could argue that this relationship between men and the means of production enables the owner to exploit the worker. As an observant human being, he saw children dying in mines, women collapsing in sweatshops, men unable to support their families even by working a sixteen-hour day. Clearly there was room for change.

Marx attacked this problem by studying total society, which was, in his view, a combination of economic, political, and ideological structures; that is, a combination of institutionalized behavior patterns serving economic, political, and ideological needs. Always he started with economic needs as they pressured human beings and shaped their behavior. He believed that the interests of the dominant class group influence each member of society, shape his thinking, affect the way he worships his god, obeys his ruler, cares for his children. More to the point, a person's economic position limits his power and that, in turn, limits everything else. Perhaps for Marx sociology was the study of power structures as affected by economic circumstances — or more abstractly, the study of institutions within a society.

SUBJECT FOCUS

Scattered references reveal that institutional change forms the subject matter of Marx's sociology. To understand this approach, we should consider which institutions he studied, how he defined society, and where he predicted change in the system.

Marx concentrated on the economic and political structures. In his "Preface to *A Contribution to the Critique of Political Economy*" (1859:181), he listed the specific features he had investigated for his lifework on capitalist society: capital, landed property, wage labor, the state, foreign trade, the world market. However, he did more than simply describe these economic and political forms, he envisioned a system (half-conceived, never carefully written out) of society, interlocking institutions and their basic economic conditions all responding to laws. And always he looked for the possibility of revolutionary change.

In a letter attacking Proudhon, Marx defined society and stated that economic forces shaped the other social institutions. Throughout his discussion, men — interacting men — lived their lives, thinking and acting as both causes and results of their economic conditions:

> What is society, whatever its forms may be? The product of men's reciprocal action. Are men free to choose this or that form of society? By no means. Assume a particular state of development in the productive faculties of man and you will get a particular form of commerce and consumption, . . . and you will have a corresponding social constitution, a corresponding organization of the family, of orders or of classes, in a word, a corresponding civil society. Assume a particular civil society and you will get particular political conditions which are only the official expression of civil society. (1846b:670)

The German Ideology (1846a:6-16) elaborates this further. Here Marx argued that man, unlike other animals, has consciousness, a mental awareness produced by his economic activity, which, in turn, is conditioned by physical organization. These physical conditions, the working materials, form the base of social life. Then increased population (a factor later developed by Durkheim) leads to increased interaction, the divison of labor, new economic practices, and finally, new ideas appropriate for changed conditions.

Of course, the new ideas may later inspire people to tamper further with the economic situation. Now we have returned to Marx's main point — science in the service of the revolution. Made aware of our economic situation, we can work to improve it. We cannot control our social destiny completely, of course; we must wait until the time is right, until the old economic order has matured and is ready to die. When that time comes, however, we will discover new material conditions allowing us to change the other conditions of society (1859:183).

Thus Marx centered attention on progressive change in the institutions of society. We know the old productive forces are fully developed and, hence, ready for such change because that is the point at which we can successfully introduce such improvement. This circular argument lead to one of Marx's faults as an empirical researcher. Since he could explain change, or lack of it, by claiming economic conditions were or were not ready for revolution, he never needed to analyze his system for the effects of other (non-economic) variables.

SCIENCE — THE PLAN

Looking for Marx's ideas on social science and research, we can reconstruct his system from scattered references. He wrote many of his remarks as critiques of the current philosophical trends, attacks against the post-Hegelian idealists. He had no need to detail the day-to-day problems encountered by the empirical researcher. However, while defending his philosophical position, he did write about the nature of science, the operation of causal laws, and, in passing, a few research techniques.

Marx believed that social science was the search for causal laws of societal development. At the beginning of his greatest research effort, *Capital* (1867:19), he defined this emphasis by comparing his thought to Hegel's. For Hegel and his followers, the idea was an independent entity transcending the objective world. For Marx, the idea was "nothing else than the material world reflected by the human mind, and translated into forms of thought." Therefore, Marx argued, change appears first in the real world, not in man's mind. Abstract thought, divorced from historical-economic situations, is an absurd analytic tool in his scientific system. How can we analyze the composition of a house, he asked, if we ignore the materials, the shape, the size, all the individual features and consider only the abstract idea of "house" (1847:105-06)? Reasoning this way, he insisted that we must study societies as they exist in a specific situation and thereby develop our ideas from the situation. Beyond the detail of the historical moment, we must account for economic laws that govern social change. Before the revolution, capitalism must follow a sequence of events, a series of "tendencies working with iron necessity towards inevitable results. The country that is more developed industrially only shows, to the less developed, the image of its own future" (1867:8-9). The basic function of science is "working out *how* the law . . . operates" (1868:246).

Working out the law of social change, Marx considered a number of important research problems, among these the nature of causality in history and techniques of judging the important states of man's consciousness. To improve Hegel's idealistic theory of causality, Marx suggested that we examine different epochs and watch men as "both the authors and the actors of their own drama" (1847:115). Ideas and objective activity are both important, neither changing without the other. To judge causal priorities between them, we should first observe immediate reality instead of beginning with a search for some ancient starting point. For example, looking at the nineteenth-century worker, we can see him becoming poorer as he produces more. Tracing the sequence backward, we can understand the cause; alienation of labor power (1844:106-10). Through *alienation* humans lose an essential part of themselves, that is, something they have created becomes an alien power. When workers sell their labor time to enrich a capitalist entrepreneur, the labor then produces goods that the workmen themselves cannot afford to use. Worse, the very process of labor becomes alien, an external activity divorced from the personality of the worker. After positing this alienation of labor as a key factor in social situations, Marx faced the challenge of measuring the subjective aspects of this state with objective indices. Marx did not debate whether there could be a positive study of subjective states, he simply used behavior as an objective measure of intangible human conditions. We know that labor in a capitalistic system feels alienating and unsatisfactory, he explained, because "as soon as no physical or other compulsion exists, labor is shunned like the plague" (1844: 111).

In sum, Marx advocated research investigations of man's behavior in various economic-historical situations. He centered attention on objective economic conditions and their effects on behavior. Thus, even when he examined subjective states, he first determined how people in such a state would act and then observed objective behavior. In his studies, he tried to detail the laws of social change, of economic-social growth. Marx assumed that the laws exist. He never recommended testing hypotheses based on these laws but simply described them in operation without admitting that they did not always work. As we shall see in the next section, this outlook underlies both the strengths and weaknesses in Marx's empirical work.

RESEARCH — THE PRACTICE

Marx researched two general areas: social change in Western Europe and the capitalist system operating in England. Considering his works in topical order, we can appreciate why Marx-the-Social-Scientist lives on even though the Prophet has been proved wrong. Dealing with historical data, he outlined causes, effects, and, a much more subtle item, the special conditions modifying effects within total societies. Given this set of circumstances, he predicted, we will get that result; given economic needs exacerbated by misery in the capitalistic system, we can predict an uprising of the workers. The Prophet failed partly because he misinterpreted the data (which we, in the wisdom of hindsight can read more clearly) and partly because he believed in the revolution so firmly that he could not use his insights to modify his faith. Here we will consider his basic line of argument along with some biases that invalidated part of his analysis.

In his early work, Marx displayed a sure sense of the difference between antiquarian fact-gathering and social science. Historians have done both. Marx clearly preferred the latter approach. Even while detailing the minutiae of a unique event, he seemed to be asking himself two questions: Is this event part of the normal pattern? and What are the implications of this pattern? In *Manifesto of the Communist Party,* he compared early social movements — "movements of minorities" — with the growing proletariat movement — "the self-conscious, independent movement of the immense majority" (1848-45). Later he compared the bourgeoise meaning of freedom — "free trade, free selling and buying" — with the communist meaning of freedom from the economic restrictions imposed on the lower classes by this free trade system (1848-48). In the *Manifesto . . . ,* Marx outlined his broad vision. Four years later he wrote a detailed analysis of political change in France from 1848 to 1851. Once again he located a unique event within the general pattern of events. For example, he noticed how people make new history with old tradition: "Thus Luther donned the mask of the Apostle Paul, the Revolution of 1789 to 1814 draped itself alternately as the Roman republic and the Roman empire, and the Revolution of 1848 knew nothing better to do than to parody, now 1789, now the revolutionary traditions of 1793 to 1795" (1852:97). Marx also searched for the implications behind surface events. He observed that the new French Constitution (of 1852), guaranteed a host of liberties for each citizen as long as these did not interfere with public safety. But in the crunch, public safety meant "the safety of the bourgeoisie" (1852:107). He continued in similar fashion to detail the rule of Louis Bonaparte and analyze its implications about the relationship between peasants and workers, the place of the proletariat in a bourgeoise state, and the role of political parties in society (1852).

In *Capital,* Marx changed his data and his line of argument to provide a new perspective on his problem. Instead of analyzing recent political change in social-class terms, he produced a thorough description of the economic and social conditions of contemporary industrial England. Exiled in London, he gained admission to the British museum in 1852. For years he spent his days there reading everything connected with his interests — economic treatises, reports of Her Majesty's Inspector of Factories, newspaper stories. In the end, he detailed his interpretation of the capitalistic economic system and its effect on industrial wage-laborers.

It is his description of the workers' plight that interests us here. And it is just that: a detailed account of human misery, the sins of capitalism exposed. Capital becomes a social force only when the owner of a means of subsistence and production (Moneybags) meets a free laborer willing to sell his labor. Once the proletarian has *alienated* his labor power (used it as a sellable commodity) he is at the mercy of the capitalist (1867:167-76). The results: misery for the worker. The capitalist who buys labor power provides the working conditions that a laborer must accept. These conditions fascinated Marx. For example, he described the "working day" (1867: 231-302) in horrible detail: "death from simple overwork," head-lines from the story of Mary Anne Walkly, age 20, who died after working twenty-six and one-half hours during the "busy season"; according to the London *Morning Star* (June 23, 1863), she was one of "our white slaves, who are toiled into the grave, for the most part silently pine and die." At times Karl Marx sounds like Charles Dickens. In the third volume (1867-79:87-96), he handled similar material more systematically, comparing death rates for workers in certain industries with the death rate for the whole population.

Throughout *Capital* Marx made two statements: 1) this is how capitalism works economically and socially; and 2) the social results are so bad that there has to be social change. But did the change have to be a revolution of the proletariat? The total argument pro-vided by all of Marx's work points to violent revolution as the only answer. Actually, in the case of England, to take one example, gov-ernment regulation (based on information from the same materials Marx had read) eliminated the worst factory and mine abuses.

Examining the flaws in his research, we can uncover some clues about why his prediction missed the mark.

First, he sometimes defined terms to suit his analytical framework without fitting them to the data. In section I, the *Manifesto of the Communist Party* (1848:35-46) traces the growth of a unique class structure, a society with only "two great hostile camps. . . . two great classes directly facing each other: Bourgeoisie and Proletariat." Previous societies had contained more complicated arrangements, gradations of social rank. In his later discussion of English social classes in *Capital* (1867-79:884-86), Marx subdivided his owners and workers into numerous smaller categories (owners of mines, owners of forests, and the like) but he never analyzed the implications of this similarity between modern gradations in stratification and ones he noticed in feudal and ancient societies. Instead, he concentrated on two "great classes"; that is, those who owned the means of pro-duction and those who did not. Marx's general concept of *social class* — groups who share the same economic situation and, by virtue of that position, also share the same degree of power — highlights a dynamic force behind social change. But, we may want to find a better empirical definition of the powerful and powerless groups.

With his insistence on the importance of social class as a cause of revolutionary change in the direction of a proletarian victory, Marx also refused to handle three alternative possibilities: 1) that other groups, non-proletarians, might spearhead a real revolution; 2) that the revolution (if any) might be heading in the "wrong" direction; or 3) that there might be no revolution.

Throughout his work, he described and interpreted political change in terms of a class-based power struggle — in nineteenth-century Europe, a struggle between wage laborers and capitalists. All social groups were either allied with the oppressed class or enemies of the revolution. In his era, when a non-proletarian group rebelled, the members did so for "reactionary" reasons, specifically to secure their own position instead of forwarding the true cause. For example, the "social scum" who occasionally fought with the workers and occasionally against them were bribed tools of reactionary forces (1848:44). And what groups constituted the "social scum"? One suspects: wage laborers who sometimes joined the wrong side and therefore were not true proletarians.

In spite of evidence to the contrary, Marx anticipated the ultimate victory of the proletariat. It is true that revolutions tend to produce a stronger centralized government, usually srtengthened to repress the unruly lower classes (1852:171). And normally a scientist predicts future events on the basis of past ones. Marx, however, offered another explanation: each successive political *coup* drove more men into the proletarian camp, thus creating a counter-revolutionary force that would win in the end (1848:43; 1850:33). But, as Engels explained later when predicted events did not occur: "History has proved us . . . wrong" because "time was not, by a long way, ripe for the elimination of capitalist production" (1895:656). To the end, Marx and his disciple did not admit that the revolution might not come at all; instead they assured us that the time was not yet "ripe."

In effect Marx was describing something that he knew must happen a certain way. When evidence proved him wrong, he simply referred to the setback as another phrase preceding the inevitable revolution. He maintained this conviction even though both his theory and his research contained clues about other possibilities.

In other words, Marx persistently ignored the importance of variables that could explain why the hoped-for conflict did not occur to change society. He recognized "national class interest" (1848:39), for example, but failed to incorporate nationalism into his system. Nation states, he told us, would not achieve independence until each country solved the problem of its proletariat: "The Hungarian shall not be free, nor the Pole, nor the Italian, as long as the worker remains a slave!" (1850:59) Why did Marx predict that class would prove more important than nationalism? He did not justify his position, he stated it. Indeed, in a later statement he contradicted this rhetorical claim. In *The Eighteenth Brumarie of Louis Bonaparte,* he acknowledged the weight of a cultural tradition that constrains men to hide behind the "names, battle cries and customs" of the past while they are trying to create new ways for the present (1852: 97). But he did not analyze this cultural tradition as a force that might, just possibly, prevent economic revolution or redirect its ultimate course. In similar fashion he explained the lack of *class consciousness* among isolated peasants, who could not interact enough to form a "community" in spite of their common class interests (1852:170-72) but he did not see how the lack of a common cultural community could prevent English mineworkers from allying themselves with Parisian seamstresses.

Marx could have improved his theory by placing more stress on one of his own key variables — the interaction of living men. If peasants from the same French provinces could not interact enough to form a community, neither could factory workers living 300 miles apart, speaking different languages, holding different traditions. While the British M.P. and the cockney laborer may not have shared social-class concerns, they did pass each other on the street; and eventually they began to vote in the same elections, and value the governmental system they both shared. In the end, they revolutionized their society by passing laws within their common-law tradition. They did not need class war.

CONCLUSION

Marx practiced social science as he defined it and left a legacy of research reflecting the weaknesses and strengths of his outlook. For him, science was not destined simply to interpret the world, but rather to change it. Holding a theory of revolutionary change (reinforced by data documenting the need for some change), Marx was loath to consider variables that might produce the social rearrangements without violent class revolt. So he insisted on using the means of production as his only important independent variable, discounting cultural tradition, nationalism, and other similar forces he had noticed in society. Further, he confused the moral need for change with an empirical one. Is there a natural law against injustice?

In spite of his faults, however, Marx produced valuable theoretical and empirical work. In an age when many were looking for cosmic laws of evolution, stages in human development, and other descriptive labels for forms of societal development, he pioneered a more fruitful way to conceptualize change in a total society. While others searched for the basis of stability in society (fearful, they hoped to prevent the French Revolution of the future), Marx pointed to the conflicts that inspire such upheavals. Looking at the interest groups within a social system, he could discern who really wanted change. Comte advised us to educate the lower classes: truth will make them peaceful. Marx suggested another possibility — the disconcerting idea that truth may inspire revolt. Made aware of their misery, the lower classes will seize their share from the upper classes. By isolating these interest groups conceptually, Marx created a powerful analytic tool. Using his framework we can observe the relationships between these groups, note the sources of strain, and anticipate the inevitable social change. With an additional century of data, we can improve on Marx's hypothesis by describing the conditions (nationalism, government planning, and other intervening variables) that affect the course of such change.

Bibliography

Marx, Karl
  1844 *Economic and Philosophic Manuscripts of 1844.* New York: International Publishers (1964).
  1845 "Theses on Feuerbach." Pp. 28-30 in *Karl Marx and Frederick Engels: Selected Works.* New York: International Publishers, 1968.
Marx, Karl and Engels, Frederick
  1846a *The German Ideology, parts I and III.* New York: International Publishers (1960).
Marx, Karl
  1846b "Marx to P. V. Annenkov in Paris." Pp. 669-80 in *Karl Marx* ... Also Pp. 179-93 in *The Poverty.* . . .
  1847 *The Poverty of Philosophy.* New York: International Publishers (1963).

Marx, Karl, and Engels, Frederick
   1848 *Manifesto of the Communist Party.* Pp. 31-63 in *Karl Marx* . . . .
Marx, Karl
   1850 *The Class Struggles in France* (1848-1850). New York: International
      Publishers (1964).
   1852 *The Eighteenth Brumaire of Louis Bonaparte.* Pp. 97-180 in *Karl
      Marx* . . . .
   1859 "Preface to *A Contribution to the Critique of Political Economy.*"
      Pp. 181-85 in *Karl Marx* . . . .
   1865 "Marx to J. B. Schweitzer." Pp. 194-202 in *Poverty.* . . .
   1867 *Capital: A Critique of Political Economy.* Vol. I. New York:
      International Publishers (1967).
   1867-79 *Capital.* Vol. 3. New York: International Publishers (1967).
   1868 "Marx to Kugelmann." Pp. 245-48 in *Selected Correspondence.* . . .
Engels, Frederick
   1895 "Introduction to Karl Marx's work *The Class Struggles in France,
      1848-1850.*" Pp. 651-68 in *Karl Marx.* . . . Also Pp. 9-13 in *The
      Class Struggles.* . . .
Secondary sources
Aron, Raymond
   1965 "Karl Marx." Pp. 145-236 in *Main Currents of Sociological Thought:
      Volume I.* Garden City, N.Y.: Doubleday and Company (1968).
Coser, Lewis A.
   1971 "Karl Marx, 1818-1883." Pp. 43-87 in *Masters of Sociological
      Thought.* New York: Harcourt Brace Jovanovich.
Marcuse, Herbert
   1954 *Reason and Revolution: Hegel and the Rise of Social Theory.*
      2d ed. Boston: Beacon Press (1960).
Mills, C. Wright
   1962 *The Marxists.* New York: Dell.
Zeitlin, Irving M.
   1968 *Ideology and the Development of Sociological Theory.*
      Englewood Cliffs, N.J.: Prentice-Hall.

Herbert Spencer

Auguste Comte served as the founding father of sociology; Karl Marx originated a line of analysis that still intrigues social theorists; but it was Herbert Spencer (1820-1903) who provided the catalyst to transform a new approach to social thought into a popular academic discipline. Some commentators later judged that Spencer's work as a promoter of sociology was the limit of his contribution. More recently, however, sociologists have, once again, come to appreciate the key insights developed by this theoretical pioneer.

The real heart of Spencer's theory lies in his concepts of *evolution* and society as a *super-organic evolutionary entity*. Nowadays we dismiss the notions that society somehow grows toward a preordained end or that it has the same needs as a giant animal. However, these caricatures deny justice to Spencer's more subtle ideas. He did not simply label social change as part of a natural evolutionary process. Like Comte and Marx he examined a particular mechanism of change. As Comte had outlined the forms of social consensus and Marx had analyzed economic-power structures, Spencer highlighted the increasing heterogeneity of social life. Borrowing and expanding ideas from Malthus, he suggested that increasing population leads to the necessity for more efficient use of resources, the differentiation of social functions, and, finally, a more complex and (by definition) more advanced society. Further, society, like any living entity, contains structures that perform functions for the whole. Certain behavior patterns promote certain areas of societal welfare. As society evolves, these patterns become more specialized, more complex, more advanced. Later Durkheim developed and refined this idea about functional complexity in his explanation of the division of labor as the key structural feature distinguishing types of societies. And others, sociologists like Simmel, elaborated on the relationship between structures and functions within all manner of social groups.

55

In the United States Spencer spurred the growth of academic sociology. Sumner used Spencer's *The Study of Sociology* as a text for the first American sociology course. Cooley discovered the field when he read this book. And many others who read Spencer's works or heard his American lecture series in 1882 also acquired an enthusiasm for the new science. Indeed, during the American era of big business and little government (more or less), Spencer's gospel of the noninterfering government touched something responsive in many American minds. But, just a little later, Americans attacked Spencer for his social-darwinist philosophy and his use of empirical evidence to "prove" misconceptions. By that time, however, sociology had grown to an established — if not altogether respectable — academic discipline in the country where it eventually flourished into a scientific big business.

Unfortunately while berating Spencer for failure to accomplish his research goals, sociologists have often forgotten that large-scale failure presupposes ambitious aims. Spencer had hoped to build data banks of information for comparative studies of total societies. He failed to complete his program because, like Comte, he focused on society as a consistently coherent whole and, therefore, missed the important relationships that did not fit the predicted mold. Nonetheless, we can consult Spencer to learn some of the problems that confront any scientist who attempts to grasp the entire social panorama in a single vision.

INTELLECTUAL BACKGROUND

Several nineteenth-century intellectual currents affected Spencer's sociological work: the belief in evolutionary change toward progress, the political-economic doctrine of *laissez-faire, the positive-inductive* approach to research, and the use of biological models in social science.

As we have seen with Comte, the notion of evolutionary progress (popularized during the Enlightenment) had become a standard intellectual fad by the mid-nineteenth century. This stress on evolution provided Spencer with a stand on another scientific issue of his day: knowledge of society could be useful in social reform — useful indirectly:

. . . if there does exist an order among those structural and functional changes which societies pass through, knowledge of that order can scarcely fail to affect our judgments as to what is progressive and what retrograde — what is desirable, what is practicable, what is Utopian. (1873b:64)

For Spencer progress simply occurs; it is our duty to learn what should happen in the natural course of events and then to stay out of the way, to let progressive practices supplant the "retrograde" and "Utopian" ones. In one sense, this opinion resembles that held by Comte: both men believed that sociology could provide a description of natural progress. But, Comte expected men to use this knowledge to encourage progress along natural lines, and Spencer hoped man would learn how to avoid interferring with normal events. Under the label "social darwinism," this *laissez-faire* doctrine applied to social issues as well as economic ones and became very popular in England and the United States during Spencer's heyday.

Like many of his contemporaries, Spencer recognized the value of inductive thought. He even claimed that most of his ideas were built directly from empirical observations. In fact, he dismissed most nineteenth-century beliefs (other than his own) as a set of obvious errors, useful only when someone like himself would criticize these mistakes and point out the real truth (1899).

An examination of his work, however, shows that Spencer assimilated key ideas current among his contemporaries. Many held biology to be the model science: a science that classifies, relates parts to the whole, traces evolutionary change. Despite his protests to the contrary, Spencer did borrow ideas from other contemporary thinkers to construct a deductive framework based on the biological model for his description of universal evolution. He was not, however, directly inspired by the most famous biologist of his era, Charles Darwin. Although Spencer admired the other man's work, he published many of his main ideas well before *The Origin of Species* appeared in 1859. In fact, both men borrowed from Malthus and posited population pressures as the principle causal mechanism behind species change. But it was Spencer who also applied this idea to societal development.

DEFINITION OF SOCIOLOGY

Spencer did not define sociology; rather he hinted at a definition when he described *inorganic, organic,* and *superorganic evolution* (1888b:3-7). Evolution forms the heart of Spencer's science. His attempt to summarize all aspects of evolution under the rubrics of a single "law" forms the basis of his theory. Naturally enough, he conceptualized sociology as the study of how this law operates in human society. He suggested that inorganic evolution controls changes in the stars, the earth, and other lifeless things. Organic evolution shapes the development of vegetable, animal, and even mental states. Super-organic evolution delimits the formation of more complex items "including all those processes and products which imply the coordinated actions of many individuals" (1888b:4). In other words, when potentially autonomous organisms band together to form a group, the group, in turn, possesses life and develops through a series of processes. Spencer elaborated his explanation of this thesis by describing the coordinated group action of ants, rooks, higher primates, and other social animals. His real interest, however, lay in examining more sophisticated evolving groups, that is, human groups:

> Having observed this much, we may henceforth restrict ourselves to that form of Super-organic Evolution which so immensely transcends all others in extent, in complication, in importance, as to make them relatively insignificant. I refer to the form of it which human societies exhibit in their growths, structures, functions, products. To the phenomena comprised in these, and grouped under the general title of Sociology, we now pass. (1888b:7)

In sum, Spencer's sociology is the study of super-organic evolution or the study of evolution in society — its forms, its processes, its correlates.

SUBJECT FOCUS

To study societal evolution, Spencer suggested that we examine changing facets of group life. Specifically, we should look for societies in different stages of evolution, gather comparative data and, finally, reach an inductive grasp of the universal relations and sequences of social growth (1888b:424-36). But, since evolution is neither automatic nor unilinear, we must learn how to recognize it, to tell progress from mere change, to know just where evidence of such progress lies.

A simple increase in human happiness does not constitute progress. Progress does increase happiness, but judging progress from this emotional state is like judging the political history of Chicago by looking only at the Daley Machine. Happiness is a result, not a teleological cause. Progress, rather, consists in a change in structure from homogeneous to heterogeneous form: the seed becomes a tree, the ovum an animal, the simple tribe a complex civilization (1857: 9-10). So, as sociologists who chart the evolutionary progress of society, we observe the development of a more and more complex social structure.

What data about society should we be collecting? Spencer appears to be recommending field studies appropriate to anthropology. Indeed, the study of social "growths, structures, functions, products," could be defined as the descriptive study of culture, although Spencer did not use that term or appreciate the great variety of cultural forms possible in societies with the same degree of complexity. Actually, his concept of data pertinent to any object — inorganic, organic, or super-organic — included internal forces within the object and external forces in the environment. Consequently, to study a super-organic aggregate of men, sociologists should consider the traits of the individual units (like intelligence, stability, strength); the characteristics of the group (size, density, division of labor); the group products (language, technology, knowledge); and the external environment (for example, climate and the activites of other societies) (1888b:8-15).

In other words, Spencer envisioned sociology as a study of change in culture and society. But he also considered it a science and it is this aspect of his definition that we will examine in the next section.

SCIENCE — THE PLAN

Spencer, philosopher as well as research scientist, speculated about the essence of science and — like Comte before him — wrote about many basic philosophy-of-science problems: the forms of scientific knowledge, the problem of simplifying reality for scientific understanding, and the relationships between theory and research.

According to Spencer, science evolves from ordinary knowledge. Like everyday knowledge, science organizes ideas, makes predictions, and enjoys varied degrees of accuracy in these predictions. Hence science and ordinary knowledge are, at root, the same (1854:1-4). To take a modern example, a teen-age boy may know the various automobile models on the market and can often predict how engineers in Detroit will modify next year's model; similarly a seismologist can map the San Andreas fault and predict the occurrence of an earthquake in California. What, then, is special about science? It requires more reasoning. Scientific knowledge includes an understanding of complex sequences, of behind-the-scene events, of actions that can be known only through reason, not through direct observation. For instance, drawing on his memory of earlier observations, a country man can describe and identify a bird whistling behind a hedge. Reasoning beyond mere observation to something he will never see, an astronomer can trace the path of planets passing behind the sun. Spencer wrote, "In brief, regarded from this point of view, science may be called *an extension of the perceptions by means of reasoning*" (1854:3). To return to our modern example, the car buff knows that the Ford engineers will modify this year's model to design the "new" version for next year, but the seismologist must estimate pressures of the earth and the strength of the fault before he can predict if another quake will occur.

Spencer divided this reasoned scientific knowledge into categories based on different forms of reasoning. All science abstract information, make general statements. But some center on abstract forms and others locate common patterns in concrete situations. The truly abstract sciences, like logic and mathematics, study forms without reference to particular objects. As we have already seen, syllogisms and equations retain their structure regardless of where they appear or what objects they purport to describe. In contrast, concrete sciences like astronomy and biology consider the phenomena themselves. In these studies, we must observe sensible reality; if a building is square, labeling it a "pentagon" does not change its shape (1864:6-8).

The preceding comments suggest a basic problem in science, especially in the concrete studies that generalize from specific situations. As Spencer correctly observed, scientists can only provide laws about the normal course of events; they cannot predict individual actions or events because they cannot collect enough data to cover all aspects of a specific situation. Elaborating on this problem, he compared biography to anthropology, history to sociology. Both biography and history can detail the nuances — often quite unimportant — of Charles I's relationship with Parliament without generalizing about the type of society that produces a strong representative assembly. Anthropology and sociology provide abstract predictions based on general laws but cannot consider the exceptional problems of each situation (1873b:43-64). In other words, scientists uncover abstract, general knowledge about types of situations. They map the San Andreas fault, explain why such geological conditions occur, but do not detail the damage done by each quake. In effect, scientists create artificial theoretical models of the world when they omit some variables in order to explain types of circumstances instead of just specific events. Spencer did not fully explore the implications of this idea, however, probably because he assumed that his holistic framework solved the choice-of-variables problem.

Sociology, he noted, studies "a complete plexus of antecedents and a complete plexus of consequents" that occur in a total social situation (1864:18-19). Some sciences — mechanics, physics, chemistry, and the like — artificially isolate elements and trace the causal links between them. Other sciences, however, examine objects that cannot be fairly analyzed in such a fashion. Society is such an object (1864:6). Further, if we are to conceptualize society as a whole, we need a framework. Considering the arrangement of structures within society, the ways in which component parts serve the whole, we may examine the patterns and purposes in society by making an analogy between them and the structures and functions of a living body (1876:134-41). Although Spencer did not adopt the big-animal analogy *in toto,* he did insist that society is a life-like coherent unity, that parts of this unity — however varied and divergent — should be studied as part of this whole, and, finally, that aspects of society which do not illuminate the normal structures and functions are not relevant to sociology (1861:86-89). In other words, sociologists view the totality of behavior and consequences that make up the action in a social group. Whatever data illuminate this totality — religious rites, laws, incest taboos — are relevant. Other data are not.

Without more specific guidelines, unfortunately, this reasoning can lead us to all manner of falsehoods. We observe certain types of data because the analogy tells us that specific facts are "relevant." Then we judge the relevance of our observations by whether they fit the analogy. In short, we can illustrate any thesis by choosing examples that fit and by discarding the anomolies. Spencer recognized the theory-research dilemma behind this problem: if we form theoretical preconceptions before we observe, he said, then we are "liable to see things not quite as they are, but as we think them"; but, if we observe without preconceptions, "we are liable to pass over much that we ought to see" (1853:166-67). Clearly we must form the right "preconceptions." Spencer stressed the inductive side of this inductive-deductive process. He insisted that we should build theoretical ideas after observing the real world (1888a:375-78). Induction, in other words, must preceed deduction. *Inductive research,* he stated, requires us to begin without assumptions, to collect numerous cases, to perceive similarities in some cases, to test the suggested possibilities in other cases (using the "method of difference" and "other tests"), and finally to accept the laws that survive these tests. Only after establishing laws through induction, can we deduce logical consequences and accept these as true (1888b: 818). Of course, this process still leaves us with the problem of deciding what areas to observe in the first place.

Spencer chose to begin with social change in society. Then working inductively (a *modis operandi* which, all his life, Spencer insisted was *the* principle research strategy), he noticed that society, like other complex unities, generally evolved in a consistent pattern. The uniform became differentiated; the simple, compound; the uncoordinated, integrated (1904:71). Society, he concluded, can be judged against this universal pattern. Once we recognize the pattern, we need simply observe processes and assess them against this norm.

The flaw in this approach lies in Spencer's strategy of combining an evolutionary framework and a holistic vision of society with the practice of rejecting "irrelevant" data. Once Spencer had decided (by whatever method) how society must evolve, he naturally could proceed to select "relevant" data illustrating that growth. Further, assuming that he must study society only in its totality, he could explain any observation by defining it as part of the whole. On the same basis, Spencer could reject "irrelevant" indicators of regression and counter trends that disturb the relationships within this whole.

RESEARCH — THE PRACTICE

Spencer's research reveals the strengths and weaknesses of work based on thorough, systematic observation marred by the conceptual problems we have just considered. To appreciate his strengths, we must consider his encylopedic approach to fact-gathering, his exposition of societal types, his insight into institutional functions. To understand the weaknesses, we must consider the remaining, untravelled steps that Spencer could have taken to develop his theory.

Certainly data-collecting was one of his research strengths. While planning *The Principles of Sociology,* Spencer employed three other men to collect data about uncivilized societies, extinct or dying civilizations, and flourishing civilizations. These men extracted information from a prodigious variety of written sources — ranging from Admiral Cook's *Voyages toward the South Pole* to J. S. Mills's *A System of Logic* and E. A. Abbott's *Shakesperian Grammar* — on literature, law, custom, and a host of other topics. Spencer himself arranged some of the data in eight volumes of *Descriptive Sociology* (published between 1873 and 1881) before he died; afterwards his admirers published the rest. In this work he created an organized data bank with as much information as he could compile — eye color, prevailing emotional temperament, tattooing practices, use of currency, and so on. He referred to his data as "facts without hypotheses" and hoped that *Descriptive Sociology* would provide information for many social researchers (1873a:iii). It was from these facts, not from the theories of other social thinkers, that Spencer argued his theses about social structures, functions, and change.

Spencer used this data to detail two kinds of evolutionary processes: a process of differentiation and a process of coordinated adjustment to the external environment.

To explain the process of differentiation, he compared society to a developing animal. Some societies remain simple in structure like a one-celled animal; others, like the higher primates, have developed from an undifferentiated mass to a complex coordinated whole (1885-6:9-13). As the component units increase in number, the density and the need for coordination expand apace. Using his *Descriptive Sociology* data, Spencer catalogued a large number of societies ranging from the Homeric Greeks to the modern Bedouins. He documented trends of increasing complexity: the growth of political hierarchies, the separation of religious and political establishments, the growth of industry. Although the details of Spencer's classifications need not concern us, we should remember his key points: (a) in general, societies become more complex with age; (b) societies with a similar degree of complexity tend to resemble each other structurally; and (c) there seems to be some order to the increasing complexity.

In explaining the forces of adjustment, Spencer examined relations between a society, its external environment and — as a correlate — the basis of cooperation within the society. On the basis of these relations, he posited two main types of society, militant and industrial. These types were not exhaustive categories; in addition, Spencer predicted a future type, a society based neither on military strength nor on material aggrandizement. At present, however, societies tend to fluctuate between the militant and the industrial. The *militant* type, often a response to threats from war-mongering neighbors, exacts close cooperation from citizens organized under a strong political rule. Other institutions reinforce the political-military regime: religion stresses enmity; industry serves as a commissariat; families train disciplined children. In the *industrial* society, a less centralized government encourages private enterprise, personal religious beliefs, independence rather than discipline. However, given the existence of peaceful simple societies and warlike complex ones, we cannot argue that industrial cooperation is replacing military force. Indeed, military conquest is often required to organize a society for future industrial growth. Although there may be — let us hope — a long-term trend, first toward industrial society, then toward a complex, peaceful, non-materialistic society, we are not progressing there in straight-forward fashion (1885-6:48-62).

Throughout his work, Spencer relied on the example of biological growth as a standard against which he measured progress in society. To mention one minor illustration, in his *First Principles,* he discussed the evolution of language (a social product) from simple to complex forms. As language develops, it acquires more and more complicated tenses, new parts of speech, and other nuances. English he concluded, is the superior language in this respect (1888a:347). In truth, the sequence often leads the other way. English may be more complicated than the speech used by Australian aborigines, but is a relatively simple language compared to classical Latin which was a younger language (at the time its form was frozen).

Modern Mandarin, however, is a much older language but it employs simple sentence construction with fewer parts of speech. In sum, Spencer failed to account for those backward movements that might disturb his evolutionary sequence. The simple assumption that a more complex social product is *ipso facto* a more progressive one is inadequate. On the broader societal level Spencer searched for types of societies but neglected to trace the growth processes of any single group (as Marx had already done, for example). Given his nineteenth-century biological framework, such studies would be inappropriate — the personal history of a plant, after all, is quite unimportant. However, we may argue, conditions do affect social change. Detailing the evolutionary processes of a single group might have forced Spencer to reevaluate his ideas in order to explain the stubborn facts that simply would not fit his model. As they stand, his types have often been illustrated by facts about the same society during different periods of development and different societies during the same time period, a practice similar to illustrating adult male muscle development by examining a child and a man or, alternatively, examining a man and a woman of the same age.

Nevertheless, despite his desire to explain an immense whole by citing disconnected details existing in the parts, Spencer noted many important relationships between major sectors of society. He observed, among other things, that the same social structure can serve different functions: one at the beginning, another later on in its development (1897:3). For example, priests first appear in a society to conduct worship; later they use their religious authority to regulate broader areas of conduct (1897:152-55). This idea — that the same activity may serve various social purposes — reappears in the work of Simmel, Durkheim, and several other sociologists. Spencer also observed that the position of women tends to improve when they begin to pursue "male" occupations (1897:342-46) — certainly a pregnant insight about caste and class structures. Spencer's work contains numerous such low-level hypotheses, many only tenuously related to his laws of evolution, but valuable nonetheless.

Pursuing his functional line of analysis, especially in historical studies, Spencer could have strengthened his research. Instead of assuming that certain institutional patterns accompanied particular evolutionary types, he could have focused on the relationships between the institutions themselves, especially during times of social change. This line of research (later used by Talcott Parsons) would have forced him to deal with the anomolies, as well as the expected relationships, in a specific situation. For example, he often commented on sacrificial rites, noting particularly that they placate the war gods of a militant society (1897:142, 182). What, we may wonder, are the sacrificial rites of modern, irreligious, warring peoples?

Spencer's holistic approach and his desire to avoid concrete historical situations, created a sociology that overlooks such questions. He discovered societal types (whether inductively or deductively is at this point unimportant). Then, dipping into his data bank, he chose examples of the institutional forms characteristically found in various types of society. Among other things, he discussed law in a simple society with unstable "headship" and religion in an industrial society. But since he did not systematically examine the growth and inner workings of any one society, he could choose examples without regard for the way they fit within a given society at a particular time.

CONCLUSION

Spencer's definition of sociology perverted his research practice. He used empirical data to provide examples of his evolutionary law — and ignored some of his own scientific ideas about "the method of difference" and other tests that could examine separate variables. As a scientist, Spencer lacked one of the important insights developed by Marx. Marx had singled out one institution and examined its effects in different types of society; Spencer tried to examine and classify whole societies, to trace the evolution of social bodies without systematically comparing the effects of variations in one institution with variations in another.

Nevertheless, Spencer has left us several important statements about scientific technique: statements about inductive theory building, simplified models of reality, data banks, comparative studies, functional analysis, and other research tools. If Spencer had pursued some of his own scientific leads, he might have written a more complete sociology. We should remember, however, that sociology was only a sideline for this man. Thinking out the details of social science research would have distracted him from his more global concern, the descriptions of the cosmic evolutionary progress in all phenomena.

Bibliography

Spencer, Herbert

1853 "The valuation of evidence." Pp. 161-67 in *Essays: Scientific Political, and Speculative*. Vol. 2. London: Williams and Norgate, 1901

1854 "The genesis of science." Pp. 1-73 in *Essays*. . . . Vol. 2.

1857 "Progress: its law and cause." Pp. 8-62 in *Essays*. . . . Vol. 1.

1861 *Education*. London: Williams and Norgate. (Parts reprinted in J. D. Y. Peel, (ed.), *Herbert Spencer on Social Evolution*. Chicago: University of Chicago Press, 1972.)

1864 *The Classification of the Sciences: To Which Are Added Reasons for Disenting from the Philosophy of M. Comte*. New York: D. Appleton and Company.

1873a *Descriptive Sociology; or, Groups of Sociological Facts*. Vol. I. London: Williams and Norgate.

1873b *The Study of Sociology*. Ann Arbor: Ann Arbor Paperback (1961).

1876 *The Principles of Sociology*. 1st ed. London: Williams and Norgate. (Parts reprinted Peel, *Herbert Spencer*. . . .)

1885-6 *The Principles of Sociology*. 3rd ed. London: Williams and Norgate. (Parts reprinted in Robert L. Carneiro (ed.), *The Evolution of Society*. Chicago: University of Chicago Press, 1967.)

1888a *First Principles*. 4th ed. New York: D. Appleton and Company.

1888b *The Principles of Sociology*. 3rd ed. Vol. 1. New York: D. Appleton and Company.

1897 *The Principles of Sociology*. 3rd ed. Vol. 3. New York: D. Appleton and Company.

1899 "The filiation of ideas." Pp. 533-76 in David Duncan *The Life and Letters of Herbert Spencer*. London: Methuen and Company, 1908.

1904 *First Principles*. 6th ed. London: Williams and Norgate. (Parts reprinted in Peel, *Herbert Spencer*. . . .)

Secondary sources

Barnes, Harry Elmer

1948 "Herbert Spencer and the evolutionary defense of individualism." Pp. 110-37 in Barnes (ed.), *An Introduction to the History of Sociology*. Chicago: University of Chicago Press (1965).

Carneiro, Robert L.

1967 "Editor's introduction." Pp. ix-lvii in Carneiro (ed.), *The Evolution of Society*. Chicago: University of Chicago Press.

Coser, Lewis A.

1971 "Herbert Spencer, 1820-1903." Pp. 89-127 in *Masters of Sociological Thought*. New York: Harcourt Brace Jovanovich.

Parsons, Talcott
    1961 "Introduction." Pp. v-x in Herbert Spencer, *The Study of Sociology.*
        Ann Arbor, Mich.: University of Michigan Press.
Peel, J. D. Y.
    1971 *Herbert Spencer: The Evolution of a Sociologist.* New York: Basic
        Books.
    1972 "Introduction." Pp. vii-li in Peel (ed.), *Herbert Spencer on So-
        cial Evolution.* Chicago: University of Chicago Press.
Rummey, Jay
    1934 *Herbert Spencer's Sociology.* New York: Atherton Press.

Gabriel Tarde

Gabriel Tarde (1843-1904) developed his sociological perspective by focusing on the problem of how to apply scientific techniques in social studies. Comte, Marx, and Spencer had all considered this problem, but they placed top priority on researching a particular subject matter. Tarde, in contrast, began with the nature of science and then defined a subject matter suitable for scientific analysis. All science, he stated, studies repeated actions — continuous vibrations, common chemical reactions, hereditary patterns. To be scientific, sociology must study repetitious patterns in social life. Unlike chemicals, however, social beings act from interior motives growing out of subjective meanings. Therefore, Tarde concluded that the repetitious social acts would have to represent some personal orientation. He chose to study *imitation*, the behavior that occurs when one person deliberately copies the action of another and *inter-mental communication*, the interpersonal exchange of thought that prompts this imitation.

Tarde then designed a methodology to examine both the subjective and objective facets of imitation. In contrast to Comte and Spencer, who discussed entire societies, Tarde described societal life in terms of the individual actor. Instead of depicting a cultural **Geist**, he measured the personal motive. Once he had chosen this psychological level of analysis, he looked for instances of repetitious action and separate data that would reveal the motives behind this action. Marx, who used the group level of analysis to explain individual feelings, had observed historical situations and then argued that subjective states like alienation and class consciousness would arise in individuals because of their objective conditions. Tarde, in contrast, studied the individual by counting his actions and looking for direct clues about his motives.

In other words, Tarde recommended a distinctly different approach to social research, an approach that has not been heavily

69

travelled by other sociologists. Nevertheless his ideas on interaction have had a profound impact because they provide a plausible explanation for ideational change ranging from the spread of criminal fads to the growth of cultural values.

INTELLECTUAL BACKGROUND

There is nothing peculiarly original in Tarde's thought. His contribution stands, instead, on a synthesis of elements and on the thoroughness of his analysis. Like many of his contemporaries he tried to unify scientific explanation, to find an analogous feature of physical, biological, and social phenomenon. For Tarde, repetitions (and oppositions) provided the basis for this scientific unity. Building on the work of Augustin Cournot (who had written about repetitions as a proper subject matter for science and imitation as a form of repetition in social life), Tarde developed his theory of social life based on imitation: as the physicist records vibrations, as the biologist records hereditary traits, so the sociologist looks for frequent patterns of repeated interaction. Tarde also believed that the evolutionary mechanisms of the physical world had counterparts in society. Linking his ideas to Hegel's explanation of dialectical change (thesis, antithesis, synthesis), he formulated his theory of social change involving imitations, oppositions to them, and new imitations. Finally, as a trained statistician, he could use time-series analysis to trace this change as a continuous process instead of just observing two stable situations labeled "before" and "after." In combination these techniques and ideas enabled Tarde to produce his special brand of sociology.

DEFINITION OF SOCIOLOGY

Many nineteenth-century sociologists — Comte, Durkheim, and others — examined total societies, and often treated the person as a simple component of a large group. Tarde's conception reversed this focus to center on the individual as the creator of the group, and personal communication as the process through which the creation takes place:

> Collective psychology, *inter-mental* psychology, that is, sociology, is thus possible only because individual psychology, *intra-mental* psychology, includes elements which can be transmitted and com-

municated from one consciousness to others, elements which, despite the irreducible hiatus between individuals, are capable of uniting and joining together in order to form true social forces and quantities, currents of opinion or popular impulses, traditions or national customs. (1898b:95)

In other words, sociology is the study of inter-mental communication or, more precisely, the study of repetition in inter-mental communication.

SUBJECT FOCUS

When Tarde chose imitation as the object of his scientific research, he was looking for visible signs of this inter-mental activity. He defined *imitation* as "the mental impression from a distance by which one brain reflects to another its ideas, its wishes, even its ways of feeling" (1898b:94). First, two conscious active partners signal each other (1902:1-2). As a result, they tell each other how to act: they eat the same foods, say the same words, salute same flag — they produce the accepted behavior patterns for a society. Occasionally, however, some social maverick will change the pattern slightly: bite into a different kind of apple, add two words together, start a political sect — and produce an *innovation* (or a *discovery*) that can be imitated by other men (1895a:1-13). When others learn about this change (through inter-mental communication, of course), they believe in the innovation and desire it. Soon they eat the new apple, say the new word, follow the new leader — and start a new sequence of imitation (1895a: 144-46). In other words, imitation is a repeated pattern of behavior produced when one human being consciously acts to copy some new way or old custom he has learned from another person through inter-mental communication.

Tarde's stress on imitation locates the source of social change in the creative individual, the maverick inventor or discoverer. This conceptualization offers us an alternative to some other explanations of social cohesion and change current in Tarde's day. Imitation can replace heredity when we try to explain the similar behavior of men in families, nations, or ethnic groups, and thus break the "umbilical cord" tying sociology to "biology, her mother" (1893a: 619). Imitation also challenges the great-cause theory of evolutionary social change. The study of invention and subsequent imitation can explain the gradually changing patterns of language, religion, politics, industry, and art better than any general law about natural force, energy, or other overarching causes (1895a:1-3).

But what if we refuse to imitate? The inter-mental rapport that produces imitation can also produce other, far less friendly, activities, for example, the actions inspired by contradiction, contempt, or hatred. However, these also shape the social group: hatred can define the course of regular action just as surely as other beliefs and desires (1901b). Indeed, we even imitate the ways in which we refuse to imitate. In France, for example, between 1761 and 1789, citizens repudiated the traditional reverence for the king, the village seigneur, and their own fathers only to replace these models of decorum with writers, philosophers, and educators (1898b:98). Thus even when we refuse to follow traditional fashion, we simply substitute one form of imitation for another. So, in the end, imitation explains both cohesion and change in society.

SCIENCE — THE PLAN

As we have already noted, Tarde's whole conception of imitation grew from his ideas about science. He believed that science studies repetitions and imitation produces the repetitions in social life. Here we will consider other facets of Tarde's scientific framework: first his definition of science and scientific theory, then his strategy for researching a subjective phenomenon with objective data, and, finally, his hopes for elementary theory construction.

To begin, science is a "collection of facts that can be drawn upon to prove a given theory" (1895a:180). And it is also "the coordination of phenomena regarded from the side of their *repetitions*" (1898a:3). Science begins when man records interesting facts — the arresting, the extraordinary, the accidental — just as historians chronicle the exploits of Alexander the Great or the discovery of printing. However, the oddities of life only introduce some scientific facts. Real science considers the regular, not the remarkable — the repetitions and resemblances, not the unique objects (1895a:4-12). Finally, after scientists have accumulated a sufficient number of facts, they generalize from the repetitious empirical patterns, first tentatively, then (if accumulating facts continue to support their theories) more confidently:

Only, among these master thoughts, these hypotheses or *inventions* of science, there are certain ones which receive increasing confirmation from one another and from the continual accumulation of newly discovered facts which, in consequence, no longer merely restrict themselves to not contradicting one another, but reciprocally repeat and confirm one another, as if bearing witness together to the same law or to the same collective proposition. (1895a:177)

In other words, as scientists, we gather data, summarize it, explain it, and examine other data to see if it confirms our explanation.

Tarde suggested that we look for this data in two ways: 1) we can watch people acting inter-mentally; and 2) we can notice types of inter-mental action. We can examine groups of people — families, social classes, nations — or we can isolate the group actions — languages, laws, family structures. With either approach we are simply observing patterns of imitation (1904:137-39) .

But Tarde did not recommend mere head counts of people in regular activity. He did not suggest, for example, that we simply enumerate the number of alcoholics, the sale of racy novels, or the fluctuation of seasonal and national birth rates. Instead we must link these imitations to some form of social communications, to the beliefs and desires within some specific groups — alcoholism among French professionals, reading habits of curious teen-agers, sexual desire in different areas and seasons. Tarde may not have considered all relevant variables, particularly in that last example, but he did make an important point: we can use objective indicators — the actions of people — as indices of the desires and beliefs communicated within different social groups (1880:1897b:222-24) .

After defining repetitions acts as indicators of beliefs and desires, Tarde proceeded to count these imitations and trace their spread over time. Defining statistics, as "an enumeration of acts which are as much alike as possible" (1895a:102), he used this tool to estimmate the diffusion of invention through imitation. For example, he suggested, we can trace the growing use of the steam engine and its underlying cause, the growing desire for mechanical power, by noting the yearly output of coal mines in nineteenth-century France. Thus, with a time-series tally of repetitious acts, we can measure the birth and growth of human desire.

However, Tarde conceded, desires lie in human minds long before they appear in human acts. Hatred grows long before the battle against an enemy. In similar fashion, people may continue to act supporting values they no longer cherish. For this reason, statistical information on acts can only provide the basic facts that we must supplement with other materials, especially with archeological data (1895a:102-13). As Tarde defined it, this supplementary material comes from a broad variety of data sources; for example, songs, cartoons, or other lampoons against an enemy can be interpreted as signs of a growing hatred that precede actual hostilities.

Finally, after we have accumulated this data, we should use the facts to create simple explanations, specifically ideas about imitation and causality in certain types of social situations. How, we may ask, does hatred of an enemy spread — from peasants to noblemen? from newsroom to countryside? from soldier to civilian? Later these patterns can be verified or falsified through comparisons with similar situations in other societies. And, in the future, we may use these patterns as a basis for a general theory of social life (1898b:82-90).

In sum, sociology, like any science, is a collection of facts and tentative theories about some repetitious phenomena, in this instance repetitious imitation and changes in imitation. Statistical data record these acts as they appear in different groups and as they occur over time. Finally, statistical information can be combined with other data as a basis for low-level theory or simple generalizations about the spread of imitation.

RESEARCH — THE PRACTICE

Tarde's conception of inter-mental communication centered his attention on the process of change, specifically the process of communication change linking people in interaction sequences. Sometimes he delineated simple sequence like the spread of dueling fads. Sometimes he speculated about culture-wide ideational change like the growth of Christianity. But, throughout his work, he utilized statistical records and other data that would reveal both the chains of imitation and their underlying beliefs and desires. Here we will consider several examples of Tarde's work, first research about simple time changes in limited situations, then his analysis of more complex problems involving change in cultural values.

When Tarde systematically investigated a limited research problem — the progress of a specific imitation pattern — he collected and reviewed a mass of pertinent data instead of simply citing convenient historical examples. For instance, in *Les transformations du droit* (1893b), he compared different legal codes and noted that people with a common social inheritance will enact similar laws. To mention two examples, colonies frequently make land laws like those found in the mother country and neighborhood areas often create similar criminal codes. In another work, *Études pénales et sociales* (1900:31-53), Tarde used official statistics and historical accounts to record the incidence of dueling fatalities in France, Italy, and England. Then, after reviewing written material about the problem, he mentionel personal causes — like political quarrels, insults, and *raisons d'ordre intime* — that might prompt men to desire dueling. Finally he suggested that imitation fanned this desire among people who interacted with each other and, therefore, distance could prevent the spread of this dangerous fashion: "Lucky England! Because she is an island, she escapes continental epidemics" (1900:50-51).

Penal Philosophy (1903:322-47) illustrates Tarde's use of similar data to test one of his *non-logical laws of imitation*. With statistics, he argued that criminal fads (smoking, poaching, poisoning, and the like) spread from more prestigous areas to less prestigous ones — from the nobleman's court to the peasant's cottage, from Parisian sidewalks to the fields of Normandy. Here Tarde examined two variables, social prestige as it affects imitation. He mapped the current crime rates in France showing that they rose in the Seine Valley around Paris and fell in the rural outer regions. He cited historical examples — the drunkenness, debauchery, violence, and indolence of monks in a thirteenth-century Norman monastery — and compared the behavior of these prestigous people from the past to the life-style of less prestigous people in the present. However, we may wonder if the chain of imitation could spread from monk to peasant across six centuries. Perhaps both groups simply participated in a culture that was common to their area during both eras. We may also argue that Paris, France, like Newark, New Jersey, has urban crime problems that may never spread to rural areas.

In *La criminalité comparée* (1890), Tarde used falsification to support his hypotheses about imitation by eliminating other explanations like national culture and urban residence. Reviwing statistics from several European countries along with secondary accounts of prostitutes, members of the *maffia sicilienne,* and other criminal types, Tarde noted the spread of criminality within geographical areas and the sharp differences between them. He observed that crime rates varied from city to city and concluded that urban residence alone cannot explain criminality. He noticed the different levels and varieties of crime existing within the same country and argued that national culture does not produce a specific criminal mentality. After eliminating various other possibilities, he concluded that imitation was the only important cause: "every time we find a regularly ascending statistical series, we may be sure that it explains an imitative spread. . . . " (1890:175). We may wonder, of course, if Tarde may have missed a cause or two. It is impossible to falsify *all* alternatives. For that reason, this strategy works best in tandem with critical experiments — a combination methodology we will consider later when reviewing the research of Durkheim.

All of Tarde's work considered so far stresses the development of some simple imitation pattern over time. However, Tarde's interest extended well beyond the superficial fads of the moment. Assessing long-term trends, he sought a universal law of change, some consistent principle describing both social and physical movement. He hypothesized that social change, like all natural forms of change, occurred in dialectical form: the thesis (existing pattern of imitation) could be challenged by an antithesis (or opposition from a new invention) and resolved in a synthesis (or new imitation) (1895a:154-73). Straight from Hegel. In the first few chapters of *L'opposition universelle* (1897a), Tarde reviewed mathematical, physical, biological, and psychological "oppositions" to argue that new developments in these phenomenon were analogous to the patterns of social change. In *La logique sociale* (1895b), he analyzed change patterns as they affect social institutions like language use, worship, and artistic expression. These human behavior patterns, he stated, originate and spread in similar manner: "Like language, religion is an activity we imitate following an original leader. Not only is it clear that it spreads through habits in a family heritage, but it is just as certain that it begins in all lands by spreading in a contagious, invading fashion" (1895b:257). Dialectical religious change may occur when different faiths compete for men's allegiance. For example, in the third-century Roman world, when many men felt the need for a strong, uniform belief, they worshipped instead with a syncretic religion, a patchwork of local gods and local customs united under Roman auspices. Christianity, which combined some local practices with its more consistent theology and more universal appeal, served the social need for religious synthesis and spread through the old Roman empire (1895b:257-87).

We may not share Tarde's Hegelian vision. Nonetheless, we must agree that his concepts of communication and imitation help explain the spread of far-reaching cultural change. Applying this framework to his own era, Tarde explained why modern society experiences peculiarly rapid change. Swift impersonal communication has replaced the traditional word-of-mouth. In "The public and the crowd," he wrote that a "public" forms when large numbers of people who have common concerns but do not know each other personally nevertheless feel bound by "impersonal communications of sufficient frequency and regularity" (1901a:280). Tarde (who never saw television) named the press as the most potent means of "impersonal communication." With newspapers, writers could sit in a Paris office and spread their ideas across France. Anti-Semitic journalists, for example, could rouse anti-Semitism among readers who lived in areas where no one had any personal contact with Jews (1901a:277-86). Journalists could also exacerbate popular trends by unifying the ideas of people in different groups. In war times reporters could describe the anti-enemy hostility existing in widely separated regions throughout the country and explain these feelings as part of a national desire for war (1897a:388-91).

Tarde used his examples to argue that the press promotes intermental communication and thus serves as a source of imitation. He assumed causality: anti-Semitic journalists cause the flowering of anti-Semitic sentiments in remote areas; provocative writers unite public opinion for the cause of war. Other scientists might suggest that newswriters follow rather than lead, that they pander to public interests rather than create them. Perhaps we could speculate that anti-Semitism has festered in Europe since the Middle Ages. Perhaps a war is merely the temporary flare-up of hostilities that date back beyond memory. To support Tarde's hypotheses further, we need data on national opinions existing before and after the media publications. Nonetheless, Tarde has pointed out an important area of sociological interest — the relationship between popular media and public opinion.

In general Tarde researched the spread of ideas. He posited causal sequences — the dialectical development of new inventions and the non-logical laws of imitation among others — and traced these sequences over time. However, he did not often conduct rigourous comparisons of key groups that might deflect the course of imitation. Instead, he generally supported his ideas with more limited comparisons; comparisons of spreading imitation within geographical areas but not between them, to show that physical barriers like the English Channel prevent such spread; or comparisons of urban and rural crime rates to show that criminal fads start in the city. The comparisons he chose varied with the discussion, usually by pointing up the crucial variable under his consideration. If he wished to eliminate cultural variables as an explanation, Tarde would compare two countries. If he wished to highlight non-logical spread from urban to rural areas, he compared Paris with the surrounding countryside. However, he did not expand his comparisons to produce critical natural experiments. For example, a study comparing Paris and London, Normandy and Northumberland would help separate rural-urban differences from cultural ones. Tarde's theory did not demand such experiments. Since he had deliberately chosen to explain social life in terms of individual motives, he did not need to consider the peculiar properties of social groups, properties like the class distinctions between nobility and peasants and the values that separate Frenchmen from Italians. Instead he explained rural-urban differences in terms of prestige — rural people imitate the more prestigous urban ways. And he explained cultural differences in terms of opportunities for imitation — people from distant areas are not always exposed to the same innovations. In his theory, group properties as such were not important. So he compared groups only to eliminate them as causes, not to discern their effects on the course of imitation.

CONCLUSION

Tarde's research practice grew naturally from his ideas about science and the appropriate subject matter of sociology. Tarde believed that, as scientists, sociologists must study some repetitious phenomna, specifically the phenomena of imitation following inter-mental communication. When he used descriptive statistics, includ-ing some time-series analyses, he was trying to describe his subject by counting its observable indices, that is, the actual imitative be-havior. In other words, Tarde conducted his research the way he urged us to conduct ours. He built his entire sociology, theory and practice, around inter-mental communication.

However, most sociologists would prefer a broader range, one that encompasses social groups. By stressing inter-mental communication, Tarde ignored the traits that distinguish these groups. He chose this methodology deliberately because of his efforts to solve a problem that had also challenged Comte, Spencer, and every other theorist of their era. He was trying to define a limited number of variables, a manageable set of observations, something more understandable than "society as a whole." As we shall see in a later chapter, Durk-heim solved this problem in a way that is much closer to the main trend of modern sociology.

Even so, Tarde has left sociology an important message: norms and institutions are not elements in a universal evolutionary se-quence, nor the results of inexplicable human instincts, but rather they are the products of communication and interaction within social groups.

Bibliography

Tarde, Gabriel

1880 " 'Belief and desire:' excerpt from *Essais et mélanges sociologiques.*" Pp. 195-206 in Terry N. Clark (ed.), *Gabriel Tarde on Communica-tion and Social Influence.* Chicago: University of Chicago Press, 1969.

1890 *La criminalité comparée.* 8th ed. Paris: Librairie Felix Alcan (1924).

1893a "Revue général: questions sociales." *Revue philosophique* 35 (July): 618-38.

1893b *Les transformations du droit.* 8th ed. Paris: Felix Alcan (1922).

1894 " 'Sociology, social psychology, and sociologism': excerpt from *Etudes de psychologie sociale.*" Pp. 112-35 in *Gabriel Tarde. . . .*

1895a *Laws of Imitation.* 2d ed. Gloucester, Mass.: Peter Smith Press (1962).

1895b *La logique sociale.* Paris: Felix Alcan.

1897a *L'opposition universelle.* Paris: Felix Alcan.

1897b " 'Quantification and social indicators:' excerpt from *L'opposition universelle.*" Pp. 222-41 in *Gabriel Tarde.* . . .

1898a *Social Laws: An Outline of Sociology.* New York: MacMillan (1907).

1898b " 'Sociology': excerpt from *Etudes de psychologie sociale.*" Pp. 73-105 in *Gabriel Tarde.* . . .

1900 *Etudes pénales et sociales.* Paris: G. Masson & Cie.

1901a " 'The public and the crowd:' excerpt from *L'opinion et la foule.*" Pp. 277-94 in *Gabriel Tarde.* . . .

1901b "La réalité sociale." *Revue philosophique* 52 (November): 457-77.

1902 *Psychologie économique.* Vol. 1. Paris: Ancienne Libraire Germer Bailliere et Cie.

1903 *Penal Philosophy.* 4th ed. Boston: Little, Brown, and Co. (1912).

1904 "A debate with Emile Durkheim." Pp. 136-40 in *Gabriel Tarde.* . . .

Secondary sources

Barnes, Harry Elmer

1948 "The social and political theory of Gabriel Tarde." Pp. 471-80 in Barnes (ed.), *An Introduction to the History of Sociology.* Chicago: University of Chicago Press (1965).

Clark, Terry N.

1968 "Gabriel Tarde." In David L. Sills (ed.), *International Encyclopedia of the Social Sciences.* New York: MacMillan and Free Press.

1969 "Introduction." Pp. 1-69 in Clark (ed.), *Gabriel Tarde on Communication and Social Influence.* Chicago: University of Chicago Press.

Hughes, Everett C.

1961 "Tarde's *Psychologie economique*: an unknown classic by a forgotten sociologist." *The American Journal of Sociology* 66 (May): 553-59.

Georg Simmel

Georg Simmel's (1858-1918) legacy to sociology contains suggestions, hints, clues, approaches — not a great synthesis, not a cogent causal explanation but a series of illuminating insights. Comte and Spencer had synthesized facts about social life in their explanations of society-as-a-whole and in their accounts of the relationship between a major institution and society itself. Simmel, in contrast, analyzed small parts of the social system. Rather than describe the religious mentality in a positivistic society, he dissected religious activity into acts of worship. Then he observed worshipful acts in various situations to learn what objects besides a god elicit our worship. Some other nineteenth-century theorists had traced major causal sequences. Marx, for example, had noted how economic structures shape other institutions and Tarde had discussed how imitation spreads social actions. Simmel centered his analysis on the conditions that limit a given causal sequence. If a relationship exists between three people, or between three groups for that matter, there are a limited number of possible coalitions that can be formed — regardless of who is in those groups or what prompted the members to form an alliance. Pursuing this mode of analysis in depth, Simmel described types of social interaction both from the point of view of the actor and from the perspective of the group. He delimited the possible behavior patterns of social actors like the pauper, the coquette, and the subordinate. Within the same discussion framework, he listed social interaction possibilities inherent in poverty, in flirtation, in subordination under a law and under other people. Using modern parlance, we would say that he defined roles and processes — social structures: not static positions, not social anatomy, but types of interaction patterns with outer limits that contain ample room for change and variation.

Simmel's analysis grew from a methodological approach. Although theorists like Comte and Marx had designed scientific techniques to investigate important problems, Simmel built a methodology and then sought problems to analyze. In the end, he left a three-fold legacy for sociology. First, he presented a way of looking at social life by describing the typical behavior in a situation. (Max Weber later extended Simmel's typical forms into one of his analytic tools, the ideal type). Second, Simmel supplied numerous examples of what he saw — a parade of nobles, antagonists, flirts, city dwellers, workers, strangers, and many others. Finally, he suggested how men could play their typical parts in these social dramas and, somehow, remain free to vary the script.

INTELLECTUAL BACKGROUND

At the time Simmel began his sociological work, most Germans identified this discipline with the doctrines of Comte and Spencer and with their biological model of society. This approach requires us to view each society as a whole, to search for common patterns of societal development. The Germans preferred a different approach. Instead of viewing societies as organic realities with common traits, they stressed the unique cultural *Geist* of each nation. In this conceptualization, society itself had no distinct reality. It was simply a collection of individuals who shared ideals and thus shared the peculiar culture of their group. And each culture was a unique configuration that must be studied as a separate entity. Both of these approaches narrow the sociological vision. Using the Comte-Spencer models, we can outline the rise and fall of feudalism, but we cannot describe or examine obedience between a lord and his vassal in Normandy except by reference to an historical stage. Using the *Geist* approach, we can discuss the mystique of Frederick Barbarossa, but we cannot systematically compare the role of king in a unified England with the role of Holy Roman Emperor in a Germany where each great lord acted like a king.

Borrowing some ideas from the philosopher Kant, Simmel built an alternative to both camps. Analytically, Kant had separated the actual reality of nature (the content of life) from the categories we use for our understanding of it (the forms). When we view reality, we organize it: first we see a complex of color and we hear a cacophony of voices and then, imposing our forms on this confusion, we see a convention crowd and we hear a chant. Simmel argued that we can study society in somewhat the way Kant had studied nature — in terms of form and content. We can observe typical patterns of association (*forms*) that persist along with the individual psychological underpinnings (the *content*) of an event. Thus we observe something smaller than total society; we anlayze the relations among the parts in a society instead of grasping at the whole (1908b:337-41).

However, although Simmel rejected the biological-model view of society as a reality in itself, he did not reject all concepts from that school. Like Spencer, Simmel saw increasing differentiation, increasing heterogeneity in modern social relations. And like Spencer, he looked beyond structures to locate their functional consequences. Indeed, this is his key question: If a behavior pattern persists, what are the likely results? What functions does the behavior serve?

DEFINITION OF SOCIOLOGY

Given his Kantian framework, Simmel naturally chose social forms as the defining subject matter of his sociology (1917:3-25). He discarded the popular notion that sociology might be a general "science of society" or, worse, a new name for all studies of social life thrown into the same pot and labeled "sociology." In fact, for Simmel society itself is merely "the name for a number of individuals, connected by interaction" (1917:10). This concept located a subarea somewhere between the total-society view of the organicists and the individualism of the German idealists. Thus, Simmel suggests, if we are interested in the peculiar features of social life that exist throughout society, we should study typical patterns of human interaction — the forms that impose order over the content of human association. Indeed: "If, therefore, there is to be a science whose subject matter is society and nothing else, it must exclusively investigate these interactions, these kinds and forms of sociation" (1908d:315).

SUBJECT FOCUS

The meaning of "content" and "form" shift subtly between Kant's theory of knowledge and Simmel's science of society. Kant wrote about mental constructs (forms) we use to organize the sensual impressions (content) coming from the "real" world. Generally, when we recognize a friend, we do not need to count the hairs on his head. Simmel tells us that in society, we not only recognize the typical patterns of interaction, but these patterns actually exist and we have created them. Forms of action exist because we, as members of society, chose to act in a consistent fashion and, on occasion, chose to change the regular course of action (1908b:351-56).

These interaction patterns — Simmel called them *sociations* — form the living tissue of society. Major social organs — the language, religion, law, and other institutional patterns that would fascinate an organicist like Comte — could not exist without the network of minor sociation patterns (1917:9-10). People want to influence their fellows or to be influenced by them, to create the patterns of influence that develop into major social institutions (1917:40-41). Naturally, personal motives, that is, historical and psychological *content,* lie behind these patterns. But the sociation itself is the "mode of interaction among individuals through which, or in the shape of which, that content attains social reality" (1908d:314-15). In other words, individual concerns affect interaction. Religious needs, for example, inspire forms of worship and the desire for *lebensraum* motivates international conflict. However, although both content and form are part of interaction, Simmel stressed sociation — the *form* — as the major subject of his sociology.

Beyond that, Simmel divided the subject matter of the field into three problem areas; 1) the sociological study of historical life, or "general" sociology; 2) the study of societal forms, or "pure" ("formal") sociology; and 3) the study of epistemological and metaphysical aspects of society, or "philosophical" sociology. General sociology considers the group as an object of study and examines the historical life of a group to discern its common features recurring in diverse situations. General sociology might examine how a Christ and a Napoleon could both appear in Western society. The formal area (which Simmel considered the most sociological of the three) stresses the forms of sociation common to individuals in all groups. It analyzes the types of interaction apart from the individual interests and group history (or social content) underlying the action. Thus the types of coquetry may be examined apart from the sexual interests and ideals of etiquette producing flirtation. In similar fashion, the behavior of groups in conflict may be studied apart from the history of war. Finally, philosophical sociology examines the basis of social science and asks questions that go beyond the social facts: How can man know society? Is society the purpose of man's existence or the means through which man acquires his distinction? Is equality better than freedom? (1917:16-84)

Putting Simmel's ideas together, we may describe sociology as an abstract study of human interaction: its settings, its forms, and the philosophical questions surrounding this activity. More precisely, sociology is the study of how human beings influence each other through interaction (1908d:315).

SCIENCE — THE PLAN

To examine these patterns of influence, Simmel recommended a special method, a combination of abstraction and analysis. First, he suggested, we must abstract typical behavior from the peculiar activity of the moment. Then we can discern the psychological motives that preceed action and list the possible consequences that might occur because of the action pattern.

What are these abstractions? How do we choose some activity to observe? We look for common aspects of interaction inherent in diverse areas of life. The excited milling of a theater audience may resemble the agitation of a lynch mob. Religious self-sacrifice may be similar to the devotion of a leader who heads an important but unpopular cause. The new individualism of Renaissance artist may help explain the economic individualism also rising in that period. Sociology is a way of detecting these common patterns and then abstracting from them to build inductive descriptions of the types of interaction or types of social actors (1917:13-16).

The end product of abstraction — the *types* — describe social life in caricature. We will never see an example of pure self-sacrifice, but we can describe it as an ideal form and we can measure reality against this type (1908b:341-51). Simmel compared these types to geometric shapes that outline an object without revealing its special color, texture, and other individual features (1908d:316-17, 320). Of course, social abstractions are much more complicated than geometric ones. We can readily conceive of the Pentagon building as a five-sided figure. But how do we separate the domination of a believer by his God from the essentials of any superior-subordinate relationship? A general model of dominance applies to wide areas of social life. But as we distinguish subordination under an individual (like God) from subordination under an elite and from subordination under a law that commands everyone, we can detail more nuances of the relationship but we must limit our scope to a smaller range of situations (1908f). Even within a limited scope, however, no individual example will ever coincide with the typical form or with other examples. Domination under God resembles but does not equal domination under a classroom teacher. Neither situation stands as the proto-typical exemplar of one-person leadership. Here we see the scientist's dilemma: as we move from the description of unique events to the scientific conceptualization of abstract types, we gain insight about the general nature of social life but lose sight of the details that order this reality. The broader — the more abstract — the type, the fewer details it can contain (1908d:321).

Although Simmel concentrated on the description of types, he always placed these types within a causal network bounded by psychological predispositions and functional consequences. Personal motives, he explained, impel us into action in the first place. And once we choose a relationship, our behavior affects other people. To really understand a type of action, we should list and consider these possible consequences — in modern terms, the possible *functions* — of the relationship (1908d:331-32).

In sum, Simmel's analysis centered on types of interaction: the motives behind them, the traits distinguishing a particular type, and the results that follow from these action patterns.

RESEARCH — THE PRACTICE

Simmel's theoretical distinction between form and content permeated his substantive research. Stressing form, he analyzed two types of social phenomena: the types of social action and the types of social actors. Generally he described interaction (the form) and then explained it in terms of drives, motivations, and desires (the content). To build an empirical basis for his descriptions Simmel used examples drawn from daily life and historical events, not systematic data gathered on a narrowly defined topic. It is true that he used some questionnaire data for his study on yodeling (1882). But even in this work he did not attempt to sample representative elements or to test a series of hypotheses about yodeling. As a rule, he observed life and analyzed many, many forms of interaction — the precipitating factors and repercussions of conflict (1908a), the techniques of conversation (1917:51-53), the alliances in a triad

(1908e:145-69) — using his observations to illustrate this analysis. Unlike many sociologists, Simmel did not attempt or need to document his statements in detail: for him, the empirical world served only as a source for induction, not as a testing ground for hypotheses.

As Simmel pursued his analysis, he leapt from topic to topic, from theme to theme, from example to example in a breathtaking display of mental acrobatics. Here I will attempt to portray the sweep of his thought by tracing the causal path between content and form, by detailing the nature of a sociological type, and by showing where social forms include room for individual freedom.

Simmel assumed that content somehow caused people to act out a pattern of behavior. Somehow . . . not necessarily this way or that way. After delineating a social type, Simmel would look backwards to speculate about motivating content. In other words, the type is the empirical reality, the content simply an explanation of how people are motivated to act within the type. The same content can be used to explain many forms. Antipathy, for example, inspires a great range of hostilities. In "Conflict," Simmel showed how antagonisms can both divide and unite a group. Conflict decimates a group when members attack each other and unifies a group when members stand against their common enemy. Moreover, the total unity of some societies depends on mutual hostility between subgroups: antagonistic Hindu castes jealously guard and perform their various social duties; the multitudes living in major cities develop antipathies and aversions that enable them to survive together in a world where "contaminating" contact with many strangers is the ever-present possibility (1908a:87-123). Just as the same content can motivate action within many forms, so a similar form can shape actions motivated by diverse contents. People in a triad, for example, must choose from a limited number of action possibilities regardless of what brought them to the triad in the first place. Are the calculated machinations of a diplomat trying to create dissension between two allies very different from the tricks of a high-school sophomore trying to cause trouble between another boy and his special girl? Whatever the motives, "divide and conquer" is the game (1908e:162-69). Some of these behavior forms even become so routine that they are almost devoid of content. People often perform a social ritual without a thought about its real meaning, indeed, without any real meaning. Many times the flirt is just going through the motions. Much of party conversation is talk for its own sake — empty of meaning, information, substance (1917:48-53). In contrast, behavior can grow from compelling, driving need, from an overwhelming personal devotion to something bigger than ourselves. This devotion, this need for transcendental experience coupled with a feeling of dependence — Simmel called it a religious need — lies behind the relationship between a worshipper and his god, a patriot and his fatherland, a child and his parents (1912:11-25).

While interesting, the connection between content and form was not the main concern of Simmel's sociology. More characteristically he described types, their forms and their functions. These could be types of actors or types of actions. Here I will detail one type (one of the very many) as an example of Simmel's empirical work analyzing the many facets of social relationship.

Simmel defined the "poor" in terms of their special social interaction (1908c). In his analysis, the "poor" are not simply people without means or people in lower economic groups. Rather they are people who must seek economic assistance from others in society. This dependence creates a special social relationship, a peculiar balance between the rights of the poor to claim assistance and the duties of more fortunate citizens to dispense it. The crucial questions are: Do the poor have rights? and do other people consider helping the poor to be their duty? The poor man's situation depends on the cultural definition of his rights: "for the humiliation, shame, and *déclassment* that charity implies are overcome for him to the extent that it is not conceded out of compassion or sense of duty or utility, but because he can lay claim to it" (1908c:120). Among the ancient Semites, for example, charity was a right claimed by the poor. Paupers were dignified persons entitled to some share of the social pie. By contrast, a medieval Christian considered charity a duty to himself. The giver received grace for his generosity to unfortunates and, therefore, could dispense what he pleased regardless of the needs of the recipient. In many modern societies, help for the poor has become a duty that citizens owe the state. Poverty programs have become a way to suppress rebellion, crime, and other disorderly lower-class activities. These societal definitions not only specify the duties we owe the poor but also limit the amount of our charity. If the poor claim a right to a just share of worldly goods, then, in theory at least, our duties could continue until all wealth has been distributed equally. If, on the other hand, assistance is a tool for maintaining the *status quo,* the poor should receive just enough to keep them peaceful. Finally, if charity is a duty we owe ourselves, if we give to receive graces, social prestige, or other favors, we are limited only by our pocketbooks and our desire to acquire personal rewards. In sum, the poor-as-poor are often social objects, people without rights. As such, they do not interact with the rest of society but simply receive its favors. This relationship renders them peculiarly helpless in dealing with the non-poor world.

Implied in Simmel's analysis of the poor is his concept of human freedom. Freedom lies within the limits of interaction. Any relationship — with its rights and duties — clearly limits freedom. Given that the poor have rights to assistance, for example, we may ask just how far redistribution of wealth will extend assuming that no countertrend breaks that tendency. How free are we to say "no" when they ask for help? So in one sense, freedom means the absence of such duties, in effect, the absence of all relationships — obviously not a common situation. More often, however, freedom grows within a relationship either when a person escapes restraining social bonds or when a person exerts influence by placing restraints on others (1908e:120-22). For example, when Simmel discussed the effects of a money economy on the plight of the individual worker, he claimed that money had liberated workers from old feudal restrictions. Economic life, he argued, is based on exchange, specifically, the exchange of one value for another equal value. Labor power, room and board, money, movable goods — each of these valuables can be exchanged for something else (1900a). The newest of these, money, provides a medium for labor exchange other than traditional ones like room and board. Because of money a laborer can work for someone else without surrendering his personal life to his employer. Therefore the modern laborer often enjoys more personal autonomy than the preindustrial serf or craftsman (1900b). If conditions permit, such freedom may expand indefinitely. Freedom from domination becomes freedom to dominate. After escaping traditional restrictions, lower-class groups typically try to become the betters, not the equals, of their old masters (1908f:268-303). Of course, as Marx would tell us, members of the upper class in this situation protect their own position by paying low wages for long hours, thus enslaving the worker under a different form of domination. Freedom, in other words, grows within a balance of social relations. Ever changing, never secure, it depends on our changing power to control others and our need to obey them.

In general, Simmel tried to observe the abstract essentials of action that occurs within the particulars of a historical situation. As an unusually perceptive observer, he noted regularities, delineated types of action, and predicted the effects of different patterns. Although he did not use this term, modern sociologists speak of social *roles,* that is, sets of behavior patterns that accompany certain relationships in society: the role of the marriage broker, the role of the undertaker, the role of the student, the role of the pauper. And like Simmel, modern sociologists predict the behavior of a typical role player, behavior that occurs because society has defined the play in certain ways. These rules and the definitions behind them prescribe the patterns of influence in sociology by detailing the limits of personal freedom within the total relationships of a given group.

CONCLUSION

Simmel's contribution to sociology is a series of insights into the substance and methods of the field. His definition of sociology — and the philosophical underpinnings of that definition — colored his research practice. He defined sociology as the study of interaction; he urged sociologists to analyze the abstract forms of interaction apart from the historical episodes preceeding it and from the psychological motives behind it; then he used this technique to develop his numerous concepts about types of interaction. This research approach produced colorful insights rather than systematic verifications.

The absence of formal verification should not surprise us, however. Since Simmel concentrated on defining concepts and types, he could use empirical data to illustrate his ideas without worrying about just how representative his illustrations might be. Nevertheless, he did more than label and classify. In his analyses, he often separated key variables defining his types. For example he noted that the change from a barter economy to a money economy affects employer-employee relations and that different attitudes about the rights of the poor produce different interactions between the pauper and the prince. In effect he often described natural experiments using critical examples that brilliantly argued his point.

Perhaps if he had defined himself as an experimental scientist, Simmel might have searched for data to verify his hypotheses in cross cultural or cross-historical comparisons instead of simply recording whatever activities illustrated his logical analysis. Do cultural values affect the condition of the poor in non-Western societies? Do exchange economies in Africa limit freedom as they did in Medieval Europe? More concerned with analysis than data gathering or theory testing, Simmel did not answer such questions but left a framework in which we can pursue the answers ourselves.

Bibliography

Simmel, Georg

1882 "Psychological and ethnological studies on music." Pp. 98-140 in K. Peter Etzkorn (trans.), *Georg Simmel: The Conflict in Modern Culture and Other Essays*. New York: Teachers College Press (Columbia University), 1968.

1900a "A chapter in the philosophy of value." Pp. 47-67 in *Georg Simmel*. . . .

1900b "Money and freedom." Pp. 553-54 in Robert E. Park and Ernest W. Burgess, *Introduction to the Science of Sociology*. 2nd ed. Chicago: University of Chicago Press, 1924.

1908a "Conflict." Pp. 13-123 in *Conflict and the Web of Group-Affiliations*. New York: Free Press, 1964.

1908b "How is society possible?" Pp. 337-56 in Kurt H. Wolff (ed.), *Essays on Sociology, Philosophy and Aesthetics*. New York: Harper Torchbooks, 1965.   ,

1908c "The poor." *Social Problems* (Fall): 118-40 (1965). Also Pp. 150-78 in Donald N. Levine (ed.), *Georg Simmel on Individuality and Social Forms*. Chicago: University of Chicago Press, 1971.

1908d "The problem of sociology." Pp. 310-36 in *Essays*. . . .

1908e "Quantitative aspects of the group." Pp. 87-177 in Kurt H. Wolff (ed.), *The Sociology of Georg Simmel*. New York: Free Press, 1950.

1908f "Superordination and subordination." Pp. 181-303 in *The Sociology*. . . .

1912 *The Sociology of Religion*. New York: Philosophical Library (1959).

1917 "Fundamental problems of sociology." Pp. 3-84 in *The Sociology*. . . .

Secondary sources

Coser, Lewis A.
  1965 "Introduction." Pp. 1-26 in Coser (ed.), *Georg Simmel*. Englewood
       Cliffs, N.J.: Prentice-Hall.
  1971 "Georg Simmel, 1858-1918." Pp. 177-215 in *Masters of Sociological
       Thought*. New York: Harcourt Brace Jovanovich.

Heberle, Rudolf
  1948 "Simmel's Method." Pp. 116-21 in *Georg Simmel*.

Levine, Donald N.
  1957 "Some key problems in Simmel's work." Pp. 97-115 in *Georg
       Simmel*.

Spykman, Nicholas J.
  1925 *The Social Theory of Georg Simmel*. New York: Russell and Russell
       (1964).

Tenbruck, F. H.
  1959 "Formal sociology." Pp. 77-96 in *Georg Simmel*.

Wolff, Kurt H.
  1950 "Introduction." Pp. xvii-lxiv in Wolff (ed.), *The Sociology of
       Georg Simmel*. New York: Free Press.

Emile Durkheim

Emile Durkheim (1858-1917) ranks as an important sociologist because of his position in the academic world and his contributions to both the substance and the methods of sociology. During his career as a French sociologist, he was appointed to the chair of sociology at the Sorbonne and he founded the most prestigious French sociology journal, *L'Année sociologique*. His key concern was the cohesion holding people in a society, a concern that inspired his research on norms as they are reflected in social deviance, religion, thought structures, family life, and economic forces. Just as important, Durkheim treated several methodological problems: the use of typologies, indices, causal relationships, and comparative studies. Indeed, in Durkheim's sociology, methodology occupies a central place. He wrote a booklength treatise on the topic; he frequently discussed philosophy-of-science problems; and he experimented with different ways of handling data. In sum, he appeared to be as interested in the appropriate ways of using social data as he was in supporting a thesis.

Durkheim never forgot his main objective, however. He applied his methods to the study of cohesion in society. Since cohesion implies that different parts form an integrated whole, he had to consider the relationship of part to part to whole, what one element did for another or for the entire society. His solution: *functionalism* — he studied how one social pattern (law, religious rite, family tradition) functions to instill a sense of group unity among individual members. Then he analyzed how these functional relationships cohere into social types: types of suicide, types of society, types of cohesion.

INTELLECTUAL BACKGROUND

Durkheim synthesized ideas from a wide range of sources, dwelling on or elaborating numerous ideas current in French thought.

Like his compatriot Comte, he disagreed with the rationalistic-*philosophé* vision of a world with competing individuals whose activites could be coordinated by the state. Both Comte and Durkheim admitted the possibility, indeed the reality, of individual competition, but both denied that rational state planning could manage this activity. They turned, instead, to the romanticist tradition of a transcendental social spirit — something non-rational, unplanned, intangible, that, nevertheless, holds society together. Comte had developed these ideas in his conception of a social-mental unity or consensus that transcends individual thought and gives society a life of its own. Looking for specific mechanisms of cohesion, Comte, Marx, and Spencer had each posited the division of labor in society as a force that could both unify and separate group members. Combining and rearranging these ideas Durkheim constructed his concept of *organic solidarity* (social cohesion based on interdependence of people who perform different tasks) to challenge both Marx's thesis about the necessity for class conflict and Comte's fears that social diversity must beget chaos. With these concepts he also formulated specific hypothesis (for example: forms of social organization are related to types of thought; types of social solidarity are related to different kinds of deviant acts) and tested these hypotheses in empirical research.

For his research designs, Durkheim borrowed scientific ideas also current in nineteenth-century thought, ideas about positivism, functionalism, and hypothesis testing. No doubt Comte, among others, taught him to be a positivist, to rely on observable data instead of philosophical concepts. And seeing society as a whole with interrelated parts, he could appreciate Spencer's functional analysis, particularly his suggestions about how the increasing division of labor functions to produce social cohesion. Furthermore, Durkheim's quarrels with Gabriel Tarde, who stressed the individual psychological basis of social life, forced him to defend his own stress on the group. However, Durkheim proved to be a more imaginative methodologist than these predecessors.

He examined the same variables in many situations to discern the relationship between independent and dependent variables (using J. S. Mill's test for concommittant variation). He also recognized how extreme cases can demonstrate that a situation is, or is not, universally true (a technique he borrowed from anthropology). And he employed critical experiments to isolate causes (as natural scientists do). Combining all these research tools, Durkheim produced a powerful brand of sociology.

Finally, like many other social thinkers of his era, Durkheim hoped that research into societal conditions would influence social change. In *Socialism and Saint-Simon,* he defined this desirable relationship between sociology and reform: "The problem must be put this way: to discover through science the moral restraint which can regulate economic life, and by this regulation control selfishness and thus gratify need" (1895-6:240). But he also warned us that empirical findings must never be used to support *a priori* ideas or to buttress false ideals, carefully designed research can be used, instead, to improve man's lot by suggesting how to promote the natural balance, stability, and peace in social life (1892:7-8).

DEFINITION OF SOCIOLOGY

Perhaps it was Durkheim's conception of sociology that guided him around some of the research biases that have bedeviled many reform-minded scientists. For him, the basis of sociology was not what the science would do for man but rather how it studies man's concerns. Scientists in each field study some form of determinism peculiar to their field. And so, sociologists must observe the phenomena caused (or determined) by a particular society, "phenomena which would not exist if this society did not exist and which are what they are only because this society is constituted the way it is" (1900:363). These peculiar social objects created by society are *social facts or institutionalized* patterns of interaction:

> One can, indeed, without distorting the meaning of this expression, designate as "institutions" all the beliefs and all the modes of conduct instituted by the collectivity. Sociologogy can then be defined as the science of institutions, of their genesis and of their functioning. (1901:lvi)

Thus, sociology is the science of "beliefs and modes of conduct instituted by the collectivity," the study of peculiar things we think and do because we are members of a particular social group. Because we are twentieth-century Americans most of us believe in electing government officials. If some rascal irritates us beyond endurance we eliminate him by electing someone else. Because they were sixteenth-century Frenchmen, they believed in hereditary monarchs. If the king became unbearable, they tried to depose him, sometimes by defeating him at war and then declaring the winner to be the real heir. Most of the time most of us believe in these cultural ideals and obey these ground rules — Durkheim called them social facts; we call them values and norms — of society. Durkheim was primarily interested in these moral-social rules: what they are, how they originate, and what purposes they serve. He tells us that sociology must persist "in seeking, among the different forms of external constraint, the different sorts of moral authority corresponding to them and in discovering the causes which have determined these later" (1912:239n6).

SUBJECT FOCUS

Durkheim developed his ideas about defining the subject matter of sociology to fit within a framework of determinism. Indeed, " . . . sociology could not emerge until the idea of determinism, which had been securely established in the physical and natural sciences, was finally extended to the social order" (1915:376). As long as man envisioned a social world moved by capricious human will — imagined, .to take a modern example, that a Hitler or a Churchill could deflect the entire course of a civilization — there could be no science of sociology. To study society scientifically, we must first observe how a group enforces conformity. Then, perhaps, we can perceive how Weimar Germany could produce a Hitler. The problem for Durkheim was in learning how society defines conformity and permits deviancy, not seeing the ways in which a deviant changes his society.

Durkheim's conception of social facts highlights the determinate patterns of social life (1895:1-13). *Social facts* are ways of acting, thinking, or feeling that are outside of the individual but have power over him. They are a form of group pressure delimiting the actions of individuals. These facts may, or may not, affect the behavior of each person in a group, but they have a pervasive influence on the behavior of group members as a whole. For example, although most people do not commit suicide, the constant suicide rate in society is a social fact, in this instance, a steady current of deviant activity within the group.

Moreover, because of their coercive power, these facts can be observed as they operate in a group. We recognize a social fact or *norm* "by the existence of some specific sanction or by the resistance offered against every individual effort that tends to violate it" (1895: 10). We look for laws, informal group pressure, forms of punishment — and we find social facts.

SCIENCE — THE PLAN

Durkheim's definitions of sociology and social facts suggest his deep interest in the philosophy and research methods of social science. With these definitions he has clearly insisted that science must deal with observable data and provide evidence about determinism. Once discovered, social facts and their causal relationships can illuminate the functional interdependence among parts of society — what is normal, what creates consensus in society, what functions to promote social cohesion. Here we will consider Durkheim's scientific approach by reviewing in more detail, first his conceptualization of science, then his reasons for insisting on social facts as the scientific subject matter of sociology, and finally the rubrics of research he laid out in *The Rules of Sociological Method*.

To begin, according to Durkheim, science produces two key products: types and causal statements (1892:8-14). Descriptive work can be summarized in *types,* that is, in constructs which define a finite number of common features present in some reality. In *Division of Labor* Durkheim compared forms of social cohesion in *mechanical* (homogeneous) societies with those in *organic* (heterogeneous) societies. But, he insisted, without *causal statements,* these types are meaningless: "There can be no types of things unless there are causes which, though operating in different places and at different times, always and everywhere produce the same effects" (1892:12). In this way, Durkheim introduced determinism, the defining characteristic of his science. Types, he stated, cannot be created from our stray notions but must be constructed as they correspond to some determining cause. They are, in other words, complexes of information that summarize some empirical cause-effect relationship. Certain types of cohesion or solidarity were caused or determined by certain forms of the division of labor; which in turn, were caused by certain degrees of population density, transportation, and communication. Empirical reality may include particular, historical features (some organic societies have kings, some have presidents, some have dictators). We may presume, however, that these variations are not an integral part of the type and therefore not determined by the causal relationship that produced it.

Further, to be part of sociology, such types must describe the persisting institutional patterns, the social facts. Just as the biologist concentrates on common structural features and overlooks the vicissitudes experienced by an individual organism, so the sociologist must concentrate on common social facts and ignore the diverting but irrelevant historical detail about Henry II's marital life or Napoleon's hemorrhoids (1898b:346). This limited range is particularly necessary in social science since, broadly defined, sociology could include an incomprehensible array of topics, in fact, all the phenomena which appear in society (1900:354-55). To avoid a chaotic dissipation of effort, and to avoid types that include a bewildering combination of details, sociologists must concentrate on this limited range of social phenomena. In different ways, the other nineteenth-century sociologists had already made the same point. Durkheim's contribution is his stress on socially created norms and institutions as the area for these limited studies.

To explicate his ideas about determinism in social facts, Durkheim wrote *The Rules of Sociological Method,* a treatise on research tactics for the social sciences. In it he discussed how we can observe and explain the social facts, not only accounting for what actually exists but also explaining the normal and abnormal relationships of social life.

The most important rule for observation of social facts is to treat them as things, objective realities, not ideas of subjective intuitions (1895:14-46). This treatment involves three processes: 1) observing data without presuppositions; 2) constructing rigorous definitions of facts based on this observed data; 3) considering the defined facts as social types, each with its own set of distinguishing characteristics. Thus the definitions of social facts are empirical, coming from observation — not ideology, not theory, not philosophy. For example, many people observe what they loosely call "democracy" in both primitive and modern societies. If we defined democracy according to the societal legal structure instead of relying on our ideological preconceptions, we would discover different types of government reflected in different types of legal arrangements. Citizens of ancient Athens did not enjoy the same democracy as citizens of eighteenth-century North America or twentieth-century Bangladesh.

Beyond observation of such facts, we must seek explanation. All social facts — forms of government, varieties of deviance, all group-regulated behaviors — fit within causal and functional relationships (1895:89-140). Durkheim distinguished the *cause* from the *function,* the force that produces a particular social fact from the end that it serves. Often this whole sequence, cause-effect-function, is composed of social facts. For example, collective beliefs may inspire punishment for a crime (a causal relationship) ; punishment, in turn, may reinforce collective beliefs about appropriate norms for the group (a functional relationship). A convent organized around the ideal of religious perfection may sanction someone for inadequate attention to prayer, thus reinforcing the religious ideal. In prison, by contrast, a convict may be beaten for failure to show proper respect to informal, inmate leaders. In either situation, violation of the group norms offends social morality and this causes the group to prescribe a punishment that functions to demonstrate just what the limits of acceptable behavior may be.

However, describing the temporal sequence of cause-effect-function does not fully explain social behavior. The fact that some punishment follows a crime does not prove causality. We must also ask whether different social facts belong together. Is death the punishment for treason in colonial society? Experiments manipulating the hypothetical cause in a variety of situations would be ideal but, in a field like sociology, arranging such experiments is usually impossible. Few researchers, no matter how dedicated, would care to arrange or commit a series of treasons in order to test their causal impact. Consequently, we must rely on comparisons (preferably cross-cultural comparisons of total situations) to see if the same effects consistently follow the facts we suspect to be the causes.

Once we have outlined the normal sequence of relations, we can detect pathological patterns. If an old custom persists after the cause has gone, it is abnormal. If normal rates of poverty and vagabondage from sixteenth-century England persist to the modern industrial era, the persisting rates are abnormal because the cause has changed. But, we may wonder, how can we be sure of cause in a changing society? Perhaps tradition or force of habit may become the cause for the continuing practice of an old, persistent pattern.

However, as Durkheim used determinism, only one cause (or constellation of causes) could be responsible for any particular effect. Thus cause and effect would have to change simultaneously; any other sequence is, by definition, abnormal. In other words, much of social change is abnormal and there are no rules for determining causality in abnormally changing situations.

Part of Durkheim's difficulty with social change occurs because he developed his notion of normalcy from a biological analogy (1895: 47-75). He reasoned that certain phenomena, like childbirth and senility, can be disruptive and unpleasant, but are normal nonetheless. To determine the acceptable social unpleasantries, we should look for the average level of the activity in a particular type of society. A certain society may maintain a certain crime rate. Constant crime is normal. A drop in strong-arm robbery, murder, or vandalism may be symptomatic of political problems, economic depression, or some other social pathology. Although as planners we may abhor crime, we should recognize these normal levels and not attempt to tamper with them. Indeed, statesmen should plan to prevent the pathological changes that disrupt normal levels of deviance.

Considering this argument from biology, we may wonder about another issue: should physicians try to solve the physical problems of childbirth and. senility or should they encourage "normal" levels for maternal deaths, arteriosclerosis, and the like? In *Rules. . . . ,* Durkheim suggested that we allow social pathology to run its normal course. Unlike many other reform-minded scientists, he believed that social good might be relative and, in any event, it could only be defined in relationship to the observed situation in a particular type of society. This view supports conservative politics. First, as long as poverty, homocide, and other ills remain at normal levels, we can — and should — accept these problems as part of a healthy society. Further, in a changing industrial society, normalcy can be an elusive state, perhaps defined to suit the convenience of a researcher or social planner. Years later, however, Durkheim hinted about a less remote relationship between knowledge and reform (1912:488-96). He argued that science, like the other mental constructs shared by members of society, can affect the social milieu. As sociology becomes increasingly sophisticated, it increases human understanding of society, and thus it becomes a social fact encouraging creative change. This suggestion, written near the end of his life, reconciles the ethical relativism of Durkheim's scientific sociology with the moral imperatives that informed the rest of his thought.

In sum, Durkheim expected sociology to explain the determinate relationships in social life, specifically the causal and functional sequences of social facts. These sequences could then be summarized in types. . . . increasing moral density causes a heterogeneous division of labor which in turn functions to promote feelings of solidarity based on interdependence and these feelings form the cohesion in organic-type societies. However, delineating these sequences proves to be much easier in theory than in practice. Often Durkheim found it impossible to isolate the components in research. Consequently, whenever he discovered one element of the sequence, he often assumed the others were present too. In the research section, we will consider this strategy in more detail.

RESEARCH — THE PRACTICE

Throughout his sociological research Durkheim analyzed the causes, correlates, and functions of social facts. In *Primitive Classification,* he examined the social origins of thought, a problem he expanded in *The Elementary Forms of the Religious Life.* In *The Division of Labor in Society,* he linked social solidarity to law and economic life. Then, in *Suicide,* he showed how this solidarity can maintain normal levels of abnormal activity. And for all these studies, he used available data (anthropological descriptions of Australian aboriginies, historical accounts of ancient legal systems, official government mortality statistics) to build his arguments about the force of group life.

Durkheim's strength and weakness as a research worker seem to come from the same source, namely, his efforts to show the determinate order in social life, to link group organization with other social facts. At his best, he delineated social types and performed careful comparisons holding one variable constant while he examined the effects of another. At worst, he defined the cause as an integral part of the effect and proclaimed causality whenever the effect appeared.

In his first major work, *The Division of Labor in Society,* Durkheim exhibited both his genius for defining types and his tendency toward tautological analysis. He boldly outlined extreme types of society based on types of solidarity. But he also assumed the existence of the functional relationship he was trying to demonstrate.

In *The Division of Labor . . .* , he presents an ingenious social paradox: as society becomes more complex, as individuals become more independent, society continues to operate as a unit. But how? Comte had started a religion to promote mental unity. Marx had predicted class conflict. Supporting his ideas with data from history and anthropology, Durkheim hypothesized: "the division of labor is the source, if not unique, at least principle, of social solidarity" (1893:62). Social solidarity is the feeling we have in common with other people either because we resemble them (*mechanical solidarity*) or because we are in an interdependent relationship with them (*organic solidarity*). In the simple society, where everybody farms, hunts, or grazes sheep, people share a sense of solidarity built on mutual sympathy for others who share the same problems, the same goals, the same ideas — the same *collective consciousness* (1893:70-110). When someone breaks this common pattern (refuses to hunt, questions the gods, breaks his neighbor's leg) the group punishes him severely. This *repressive* action both prevents future deviance and reinforces the group's feelings of solidarity — "We all know that is wrong!" (1893:49-69) As population density, transportation, and communication increase, society becomes more complicated and people begin to perform a variety of different tasks. In a society marked by a complex division of labor, the work of art, religion, food production, child rearing becomes the specialized activity of artists, priests, farmers, and mothers (1893:111-32). Here *restitutive law* binds individuals through a series of mutual agreements. The legal framework provides rules for restoring the balance of social life rather than just punishing wrong-doers. Certain crimes, like worshiping the wrong god, simply do not exist in a restitutive legal system. Indeed, if we all differ in many respects, why should we condemn someone for one more difference (1893:49-69)?

Thus Durkheim argued that the division of labor produces two extreme types of social solidarity. Further, this solidarity can be observed in the types of law found in society. In other words the legal forms caused by types of solidarity, *repressive* and *restitutive law,* also form the visible indices of the causal qualities called mechanical and organic solidarity (1893:49-69). Law, however, is not a perfect index. At times, custom alone serves as a normative guide for society. At times, custom even changes the spirit of enacted law.

"This opposition," Durkheim claimed, "crops up only in quite exceptional circumstances. This comes about when law no longer corresponds to the state of existing society, but maintains itself, without reason for so doing, by the force of habit" (1893:65). In other words, types of solidarity are reflected in types of law — most of the time. But, since the legal index does not produce an accurate measure of solidarity in changing situations, we can only depend on it when we are researching stable societies. Durkheim's statement that outdated, out-of-place laws are just symptoms of "force of habit" also raises a theoretical issue: "force of habit" may prove to produce as many feelings of solidarity as the division of labor. Further, Durkheim did not posit a progressive shift from pure mechanical to pure organic solidarity. He recognized the power of *collective consciousness* (we might call it a set of cultural ideals) to rule men's thought even in a contract-based legal system. Pure self-interest will not bind us to society: even restitutive law depends on mechanical-solidarity feature like our recognition of society's right to regulate social behavior (1893:277). Thus law, Durkheim's index of solidarity, becomes an inaccurate tool to use on etiher modern societies or changing situations.

The problems in Durkheim's conceptualization of change reappear in his analysis of abnormal forms of the division of labor (1893: 353-409). The abnormal forms, producing conflict or boredom rather than solidarity, occur when social action is not regulated or is not regulated properly. Class strife, alienation, and other ills associated with modern life can be alleviated if we substitute real division of labor for the abnormal, improperly regulated forms. However, this recommendation contradicts other postulates in Durkheim's system. Earlier he told us that types of solidarity belong in a social package linked with types of law and types of interdependence. But here Durkheim has taken situations in which solidarity and division of labor do not cohere according to type, labeled these cases abnormal, and decided that proper regulation would solve the problem. In his analyses of static situations, Durkheim described law as a reflection and index of solidarity. Instead of causing cohesion, he stated, it signals the existence of cohesion and reinforces what solidarity already exists. When suggesting law as a cure for abnormal societies, Durkheim assumed that the indices of cohension and the reinforcing functions he had observed in static situations also operated as causes, or key independent variables, in dynamic settings.

In later work, Durkheim broadened his conception of coercive collective ideals beyond law to include family custom, religious ritualism and even cognitive thought. In *Incest* (1898a) and *Primitive Classification* (1903) he used anthropological data to compare social organization with types of thought. He noticed that groups tend to display consistent cognitive patterns. To mention one, Australian tribesmen defined marriage groups on the basis of allegiance to animal totems and then used the same classifications to define animal species. Durkheim concluded: "Now the classification of things reproduces this classification of men" (1903:11). Durkheim never proved that social patterns cause forms of thought. In fact, we might suggest that the tribesmen first noticed species and then defined marriage groups. Nevertheless, Durkheim did demonstrate that types of thought tend to accompany types of social behavior patterns. Thus he countered two popular theories: one (formulated by Kant) that *a priori* cognitive forms determine perceptions and the other oppositive notion that thought is purely the product of individual experience.

In a much later work, *The Elementary Forms of the Religious Life* (1912) Durkheim continued to analyze social causes of thought, particularly the sacred thoughts that underlie religion. Noting that we cannot discover the real origins, "the very first beginnings" of religion, he decided to search out the forces that encourage religious practice among Australian aboriginies. Why aboriginies? Because it is easier to analyze relationships between institutions in a simple society than it would be to trace such patterns in nineteenth-century France. Beyond that, religion in a simple society has fewer nonessential features to distract us: no centuries of theological development, no elaborate bureaucracy, and (this last point especially interested Durkheim) no deity (1912:18-21). Durkheim carefully selected this extreme case to illustrate the functional relationship between religion and society itself.

Reviewing the anthropological data on the aborigines (and some other primitive peoples), Durkheim outlined the sources of interdependence between religion and the rest of society. The common religious rituals — the dances, the sacrifices, the chants — tend to reinforce *collective consciousness,* which is a synthesis of sentiments, ideas, and images that are, to some degree, shared by all group members (1912:414-33). The religion itself arises from group experience. As people conduct their daily lives they develop a collective sense of ground rules, a feeling of moral authority shared by group members. On extraordinary occasions, at the parade or the dance or the sacrifice, these people enjoy an exalting experience, a contact with something well beyond the mundane world. Finally these shared experience combine to form *religion*, the embodiment of society's sense of the sacred and sense of moral authority, not necessarily supported by a god (1912:235-51).

In other words, we form a sacred being in our image and we then worship it. Or do we? Here Durkheim has, indeed, explained what religion does in primitive society, but he has not told us about the first dance, the initial sacrifice, the act that begins this functional cycle. However, if Durkheim is correct his analysis suggests a reason why men continue to obey law in an organic society. Society itself has acquired some sacred-moral authority. Perhaps it is not the the modern god. But certainly it wields some of the same moral authority (1912:492-95).

In *Suicide* (1897), Durkheim researched a much more concrete activity using sophisticated comparisons to test his theory about group cohesion and its affect on deviance within the group. Although we can criticize the statistical techniques, data sources, and other technical aspects of this study, we must admire this fine example of research used to support hypotheses drawn from a major thesis.

Durkheim used mortality statistics from different regions to develop a typology of suicide based on social causes, specifically, on the forms of social cohesion. He delineated three main types of suicide caused by three different sets of social conditions: 1) egoistic suicide that occurs when men are detached from their social groups; 2) altruistic suicide that occurs when men are integrated into a social group encouraging this action; and 3) anomic suicide that occurs when social conditions change creating confusion about group norms or social rules.

To examine egoistic suicide, Durkheim observed, among other things, that urban populations and educated ones both have higher suicide rates than their rural and less educated counterparts. Further, these rates remain relatively constant within groups. In other words, rural Frenchmen have a lower normal suicide rate than Parisians. Durkheim explained that urban educated individuals are less integrated with their social group and, therefore, more inclined to commit an act proscribed by this group. Nineteenth-century European Jews were a conspicuous exception — educated, city people with low suicide rates. The reason: they belonged to a very cohesive religious community, a group that could counteract the effects of the rest of their social environment. Thus in *Suicide,* Durkheim documented the variations among his group and used the exceptional one as part of an experiment supporting his hypothesis. He demonstrated that members of less cohesive groups commit more egoistic suicides (1897:152-216).

Throughout *Suicide* Durkheim used religion, educational level, and other group properties to explain deviance. Then, in order to buttress his argument further he falsified alternative possibilities by eliminating mental condition, hereditary background, time of day, season, and Tarde's theory of imitation. In one demonstration, he averaged the temperature and suicide rates in France, Italy, and Prussia for each month over several periods. Overall his statistical analysis was crude: no tests of significance, samples involving different periods of time for different groups, the use of group data for a discussion of individuals within the group, and other irregularities. However, Durkheim's use of statistics to falsify other possible explanations of suicide strongly supports his argument that social factors produce the normal rates of deviance in various groups (1897: 57-142).

In general, Durkheim's work exhibits keen insight into the stabilizing mechanisms of society. His research defines types of social patterns and the forces that reinforce these structures. Among other things, he showed that religion provides both a way for man to probe life's deepest mysteries and a set of shared beliefs (a collective consciousness) holding men together in a group. These beliefs, in turn, inspire men to practice the religion that will reinforce the belief. But when this sequence is broken, when institutions like religion fail to promote social cohesion, then the group looses its ability to control suicide and other forms of deviance. It is during such changing, unsettled times that social pathology rises to unnatural levels. In effect Durkheim examined two basic situations: stable-normal and changing-abnormal.

This dichotomy is surprising since Durkheim clearly believed that modern society can be desirable, that organic solidarity in nineteenth-century Paris may provide a better life than mechanical solidarity in a thirteenth-century rural village. Unlike many contemporary theorists, Durkheim did not fear the very nature of modern life or the change necessary to produce it. It was not his theory but his methodology that led him to interpret changes as "abnormal." His use of a biological analogy would predispose him to think of a one-to-one relationship between any structure and its functions. So, searching for the determining elements of social life, he looked for the single cause (or unique constellation of causes) that produce a given social fact. Such a methodology simply cannot handle unsettled situations in which family life style, religious belief, government forms, and other structures are changing at different rates in different directions.

CONCLUSION

Durkheim's investigation of social cohesion led him to analyze the integrative mechanisms of society, to trace the functions of various institutionalized behavior patterns, to relate behavior patterns and belief structures, to explicate the force of norms within a social group. Comte and Spencer had also looked for the forces that hold society together. However, instead of searching through the medieval civilization or speculating about cosmic forces, Durkheim examined the subgroups of a society. Within these smaller units, he could identify mechanisms like religious belief and occupational interest that functioned to insured cohesion in the isolated tribe and the industrial nation.

Durkheim's main fault occurred when he moved from functional analysis of static situations to causal explanation of social change. He argued that a function should appear only with its cause; all other arrangements are abnormal. In effect, he confused methodological and theoretical idea of normalcy with the empirical reality; he transformed his hope for an integrated society into a scientific description of normal social life. So he has left us wondering how we can be sure that a society has normal integration — especially in changing societies where law, institutions, collective consciousness, and cohesion are not necessarily changing at the same rate or conforming to the old type.

Bibliography

Durkheim, Emile
1892 "Montesquieu's contribution to the rise of social science." Pp. 1-64 in *Montesquieu and Rousseau: Forerunners of Sociology*. Ann Arbor: University of Michigan Press, 1960.
1893 *The Division of Labor in Society*. New York: Free Press (1964).
1895 *The Rules of Sociological Method*. New York: Free Press (1964).
1895-6 *Socialism and Saint-Simon*. Yellow Springs, Ohio: Antioch Press (1958).
1897 *Suicide: A Study in Sociology*. New York: Free Press (1966).
1898a *Incest: The Nature and Origin of the Taboo*. New York: Lyle Stuart (1963).
1898b "Prefaces to *L'Année sociologique* (Vol. I)." Pp. 341-47 in Kurt H. Wolff (ed.), *Emile Durkheim, 1858-1917*. Columbus, Ohio: Ohio State University Press, 1960. (Reprinted as *Essays on Sociology and Philosophy*. New York: Harper Torchbooks, 1964).
1900 "Sociology and its scientific field." Pp. 354-75 in *Emile Durkheim*.
1901 "Author's preface to the second edition." Pp. xli-lvii in *The Rules*.
Durkheim, Emile, and Mauss, Marcel
1903 *Primitive Classification*. Chicago: University of Chicago Press (1963).
Durkheim, Emile
1912 *The Elementary Forms of the Religious Life*. New York: Free Press (1965).
1915 "Sociology." Pp. 376-85 in *Emile Durkheim. . . .*
Secondary sources
Alpert, Harry
1938 "Durkheim's functional theory of ritual." Pp. 137-41 in Robert A. Nisbet (ed.), *Emile Durkheim*. Englewood Cliffs, N.J.: Prentice-Hall, 1965.
Aron, Raymond
1967 "Emile Durkheim." Pp. 11-97 in *Main Currents in Sociological Thought: Volume II*. New York: Basic Books.
Coser, Lewis
1971 "Emile Durkheim, 1858-1917." Pp. 129-74 in *Masters of Sociological Thought*. New York: Harcourt Brace Jovanovich.
Gouldner, Alvin W.
1958 "Introduction." Pp. 7-31 in Emile Durkheim, *Socialism*. New York: Collier (1962).
Lukes, Steven
1972 *Emile Durkheim, His Life and Work: A Historical and Critical Study*. New York: Harper and Row.

Madge, John
1962 "Suicide and anomie." Pp. 12-51 in *The Origins of Scientific Sociology*. New York: Free Press.

Merton, Robert K.
1934 "Durkheim's *Division of Labor in Society*." Pp. 105-12 in *Emile Durkheim*.

Nisbet, Robert A.
1965 "Perspective and ideas." Pp. 29-102 in *Emile Durkheim*.
1974 *The Sociology of Emile Durkheim*. New York: Oxford University Press.

Parsons, Talcott
1937 "Emile Durkheim, I-IV." Pp. 301-450 in *The Structure of Social Action*. New York: Free Press (1968).

Selvin, Hanna C.
1965 "Durkheim's *Suicide*: further thoughts on a methodological classic." Pp. 113-36 in *Emile Durkheim*.

William Graham Sumner

William Graham Sumner (1840-1910) enjoyed two careers: polemicist and scholar. As a polemicist, he preached (in magazines, at banquets, in the classroom) against the evils of protective tariffs, sentimental charity, and other forms of social coddling. As a scholar, he first wrote several notable works in American history. Finally, in 1899, he began to devote full-time attention to scholarship in sociology, writing a massive treatise in the field, *The Science of Society*. Bad health prevented him from completing the work, so in the end, most of his *magnum opus* was rewritten by someone else (his student and colleague, Albert Galloway Keller) and published in 1927, seventeen years after his death. However, since one chapter (about 200,000 words!) seemed to merit special attention, Sumner published it separately in 1906 under the title of *Folkways*. Sumner's reputation stands on this book.

The book — about norms and institutions, in-groups and ethnocentrism — became a sociological classic. In it Sumner reasoned: a few basic human needs produce an endless variety of social norms prescribing how to satisfy these needs. To support this statement, he presented hundreds and hundreds of examples — a Sumner's believe-it-or-not — showing the bewildering variety of customs that humans can use to prevent starvation, to satisfy the sex drive, to gratify vanity, to allay fears. *Folkways* has established beyond question, the proposition that "right" might be relative. This overgrown chapter also provides an example of research with available ethnographic materials — a well-documented inductive argument based on field studies, law books, travelogs, and other sources that described customs in ancient Gaul, nineteenth-century Brazil, and hundreds of places between.

Spencer had used the same inductive strategy with less success, trying to explain societal evolution by arguing from "relevant" illustrative examples. Sumner, a great admirer of Spencer's, succeeded by investigating a narrower topic in greater depth. In the next few sections, we will review how Sumner built from Spencer's ideas about cosmic evolution to develop a classic research monograph on the growth of social norms.

INTELLECTUAL BACKGROUND

Like so many other early American sociologists, Sumner began with the ideas of Herber Spencer and elaborated them to create his own theories. Social darwinism, evolution, ethnographic method — these were the principal Spencerian ideas used by Sumner. The combination of social darwinism and evolution directed him to examine needs and the struggle for existence as the sources of social institutions. Borrowing additional theoretical leads from European thinkers like Thomas Malthus, Ludwig Gumplowicz, and Gustav Ratzenhofer, he analyzed the survival needs of people within groups, the institutions they form to fill these needs, and the conflicts between groups that compete for the same resources. Using ethnographic data (following the example of Spencer and social anthropologists like Julius Lippert) Sumner collected a massive quantity of second-hand accounts detailing life among the Pigmies, human customs in the South Seas, primitive ways in Australia, and other evidence of the variety of human norms. However, because of the additional theoretical insights used by Sumner, there is critical difference between his methodology and Spencer's, a difference which begins with their choice of subject matter. Spencer studied evolution within a total society. Sumner stressed human survival needs satisfied by group customs. And this difference enabled Sumner to produce his definitive work on norms and institutions.

DEFINITION OF SOCIOLOGY

Sumner never formulated his particular definition of sociology. Instead he paraphrased Spenser's ideas about the social organism with coordinated structures and functions:

> Sociology is the science of life in society. It investigates the forces which come into action wherever a human society exists. It studies the structure and functions of the organs of human society, and its aim is to find out the laws in subordination to which human society takes its various forms and social institutions grow and

change. Its practical utility consists in deriving the rules of right social living from the facts and laws which prevail by nature in the constitution and functions of sociology. (1881:167-68)

Even in this early definition, however, we can detect Sumner's own ideas about "social institutions" that "grow and change." Perhaps, had he lived to complete *The Science of Society,* he would have rewritten his definition to highlight institutional change in society. But this is speculation. Sumner's final definition simply describes sociology as, "the Science of Society, a science of generalization, using the results of Anthropology." He added that this science examines social evolution as it appears in self-maintenance, self-perpetuation, and self-gratification (1910:2213-14), but he never defined sociology specifically in terms of him own special interest in norms and institutions.

SUBJECT FOCUS

From the outset, Sumner pictured society as the arena for human struggles:

> Let us then endeavor to define the field of sociology. Life in society is the life of human society on this earth. Its elementary conditions are set by the nature of human beings and the nature of the earth. . . . Sociology is a science which deals with one range of phenomena produced by the struggle for existence, while biology deals with another. (1881:173)

The struggle for existence — the struggle for material goods needed to support life — creates the various action patterns both within a biological organism and within a society. Therefore, the social struggle is rooted ultimately in the basic economic situation, that is, in the amount of land and other material supplies available. Back to Malthus via Spencer.

Years later, after he had spent time in actual sociological research, Sumner developed a narrower, more specific idea about the subject matter of sociology. For him sociology became the science of folkways in society:

> In the present work the proposition to be maintained is that the folkways are the widest, most fundamental, and most important

operation by which the interests of men in groups are served, and that the process by which folkways are made is the chief one to which elementary societal or group phenomena are due. The life of society consists in making folkways and applying them. The science of society might be construed as the study of them. (1906a: 46)

What are these *folkways*? Regular patterns of action established by group members to handle the needs of life which spring from the four basic human motives of hunger, love, vanity, and fear. These motives inspire people with "stronger minds" to conceive of ways to satisfy basic needs. If their ideas synchronize with other socially accepted practices, the new ways spread to other members of the group. For example, men acting out of fear create taboos, curses, sacred cults, and other devices to placate powerful gods. Later a new generation learns to obey the taboos, chant the curses, practice the cults. Co-religionists also initiate society-wide searches for heretics, witches, and other ungodly people who violate group folkways defining religious propriety (1906a:17-45). The socially accepted forms of worship and the socially accepted forms of retribution exacted from infidels — these norms and institutional patterns — are the subject matter of Sumner's sociology.

SCIENCE — THE PLAN

For Sumner the key tenet of scientific methodology was the search for truth, that is, tentative truth. He defined science as "knowledge of reality acquired by methods which are established in the confidence of men whose occupation it is to investigate the truth" (1905: 18). During the course of their search for knowledge, Sumner believed, scientists should improve their methods, replace old mistakes with new strategies — but at the same time remember that they can never be sure of understanding a complete reality. In this respect, science is the opposite of religion: "A religion cannot say: I am the best solution yet found, but I may be superseded tomorrow by new discoveries. But that is exactly what every science must say" (1905:24). Although modern theologians may quarrel with Sumner's critique of religion, modern scientists must accept his description of science as a search for tentative truth using appropriate strategies and techniques.

So what are the appropriate strategies and techniques? To begin Sumner identified the necessary elements that underlie any sound scientific research: "I insist upon strictness of definition, correctness of analysis, precision in observing phenomena, deliberation in comparison, correctness of inference, and exhaustiveness in generalization" (1873:401). Looking for more specific guidelines — guidelines that would inform the routine practice of sociology — Sumner turned to the English evolutionist, Spencer. At a banquet in Spencer's honor, Sumner spoke about the importance of a "powerful and correct method," — specifically Spencer's inductive research, which we may recall was not always inductive, combined with his principles of evolution (1882). Years later, while he was working on *The Science of Society*, Sumner repeated his basic comments about method: sociology needs "a scientific method which shall descend to a cold clear examination of facts and build up inductions which shall . . . trace the evolution of society from its germ up to its present highest forms" (ca. 1900:425).

These two elements — induction and the evolutionary perspective — remained the only explicit instructions Sumner ever offered on methodology. After he had completed *Folkways* in 1906, he suggested that a stress on ethnographic material would be good in a college sociology course to show students the source of scientific inductions: without data, he said, "sociology becomes a thing up in the air" (1906b:408). Even later, in *The Science of Society*, he once again recommended that we gather masses of data — "evidence of social life" — and season it with an "evolutionary perspective" (1910: 2224-47).

When judging specific research techniques used by other sociologists, Sumner adhered to his own basic tenet that science must search for truth. For example, he described a research project conducted by his colleague Franklin Giddings, a project that demonstrated an ingenious search for data flawed by a poor operational definition. Giddings had attempted to measure the American "temper" by classifying and counting newly published American books. Very clever, Sumner commented, but "We must notice, as limiting this test, that the book-market can bear testimony only to the taste of the 'reading public,' which is but a very small part of the population, and does not include the masses" (1905:27).

In addition to this universal scientific concern Sumner also recognized two problems that weigh more heavily on the social sciences than on the physical ones: 1) the use of experiments must be very limited in studies with human subjects; and 2) it is very difficult to number, let alone control, the multitude of critical variables operating in any social situation. Although Sumner supposed that sociologists might eventually find more creative solutions for these problems, he decided " . . . at present I see no means of advancing sociology save by the cultivation of a trained judgment through the careful study of sociological phenomena and sequences" (ca. 1900:419).

In other words, when recording his advice on methodology, Sumner consistently adhered to the Spencerian formula: first observe life in society and then make inductive generalizations that fit within an evolutionary explanatory framework. And following this strategy, sketchy though it may be, Sumner produced his research masterpiece.

RESEARCH — THE PRACTICE

Sumner's masterpiece is the book titled *Folkways*, part of the corpus he wrote after he had abandoned his career as a social commentator and had retired to the library for scholarly research. However, it was not his only important empirical work. His earlier research reflects two facets of his intellectual life, his social conscience and his training in history. His later work, including *Folkways*, manifests his conception of sociology as a science based on ethnographic data. In effect, Sumner remained an historian throughout his life, simply shifting his emphasis from the history of the situation to the history of the institution. In his early writing he detailed situations like the financial support of the American revolution. Later he outlined features of human economic institutions.

Two examples of Sumner's pre-*Folkways* writing will serve to illustrate his early interest in social commentary and historical research. In his famous *What Social Classes Owe to Each Other*, he argued that we help the weak by stepping on the strong. A law against liquor does not affect the alcoholic (who ignores it) but rather deprives the social drinker (1883:132-33). This whole discussion is backed by illustrations — largely manufactured by Sumner — that demonstrate the futility of protecting misfits by penalizing everyone else. Another early book, *The Financier and the Finances of the American Revolution* (1892), demonstrates the thorough-going approach to historical research that served Sumner so well when he later turned to investigating social norms. Here he presented a scholarly biographical exposition (of Robert Morris, stressing his role in American Revolutionary finance) backed with congressional records, state legislative journals, diaries, letters, memoirs, diplomatic correspondence, and other primary sources describing Morris and other important figures in the revolutionary drama.

For his mature sociological works, Sumner followed the example set by Spencer in *Descriptive Sociology*. He assembled and classified thousands of "cases," descriptions he had found in ethnographic and historical sources, in primary and secondary writings, in "The natural history of a Chinese girl" by an anonymous informant and "The sniff kiss in ancient India" by E. W. Hopkins. Just collecting this material was the labor of many years. In fact, although Sumner did most of the collecting, Keller later added "many thousands" of cases needed to complete the work (1927: xxv). A great deal of this data was eventually arranged in volume four, (the *Case Book*) of *The Science of Society,* by topic and geographical area, starting with destitution in primitive Australia and ending with war trophies in historical Europe.

In *Folkways,* Sumner used this material to detail the nature and variety of human customs and to speculate about their sources and implications. Rather than measure the relationships between two or more variables, Sumner preferred to describe types of habitual social activity: wife-lending among the Eskimos, torture in ancient Assyria, fishing habits along Polynesia. He organized his *Folkways* (1906a) to explain the origin and development of these various social habits. Man's struggle for existence necessitates that he develop expedient behavior patterns. Among other patterns, our ancestors learned ways to hunt, to fish, to plant seeds, to do whatver would produce necessary food supplies (1906a:114-45). Once established, social customs — the ordinary folkways and the more important customs sometimes called *mores* — become part of a group's identity, promoting *we-group* identification. As group members, we become *ethnocentric*: we tend to rate our group as "best" and to judge other groups according to how much their members act like us (1906a:27-29). Furthermore, our social habits become so much a part of social life that they persist through governmental upheaval and other surface changes. The French Revolution, for example, destroyed the old classes but could not eradicate the old manners appropriate for a subordinate meeting his social superior (1906a: 153-54). Throughout *Folkways* Sumner documented the existence of a variety of these customs (or *norms*) that define styles of sexuality, worship, clothing, and other facets of societal life. He argued that these norms crystallized into *institutions,* that is, into customary patterns of activity that help men solve the basic problems of group life. Sex mores, to mention one example define how men and women behave toward each other. Each society has a cluster of these mores describing what behavior is acceptable in marriage: who can claim dower rights, who can keep concubines, and so on for an endless variety of contingencies (1906a:294-354).

In the course of detailing his concepts of norms, institutions, and related group patterns, Sumner typically argued inductively, citing a series of cases and then noting some general tendency. Doing this, he often discovered intriguing relationships. Among other things, he recorded a series of situations illustrating the social position of widows: on the Fiji islands widows were strangled and buried with their husbands; Augustine considered second marriages a form of adultery; Salic law required the widow to marry at night. In the end, he noted that remarriage and "other worldliness" were inversely related. If men believed that the other world was near, if they believed the dead could view the actions of the living, then the living tried not to offend the dead by marrying their widows (1906a:330-35).

This is an interesting hypothesis: the more men fear the displeasure of dead predecessors, the more likely they will be to prohibit the remarriage of widows. In two other works on the position of women in social life, Sumner suggested other similarly intriguing hypotheses. In "The status of women in Chaldea, Egypt, India, Judea, and Greece to the time of Christ" (1909b), he cited evidence linking woman's status to her economic functions: farm men value their wives as farmhands but nomads may not value the women who sit home while men go hunting. In "The family and social change" (1909a), he suggested that a mother's need for male protection created the "inferior" status of women. Combined these hypotheses could become part of a theory about religious, economic, and protective factors in the creation of woman's status or in the formation of sex-role ideology.

Sumner's work is filled with such tantalizing possibilities. He did not pursue them himself — perhaps because they lay beyond his vision of sociology, perhaps because death halted his work in progress. Whatever his reason for not investigating his hypothesis about the sources of specific norms, he left a definitive account of the possible range of these norms — a conclusive demonstration that there exists a wide variety of institutional forms acceptable within some human group, that few acts are so bizarre men cannot adopt them as social customs.

CONCLUSION

Sumner wrote a series of historical and ethnographic accounts, one of which includes his famous book on norms and institutions. Working without a scientific strategy — except induction and the "evolutionary perspective" he had borrowed from Spencer — Sumner was forced to examine everything when he studied society. His approach required a never ending search for data. He accepted this burden and collected many thousands of cases for *The Science of Society*. If he had defined sociology differently — the study of men's interaction in society, perhaps — Sumner might have narrowed his search, looked at specific types of interaction in a selected number of societies, seen the relationships between different kinds of institutional forms within a society. But then, he did not define science; indeed, he did not distinguish it from descriptive history. So, even if he had conceptualized sociology in different terms, he would probably have continued to study his subject with purely descriptive methods.

This technique served his purposes. Sumner's descriptive accounts proved that norms and institutions exist, moreover, that they exist in great variety, and that cultural standards are relative to a particular culture. However, pure description cannot tell us about the relationships between types of norms or what constellations of patterns we might expect to find within the same society. If we wish to progress beyond simple statements about the existence of norms and institutions, we must also employ more discriminating methods than the ones used by Sumner.

Bibliography

Sumner, William Graham

1873 "Introductory lecture to courses in political and social science."
Pp. 391-403 in Albert Galloway Keller (ed.), *The Challenge of Facts and Other Essays*. New Haven: Yale University Press, 1914.

1881 "Sociology." Pp. 167-92 in Albert Galloway Keller (ed.), *War and Other Essays*. New Haven: Yale University Press, 1911.

1882 "The science of sociology." Pp. 401-05 in Albert Galloway Keller (ed.), *The Forgotten Man and Other Essays*. New Haven: Yale University Press, 1919.

1883 *What Social Classes Owe to Each Other*. New Haven: Yale University Press (1925).

1892 *The Financier and the Finances of the American Revolution*. New York: A. M. Kelley (1968).

ca. 1900 "The predicament of sociological study." Pp. 415-25 in *Challenge. . . .*

1905 "The scientific attitude of mind." Pp. 17-28 in Albert Galloway Keller (ed.), *Earth-Hunger and Other Essays*. New Haven: Yale University Press, 1913.

1906a *Folkways: A Study of the Sociological Importance of Usages, Manners, Customs, Mores, and Morals*. New York: Mentor Books (1960).

1906b "Sociology as a college subject." Pp. 407-11 in *Challenge. . . .*

1909a "The family and social change." Pp. 43-61 in *War. . . .*

1909b "The status of women in Chaldea, Egypt, India, Judea, and Greece to the Time of Christ." Pp. 65-103 in *War. . . .*

1910 "Unaltered sections." (chapter LVIII; chapter LXI; sections 458-61, 463) of *The Science of Society*. New Haven: Yale University Press (1927).

Sumner, William Graham, Keller, Albert Galloway, and Davie, Maurice Rea (Vol. 4)

1927 *The Science of Society*. 4 vols. New Haven: Yale University Press.

Secondary sources

Barnes, Harry Elmer

1948 "William Graham Sumner: Spencerianism in American dress." Pp. 155-72 in Barnes (ed.), *An Introduction to the History of Sociology*. Chicago: University of Chicago Press (1965).

Davie, Maurice Rea

1963 "Life, writings and methods." Pp. 1-11 in Davie (ed.), *William Graham Sumner*. New York: Thomas Y. Crowell.

Hofstadter, Richard
1959 "The vogue of Spencer." Pp. 31-50 in *Social Darwinism in American Thought.* Rev. ed. New York: George Braziller.
Leyburn, James G.
1968 "William Graham Sumner." In David L. Sills (ed.), *International Encyclopedia of the Social Sciences.* New York: Macmillan and Free Press.

Albion Woodbury Small

Albion Woodbury Small (1854-1926) influenced sociology primarily through his professional activities rather than through his original thought. His writings on the development of German social thought made these theories accessible to American sociologists. Further, his leadership in academic sociology helped establish the field as a respectable discipline in the United States. In 1892 he became chairman of the first American department of sociology (at the University of Chicago) and, in that capacity, trained a large number of Ph.D's who spread his ideas to other schools. He also co-authored the first introductory text for the field, published in 1894. One year later he edited the first issue of *The American Journal of Sociology*, an influencial journal he continued to edit for thirty years. A man like this was bound to affect his field, regardless of his theory-building or his research.

Small did indeed influence American sociology in important ways. His stress on scientific objectivity and on the study of group associational processes lured the discipline away from two other possible directions of development: away from social engineering and away from overarching analyses of societal evolution. Under his leadership as chairman, the sociology department at the University of Chicago encouraged a broad range of interests and theoretical viewpoints instead of promoting one "school" of sociology as European departments did. During Small's tenure as chairman, the Chicago faculty also encouraged empirical research, most notably research on the facets of city life which took place all around them. Though Small (and most of his compatriots at Chicago) never forgot the human values that inspired a series of welfare-reform movements during their era, they used these values to inspire empirical research, not settlement houses, not grand schemas of societal change or reform. Instead of direct action, they searched for the knowledge that must preceed action. Instead of outlining the mechanisms of total society (as Spencer, the nineteenth-century ideal, had done) they examined specific social processes.

INTELLECTUAL BACKGROUND

Small's role as promoter of scientific objectivity in sociology is an ironic one. By encouraging rigorous methodology he highlighted the means and overshadowed the end — for Small, personally, an unfortunate stress. His values, his hopes for sociology, grew directly from the nineteenth-century reformist tradition and his own theological training. His science was intended as a religious force, as an inspiration for social action:

> Our first and largest function as academic men must always be to help our fellow-men find out what is true, and honorable, and just, and pure, and lovable, and reputable. We shall at least have done a necessary part if we do no more than keep attention fixed on these things, while other men are doing the subsequent work of more directly making these valuations bear the ripened fruits of action. (1910:270-71)

Other facets of Small's academic training shaped his methodology. His studies in social economics, political science, and history provided a subject focus for his work. He analyzed a series of specific social problems (often those with moral and economic implications) rather than society as a whole. Furthermore, two years of residence at the Universities of Berlin and Leipzig gave Small an interest in German social thought, particularly in the ideas of men like Simmel who emphasized the movements or processes of interaction. Later Small introduced these German ideas to a wide American audience and used them to supplement his own social hypotheses about the relationship between human needs and intergroup conflicts. In other words, Small focused his research on action processes within and between groups. But he did not acquire the scientific training that could lead him to the solutions of many empirical problems we encounter when researching these social processes. Instead he assumed that historians and other field workers could develop all the techniques needed for gathering social-science data.

DEFINITION OF SOCIOLOGY

Conscious of his position as an academic pioneer, Small believed that he could serve sociology by delineating the field. He wrote numerous definitions, changing them during his career to reflect the changes in his conception of sociology from a positivistic synthesis of social science to a study of human groups. In his text, *An Introduction to the Study of Society,* Small (and his coauthor, George E. Vincent) defined sociology as "the synthesis of all the particular social sciences" (1894:54) and "the organization of all the material furnished by the positive study of society" (1894:70). Eleven years later, in *General Sociology,* Small devoted a chapter to definitions, culminating in his favorite: "Sociology is the science of social process" (1905:35). His subsequent statements continued to demonstrate his enduring interest in dynamic aspects of group life. For example, in 1916 he wrote, "Sociology is that variety of study of the common subject-matter of social science which trains attention primarily upon the forms and processes of groups" (1916:825). But, we must always remember, Small's vision of sociology extended beyond subject matter to reformist ideal: "Sociology is an attempt so to visualize and so to interpret the whole of human experience that it will reveal the last discoverable grounds upon which to base conclusions about the rational conduct of life" (1905:35).

From all of these formulations, we can rephrase Small's definition: sociology is a positive (or empirical) science that studies "social process" so that planners may use this information to reform society. As we shall see in the following sections, idealism occasionally warred with science and even provided a rationale for Small's causal disregard of technical research problems.

SUBJECT FOCUS

Small naturally shifted his subject focus to reflect his changing conception of sociology. In his first major sociological work, he studied society as a whole. Later he analyzed the cause and course of social processes, a change which parallels both his own maturing ideas of social science and his increasing familiarity with German sociological thought (1916:818).

Small and Vincent's *Introduction. . . .* (1894) employed the biological analogy used by Comte, Spencer, and Americans like Lester Ward. Some sections of the book trace the "natural history" of a society from farm family to city complex. Other sections analyze "social anatomy," "social physiology," and "social pathology," comparing social phenomena to physical organisms. For example, various sections discuss communication through the "social nervous system," and the "mutilation" of a family through death. But even in this early work, Small never conceptualized society as the product of impersonal biological-type mechanisms. To supplement his biological framework, he introduced social psychology and noted that the unconscious desires of individual men often lay behind their activities in social institutions (1894:317-20). As his thought developed he expanded this psychological idea in his theory about how human interests affect social interaction.

In his later formulations, he stated that each science must be unified around some subject matter: physics around molecular process, chemistry around atomic process, and biology around organic process. Sociology is no exception: human associational processes serve as the unifying core of this science (1905:3-8).

By *process* Small meant "a collection of occurrences, each of which has a meaning for every other, the whole of which constitutes some sort of becoming" (1905:513). The *human association process* is a movement of interlocking people and groups in society, a movement from one state to another. This associational process propels mankind toward a state that will provide a good, humane life for more people. For example, several different human groups, with different interests and wants, acted in a process called the French Revolution. The revolutionary assembly rolled a few heads and rearranged French society to suit the interests of a larger segment of the population than the cliques formerly served by the *ancien régime* (1905: 513-23).

Interests and wants are the real heros of the drama above. Interests rise from unsatisfied human desires. They inspire action by motivating people to change their condition. *Social process* is the activity people employ to develop and satisfy these interests (1905:425-42). So, Small concluded, "Sociology might be said to be the science of human interests and their workings under all conditions, just as chemistry is sometimes defined as 'the science of atoms and their behavior under all conditions' " (1905:442). And, as German sociologists like Georg Simmel, Ludwig Gumplowicz, and Gustav Ratzenhofer had also noted, these interests produce group association, conflict, and other vital social activity (1905:495-500).

In other words, interests (especially economic ones) serve as Small's main independent or causal variable. Interests produce conflict which may be resolved in favor of greater happiness for more people. Since these interest are the existing human concerns that critically affect group life, they form the main subject matter of Small's sociology.

SCIENCE — THE PLAN

Nowhere is the tension between Small's scientific ideals and his reformist ones more evident than in his explicit methodology. Trying to explicate a research strategy for sociology, he also tried to reconcile these ideals within the methodology itself. He abandoned the holistic framework used by grand-schema visionaries like Comte and Ward. However, he continued to hope that sociology could solve societal problems — and he inserted that hope into his research designs.

As we have seen, Small began his scientific career by applying the biology-systems framework to society (1894). Later, as he became more familiar with German sociology, he concluded that "the central line in the path of methodological progress, from Spencer to Ratzenhofer, is marked by gradual shifting of effort from analogical representation of social structures to real analysis of social process" (1905:ix).

Beginning with the biological framework, Small could discover an intrinsic moral principle, namely, health. The orderly society is a healthy one. Given this viewpoint, his only ethical problem would be deciding whether to doctor a sick society (Comte's approach) or to await spontaneous remission (as Spencer would). But after shifting to the analysis of social process, Small was forced to reevaluate the good society.

The reevaluation became an integral part of his research strategy. He defined four phases of scientific activity: descriptive, analytical, evaluative, and constructive. The first two phases involve the conventional tasks necessary in any science, namely, data gathering and formulating simple explanations. Phases three and four, however, reveal the moral-reformist nature of socielogy: sociologists must judge the "worth" of data and decide how to control social activity. To analyze the "worth" of various findings, Small proposed that we assemble a council of scientists who could judge human values inherent in social situations. Later the same council members could direct phase four by making social policies based on their judgments (1910:149-271). These last two phases are critical. Indeed, the final task of sociology is "to interpret the meaning of human experience, and to find out how human experience may be directed in the future toward a larger output of life values " (1924:7).

This ethical spirit informed all of Small's work. His interest lay in the information we gather and the purpose we pursue, not our methods for collecting the facts. The data gathering, and the field-work stand as an incidental prelude to the real business of his sociology. Thus he could suggest that anthropologists, ethnologists. and historians might perform the actual research, freeing sociologists for the more important tasks of analysis, evaluation, and social re-form (1894:64-65).

RESEARCH — THE PRACTICE

Small, a trained historian, developed his sociological research strategy by applying historical techniques to sociological problems. Like a good historian, he reviewed primary sources in order to de-lineate sequences of events and interpret trends of thought. How-ever, like a sociologist, he examined specific variables to discover their effect on group life. And doing this, he always remembered his goal: to build the ethical science of group process.

Three historical works provide a sample of Small's research into social process. "The beginnings of American nationality" (1890), written before he moved to the University of Chicago, indicates that his concern with interests and social problems began early in his career. Using legal records, congressional journals, and other historical documents, he contrasted the legal basis of American federalism with the states-rights ideas of people in the various local areas. In effect, he recorded the struggle between human groups representing diverse interests. A less scholarly work, "The civic federation of Chicago: a study in social dynamics" (1895a), exhibits the same basic pattern. Here he chronicled the conflicts and adven-tures of several interest groups united to solve the planning prob-lems of a fast-growing, unruly city. Small wrote *The Cameralists: The Pioneers of German Social Policy* (1909) after he had formally articulated his theory of interests and social process. In this work he examined the writings and actions of German cameralists to answer one central question: What was the purpose or interest that motivated the cameralists (1909: xiv)? Concluding, Small remarked that German social planners perceived the state as a unit first and then as an aggregate of individual German people. Americans, on the contrary, visualized the collection of personalities first, then the state unit. These different viewpoints, which defined different sets of interests and led to different types of social policy, must be understood by scientists attempting to interpret the actions of either group (1909:596). In sum, Small's historical works (including the one written before he became Mr. Sociology at the University of Chicago) all recount the adventures of an interest group, or more precisely, the social history of institutions that men have built to satisfy human interests.

The Cameralists also illustrates Small's work in intellectual history, a research activity he pursued in several other publications. In *General Sociology* (1905), for example, he sketched the ideas of some major writers in sociology — Herbert Spencer, Albert G. Schaffle, Gustav Ratzenhofer — before presenting his own theory of interests. His volume on Adam Smith (1907) interprets Smith's economic writings as pre-sociology, not an account of monetary theories but rather an analysis of economic interest groups operating in a social milieu. In his last book, *Origins of Sociology* (1924), Small examined German social thought as it shaped sociological method and theory: Friedrich Karl von Savigny's discovery of historical change through continuity rather than catastrophy; K. F. Eichhorn's vision of complex, multiple causation; B. G. Niebuhr's criticism of historical evidence; Leopold von Ranke's use of documentation. In other words, Small evaluated advances in historical methodology as advances in the methodology of all social science, including sociology. Here he also explicated German political and economic theory in terms of later sociological ideas. He noted, for example, that Schaffle's ideas about men acting in pursuit of wealth were broadened later to a conception of men acting for a wide range of motives.

These theoretical interpretations, along with Small's translations of Simmel published in the *American Journal of Sociology*, brought English and German thought to the attention of American sociologists. Why did Small bother with the tedious, time-consuming task of translating and outlining these works? By promoting the ideas of European theorists, he hoped to lay a foundation — a foundation of analysis replacing sociology's early ambitions to explain everything at once — that would underlie careful empirical work. European thinkers, he argued, had already begun the important sociological tasks. Americans should review these masters before beginning their own analysis because, "To save enormous waste it is unquestionable economy to spend all the time necessary finding out what has previously been done" (1924:7).

Although Small was anxious to reconcile his ethical hopes with his scientific analysis, he never applied sophisticated German techniques in sociological studies of contemporary problems. Beyond recommending suitable topics for his ethical science — the New England Kitchens in Boston, a "pathological" family, a family living in two rooms (1894:280-82) — he did not offer concrete advice for field research. In his own historical studies he followed a simple formula: demonstrate that interests, especially conflicting interests, affect group life. In effect, he documented the existence of interest-laden situations and detailed the subsequent sequence of events. In his intellectual-history studies, he employed a similar narrative strategy, demonstrating that recent European thought had been informed by an increasing awareness of social milieus and an increasing tendency to analyze the activity of groups within society instead of simply observing society as a whole. Although he identified various research approaches (Simmel's, for example) that would isolate the essential features of group life, he did not provide examples of how to use these strategies and techniques.

CONCLUSION

Small contributed to sociology chiefly through his work as an academic entrepreneur and through his interpretations of German social science. His principle merit does not lie in his original thought and sophisticated research. It comes, instead, from his teaching, writing, editing, and activities as chairman at Chicago, all of which helped to establish sociology as a respectable discipline in American academia. Instead of pioneering new empirical techniques, Small identified the men who had, and encouraged others to follow the path of analysis rather than the dream of global, holistic explanation. Small's own research on the process through which interests affect group life consisted of straight-forward description. We may criticize Small for failing to utilize new empirical techniques in his research. But for a man whose first loves were theology, economics, and political science, he served sociology well — by stressing the importance of analytic methods and by promoting the ideas of other social scientists.

Bibliography

Small, Albion Woodbury

  1890 "The beginnings of American nationality: the constitutional relations between the Continental Congress and the colonies and states, from 1774-1789." Pp. 1-77 in *History, Politics, and Education*. Vol. 8. Baltimore: The Johns Hopkins Press.

Small, Albion Woodbury and Vincent, George E.

  1894 *An Introduction to the Study of Society*. New York: American Book Co.

Small, Albion Woodbury

  1895a "The civic federation of Chicago: a study in social dynamics." *American Journal of Sociology* 1 (July) : 79-103.

  1895b "The era of sociology." *American Journal of Sociology*. 1 (July) :1-15.

  1905 *General Sociology: An Exposition of the Main Development in Sociological Theory from Spencer to Ratzenhofer*. Chicago: University of Chicago Press.

  1907 *Adam Smith and Modern Sociology: A Study in the Methodology of the Social Sciences*. Chicago: University of Chicago Press.

  1909 *The Cameralists: The Pioneers of German Social Policy*. New York: Burt Franklin (n.d.) .

  1910 *The Meaning of Social Science*. Chicago: University of Chicago Press.

  1916 "Fifty years of sociology in the United States (1865-1915) ." *American Journal of Sociology*. 21 (May) : 721-864.

  1924 *Origins of Sociology*. Chicago: University of Chicago Press.

Secondary Sources

Barnes, Harrry Elmer

  1948 "Albion Woodbury Small: promoter of American sociology and expositor of social interest." Pp. 766-92 in Barnes (ed.) , *An Introduction to the Science of Sociology*. Chicago: University of Chicago Press (1965) .

  1968 "Albion W. Small." In David L. Sills (ed.) , *International Encyclopedia of the Social Sciences*. New York: Macmillian and Free Press.

Becker, Ernest

  1971 *The Lost Science of Man*. New York: George Braziller.

Max Weber

Max Weber (1864-1920) has a secure place among the giants in sociology, a peculiar distinction for a nineteenth-century historian. From his historical studies, he developed socological explanations of religion, economics, authority, stratification, urbanization, and a host of other concerns associated with long-term trends in Western civilization. He did not speculate about mental unity or cosmic growth. Rather, like Marx, he pointed to a powerful social mechanism. Marx had examined how human freedom depends on economic position. Weber noticed the Western stress on rationalism, on efficiency. He observed that European men had imposed control, at least some control, over nature: supporting arches, steam power, pumps, and a variety of other gadgets testified to their search for better techniques. This same passion for efficiency served political purposes. The *bureaucracy,* a rationally designed administrative machine, exerted governmental control over Weber's Germany and was extending itself into other spheres. In Weber's opinion the success of bureaucratic efficiency meant the decline of human freedom. Efficient slavery — the promise of the future.

To study this Western dilemma between efficient slavery and chaotic freedom, Weber tried to examine the causal force of subjective meanings: How, he asked, can we speak about the rationality of Western life unless we know what rationality can mean to an individual who exhibits it? Using subjective meanings as the defining subject matter of his sociology, he analyzed social situations with *Verstehen* (interpretative understanding) designed to uncover these meanings. Then he delineated the key features of meaningful situations in constructs called *ideal types.* And, finally, he used types in causal explanations of social life, including social change. This rational methodological strategy did not always operate as efficiently as an ideal-typical bureaucracy. Often Weber lost sight of subjective meanings and had to explain causality in terms of social structure or cultural values instead. No loss. He remained the consummate social scientist researching important areas of human concern.

INTELLECTUAL BACKGROUND

Working within the German tradition, Weber dealt with the same conceptual problem that had challenged Simmel. How can we create a science that accounts for the peculiar subjective elements in human life? The solution for them was conceiving of these subjective elements as part of a causal pattern. Simmel had described typical action sequences and then referred to psychological motives as a *post hoc* explanation of why people enter the action in the first place. Working from Simmel's example (and other ideas), Weber created another set of type-concepts. He focused specifically on the meanings of action. From this vantage point, he could examine typical motives or meanings and see whether or not they caused the intended results.

Weber used these types (concepts like rational economic behavior and rational religion) to challenge the Marxian thesis about social change. Marx had suggested the preeminence of economic causality, hypothesizing that the economic structure of society affects the rest of human life from the way we eat to the way we think. Weber countered with his hypothesis stating that the subjective meaning of rationality had permeated and shaped all Western institutions including economic ones. Hence rational ideas helped shape rational economic structures like capitalism. Weber did not argue one-way causality (he recognized a reciprocal exchange between meanings and structures), but he stressed the effects of ideas as part of his own response to issues already raised by Marx.

To study these issues, Weber had to examine institutions within total societies (another shift from Simmel's limited types of action). He also searched for data much more systematically than his colleague. Drawing on his own academic background in law, economics, historical research, and several Indo-European languages, he conducted masterful empirical studies comparing structures and meanings in several different societies.

DEFINITION OF SOCIOLOGY

Naturally Weber defined sociology in terms of his central concerns:

> Sociology (in the sense in which this highly ambiguous word is used here) is a science concerning itself with the interpretive understanding of social action and thereby with a causal explanation of its course and consequences. We shall speak of "action" insofar as the acting individual attaches a subjective meaning to his behavior — be it overt or covert, omission or acquiescence. Action is "social" insofar as its subjective meaning takes account of the behavior of others and is thereby oriented in its course. (1922:4)

In other words, Weber's sociology studies the subjective meanings or motives behind human behavior. Social people do not simply wander at random but rather they assess the scene and plan their activities to fit in with the behavior of others. This causal sequence — assessment followed by behavior — is the critical explanatory element in Weber's theory.

However, science must do more than delineate causal sequences (1922:19-20). The sociologist and the historian both observe the same empirical data and trace causal paths. The historian records the exotic events, the vividness of strong personalities. By contrast, the sociologist abstracts from these details to present clearly defined concepts, precise meanings:

> We have taken for granted that sociology seeks to formulate type concepts and generalised uniformities of empirical process. This distinguishes it from history, which is oriented to the causal analysis and explanation of individual actions, structures, and personalities possessing cultural significance. (1922:19)

In sum, sociology is the empirical study of social action types.

SUBJECT FOCUS

In his discussion of *social action* (1922:22-26), Weber delineated two important aspects of this behavior: causality and meaning. The person engaging in social action must act, or fail to act, because of his orientation toward some other human being or a number of other human beings.

Weber noted a wide range of causal settings for social action. An actor might orient his behavior toward one special individual or toward some vaguely conceived group of them. He might plan his activities because of the past, present, or anticipated future conduct of the other people. A modern example: a child may cut lawns to earn money not because he thinks that rectangles of green paper are inherently valuable, but rather because he knows that other people will accept the money in trade for something he really wants, perhaps a new bicycle. Since the lawn cutting is ultimately orientated to the reactions of others, it is a social action. Accidents, in contrast, are not caused by our orientations to others and, therefore, are not social actions. When two cyclists collide, that is an accident. When they start a discussion about who is blind and who is careless, that is social action.

On the other hand, an action is not necessarily social just because it was caused by one person's reaction to another human being. Imitation (as analyzed by Tarde) could be "purely reactive" behavior, a "borderline" activity caused by other people, but not meaningful. Likewise, traditional behavior is "often a matter of almost automatic reaction to habitual stimuli which guide behavior in a course that has been repeatedly followed" (1922:23). Clearly, "meaningful" action requires some thought on the part of the actor.

Weber divided these meaningful actions into four types based on the quality of thought involved. Although, of course, most real human activities do not belong completely in one type or another, the classification does distinguish conceptually between different kinds of meaning possible in social action. In their pure (or extreme) forms, the types are:

1) instrumentally rational (*zweckrational*) action based on the deliberate choice of efficient means to achieve some ends determined by the actor — We consider all the possibilities, what we want and what will happen when we get it. Then we decide the most efficient way to reach our goal.

2) value-rational (*wertrational*) action inspired by belief in some values — We may devote ourselves to some ideal (religious vocation, loyalty to a friend, social reform) and then choose the best way to please God or support our friend or serve the cause.

3) *affectual* action determined by the actor's emotional state — Often we react without rational thought: we speak sharply to someone who has irritated us; we pat the head of a nearby child.

4) *traditional* action based on habit — We eat with forks; we wear

shoes; we pursue most of our daily round doing things the way they are "always" done.

Within this system, "instrumentally rational" activity, which requires the deliberate choice of means and ends, contains more "subjective meaning" than traditional action inspired by the customs of dead ancestors. And, since Weber based his sociology on the study of subjectively oriented action, he naturally stressed transitions from traditional to rational activity. Indeed, his work contains a key theme: the increasing rationalization in Western culture.

SCIENCE — THE PLAN

Given his interest in rationalization, Weber needed a technique for judging individual subjective meanings, a method of understanding or *Verstehen*. However, since he wanted to study socially held meanings, he also needed a tool for assessing the social impact of individual ideas. For this assessment, he developed *ideal-type* concepts, descriptions of extreme social meanings and social actions that could be used to compare the subjective states of many individuals. Then, using ideal-type concepts, he experimented with hypotheses about how "typical" meanings (like rationality) affect social life. And so it is not surprising that somewhere between *Verstehen* and ideal types, Weber's sociology shifted from a study of subjective meanings in individual action to a science of cultural values held by individuals.

Verstehen, the first technique here, is Weber's method of interpreting subjective meanings (1922:3-9). To use *Verstehen* we must observe a situation and ask why the people involved acted the way they did. That youngster cutting the lawn: Was he really trying to earn money for a bicycle? When the meanings are rational, we can often understand them by noticing how an actor works toward his goals, particularly if his goals are similar to our own. Moreover, empathy can often help us understand familiar non-rational motives like pride, envy, jealousy, loyalty, love, and other assorted passions. However, it is very difficult for us to empathize with actors who display unfamiliar emotions, accept strange goals, or respond to foreign traditions. How, for example, can an atheistic political liberal, born in 1940, understand the zeal of Torquemada?

To answer such questions, Weber designed his ideal types. Even if we cannot understand individual meanings, he reasoned, we may be able to judge these meanings as departures from some arbitrarily defined norm. If we decide, for example, how a completely rational person would behave in a given context, we can compare real behavior with the rational prototype. If we decide how a person in a money economy would acquire material possessions, we can judge our lawn cutter's behavior (and the meaning behind it) by how well it coresponds to the rational ideal type.

In other words, the *ideal type* summarizes important and unique features of a meaning by highlighting the cultural values that motivate behavior (1904:62-112). When people engage in social action, each person expects the other to share ideas, to react in certain ways at least most of the time (1922:22-24). Without these mental expectations, a relationship would be fruitless. Why earn money unless someone else is willing to trade your money for his meat or that bicycle? In an ideal type, we highlight the essential or extreme elements of cultural values and the relationships they inform; we create "a *utopia* which has been arrived at by the analytical accentuation of certain elements of reality" (1904:90). For example, *bureaucracy* includes a hierarchy of control, written rules, and all the other paraphernalia of an administrative machine designed for maximum technical efficiency. Bureaucratic officials are functionaries performing specific tasks, replaceable parts in the administrative machine. *Charismatic* authority, in contrast, grows from the powerful personality of a natural leader. Although both types of leaders command obedience, it is for quite different reasons. We obey the functionary as we obey the law. However, we grant allegiance to the charismatic leader and follow him in new ways (1922:952-54, 1115-17).

The mental "utopia" — the ideal type defining the subjective meaning of a relationship — is not quite as simple to use as, for example, the ideal type of a chair. All chairs possess, or do not possess, the typical features. But men may engage in the typical actions without necessarily being aware of the subjective meanings that could be involved. As Weber noted, "Only occasionally and, in the uniform action of large numbers, often only in the case of a few individuals, is the subjective meaning of the action, whether rational or irrational, brought clearly into consciousness" (1922:21-22). A clerk in the county circuit court need not understand the rationale behind bureaucracy. However, in research, the ideal type helps us study relationships and meanings within a group. If most people in the group tend to behave as if they believed in rational-legal adminstration, we may assume that rational planning is a cultural value. But, for all we know, that clerk never gives his daily round a stray thought.

So, the ideal type solves two empirical-research problems. First, it provides some way to sort out reality, to cut down the number of things we must notice in complex situations. Second, it provides a basis for judging whether or not certain important variables exist in the situation being studied. But these types are not ends in themselves. According to Weber, scientific work requires two major tools, namely the concept and the *rational experiment* (1918:141). As he conceived them, type-concepts do not simply provide labels for reality, but also form the variables we use in experimental studies.

Clearly we cannot manipulate social reality the way psychologists encourage aggressiveness in rats. As a rule, sociologists must observe life outside the laboratory. Weber recommended comparative studies isolating important subjective meanings and examining a variety of situations with and without the ideal-type meanings (1922:9-12). His central question was this: Do certain ideal-types of cultural values encourage or permit certain types of historical development, assuming that other conditions are propitious? In comparative experiments, we should not isolate a random cause, like the scuffle on a hot summer night that precipitates a three-day riot. Rather we should compare the ideal-type cultural values that exist in riot-prone societies with those in other societies that have racial tensions (or other conditions) but no riots (1905:164-88).

In sum, *Verstehen,* the ideal type, and comparative studies were tools Weber used to define the typical aspects of individual subjective meanings and to explain the causal sequences between these meanings and other social factors. According to Weber, "The real empirical sociological investigation begins with the question: What motives determine and lead the individual members and participants in this socialistic community to behave in such a way that the community came into being in the first place and that it continues to exist?" (1922:18)

Weber used tools to research a very important problem, the changing values of communal life as he knew it, specifically, the growth of rational meaning in Western civilization. There were, we have already noted, aspects of this development Weber feared. Indeed, it was his personal fear that impelled him to study rationalization. On the other hand, he believed his hope for civilization should not affect his use of data or his interpretation of empirical reality. This is what Weber meant by his famous plea for *value-free* sociology: not that values have nothing to do with our choice of a problem, but rather that we must separate our dreams from reality, our preferences from the facts, our political commitments from the search for truth (1917). Science itself provides only practical-technical knowledge and, theoretically at least, gives man the power to analyze his world rationally. Certainly science does not produce progress or happiness: "Who believes in this? — aside from a few big children in university chairs or editorial offices" (1918: 143). So, unlike many contemporaries, Weber defined science as an intellectual enterprise not necessarily related to reform, revolution, or other planned social change. But he always remembered the love of human freedom that lead him to investigate the phenomenon of rationality in the first place.

RESEARCH — THE PRACTICE

Weber researched this problem of rationality using both primary and secondary historical sources: census statistics, the *Ramayana,* Benjamin Franklin's *Autobiography,* legal codes, the *Lun Yü (Confucian Analects)*, musical notation, the *Old Testament,* scholarly historical accounts of various societies, and numerous other records describing the economic, religious and political life of China, India, ancient Judea, medieval Europe, and modern Western civilization. With *Verstehen* he built ideal types (inner-worldly asceticism, rational prophecy, rational-legal authority) from this data. Finally he used these types in causal explanations of his key theme, the growing rationality of Western culture.

Not all of Weber's work fits this scheme quite so neatly. Sometimes he analyzed cause in terms of social structure, behavior patterns not directly motivated by the subjective orientations of the people involved. In the rest of this section, we consider both types of causal explanation; first structural studies and then those involving ideal types.

In "The social causes of the decay of ancient civilization" (1896),

Weber detailed the economic life of the Roman world. Gentleman farmers stayed in town, living the civilized life, while bailiffs supervised large, slave-manned plantations. The slaves lived a celibate life in plantation barracks and produced the wealth that supported their gentleman owners. Unlike many medieval serfs, these skilled workers did not seek freedom and opportunity in the towns. There simply were no opportunities for escaped slaves. As long as the Romans continued their offensive warfare — and its correlate, the slave raid — they procured a constant supply of new, cheap human labor. But when the wars ended, when the Romans could no longer capture new laborers for the plantation and foot soldiers for the army, their economy collapsed. In another study, "Capitalism and rural society in Germany" (1906), Weber used a similar demographic-structural explanation to contrast the German peasant with the American farmer. Germany, he concluded, is a country with too little land and too much farm labor, and therefore it could never support the rural entrepreneurs who flourished in the spacious, less populated United States. In both pieces, Weber sounds like Marx: the means of production affects social patterns. Of course, Weber never denied the validity of this argument. He just believed that Marx had been one-sided, not presenting the situations in which economic institutions appear as the effect or dependent variable in a causal sequence (1904-5:183).

When Weber treated subjective meanings — the official subject matter of his sociology — he was more cautious about presenting a causal argument. For example, in his famous *The Protestant Ethic and the Spirit of Capitalism,* Weber argued that Calvinism contributed to the growth of capitalism. Considering the historical development of both factors, he noted that a stronger argument, claiming the Protestant ethic had caused the spirit of capitalism, would be absurd:

> On the other hand, however, we have no intention whatever of maintaining such a foolish and doctrinaire thesis as that the spirit of capitalism (in the provisional sense of the term explained above) could only have arisen as the result of certain effects of the Reformation, or even that capitalism as an economic system is a creation of the Reformation. In itself, the fact that certain important forms of capitalistic business organization are known to be considerably

older than the Reformation is a sufficient refutation of such a claim. On the contrary, we only wish to ascertain whether and to what extent religious forces have taken part in the qualitative formation and the quantitative expansion of that spirit over the world. . . . In view of the tremendous confusion of interdependent influences between the material basis, the forms of social and political organization, and the ideas current in the time of the Reformation, we can only proceed by investigating whether and at what points certain correlations between forms of religious belief and practical ethics can be worked out. (1904-5:91)

To see how Weber developed this idea, we shall outline his argument stripped of detail. In brief, he covered the following points: occidental rationality as a general cultural value, the extreme religious and economic versions of rationality, the historical development of these meanings, and the economic development of societies with and without the "Protestant ethic."

In the *Ethic* . . . (1904-5:13-26), Weber explained instrumental rationality by listing its effects on occidental culture. For Indians, observation was the method of natural science; Europeans also used experimentation. Many cultures contained polyphonic music; only Western culture produced rational music with counterpoint and harmony. Asians decorated their buildings with pointed arches; Europeans used the arch to distribute pressure. Men worked in all societies; but Western businessmen were among the few employers to deploy laborers where they would produce the most instead of allowing men to enjoy their traditional work habits.

Since instrumental rationality involves defining goals and seeking the means to obtain them, rational action varies with the choice of goals. One possible form of religious rationalism is inner-worldly asceticism:

> . . . the concentration of human behavior on activities leading to salvation may require participation within the world (or more precisely: within the institutions of the world but in opposition to them) on the basis of the religious individual's piety and his qualifications as the elect instrument of god. This is "innerworldly asceticism" (*innerweltliche Askese*). (1922:542)

The Calvinists believed in a stern, demanding God. No magic, no prayers, no acts of contrition would win his favor. In fact, there was no assurance that the Calvinist could please God. However, if a believer devoted his life to hard work, success in that work might be interpreted as a sign of God's favor — although one could never be sure. Having eliminated idle enjoyment of wealth (a cardinal sin), the successful businessmen were forced to reinvest the money in more business ventures as a way of serving God and, indirectly, assuring themselves that God was pleased with their service (1904-5: 114-18, 55-59).

Just as inner-wordly asceticism is an extremely rational religious orientation, so capitalism is an extremely rational form of economic life. It cannot be equated with mere greed or considered a result of advanced commercial techniques any more than inner-worldy asceticism can be called simple piety or considered solely as a natural outgrowth of Protestant theology. The greedy Spanish hidalgos stripped resources from the New World without planning for the future. Capitalists, in contrast, systematically invested, saved, manipulated utilities, and took whatever other means they needed to increase profit and insure future income. Chinese and Indian merchants used bookkeeping, credit, and other modern commercial necessities, but they never assumed the calculated approach to renewed profit that motivated Europeans to apply these techniques in capitalism (1904-5:17-26; 1922:90-100).

To build his concepts of inner-worldly asceticism and capitalism Weber first observed an historical situation and then inductively developed ideas about characteristic, or ideal-type, patterns. Finally, he returned to the "real" world and sought other examples of actions that might resemble the type. For detailing inner-worldy asceticism he examined sermons, personal letters, diaries, and other writings about the Protestant's relationship to God and the world. Looking for the spirit of capitalism he reviewed personal letters, Franklin's autobiography, and other commentaries left by men who also exhibited successful capitalistic drives.

Weber's use of data raises an interesting question: Did Richard Baxter's sermons define the subjective meanings of an average individual or a peculiar outlook held by a few Calvinist preachers? Here is a problem inherent in historical research involving personal documents. We are forced to consider the opinions of a literate minority while we ignore the mass of people who could not, or did

not, leave letters, diaries, sermons, and autobiographies for our inspec-
tion. Perhaps the preachers spoke for most Calvinists. On the other
hand, individual Calvinists may, instead, have used a traditional
mode of social action, simply doing whatever the community and
their parents had taught them to do. In practice, Weber was examining a subjective orientation that is part of a culture, without
assessing how many people consciously valued the meanings involved.
But that may not be important. If a community follows its leaders,
their orientations may be the ones that count.

Dealing with the practice of capitalism, Weber had other evidence
to examine, most telling, the behavior of Calvinist businessmen.
Certainly these entrepreneurs acted as if they held the values defined
by this "spirit." Their no-nonsense approach to increased profits is
testimony to the existence of the "spirit of Capitalism," particularly
since their personal papers also testified to a belief in "rational"
economic planning often sanctioned by religious inspiration.

Comparing his religious and economic ideal types, Weber developed a causal argument that rational capitalism and rational
inner-worldly asceticism reinforced each other. Neither was a prime
cause, although the two variables appeared to be highly correlated
(1904-5:35-46). Both, of course, were segments of the general rational orientation of occidental culture. Weber then demonstrated
this general trend by examining the historical development of rationalization and by conducting an historical "experiment" in non-
Western cultures.

First, Weber traced the disenchantment of the world, or rationalization of the culture, back to an era when Semitic nomads envisioned God as a patriarch in a garden. This God, who controlled
nature, could suspend natural forces in a miracle but he did not
perform magic as gods did in a world without rational order.
Furthermore, He could respond to prayers and other acts of worship. He was a God who enabled the Jews to live in a somewhat
understandable world; unlike most tribal peoples, they could live
virtuous lives to attract God's favor instead of simply accepting a
totally unpredictable existence (1917-9:219-25). Early Christianity
continued this rationalization process by devaluing magical ties.
Christians were urged to treat each other like brothers, to trust and
help men outside of their families. Eventually, this practice enabled
Christians to deal equitably with a large community, instead of

viewing life as a contest between a very small group of intimates and an overwhelming number of strangers (1915:232-42). Life in medieval cities furthered this trend as people from many families settled together and formed political groups to handle trade, protection, and other social necessities. As a consequence of these historical events, by the time of the Reformation, Europeans had constructed a view of the world that permitted rational planning and trustworthy dealings with strangers — both prerequisites of capitalism (1922:1236-65).

Weber's experiment — an examination of societies that had the technical prerequisites of capitalism but lacked the religious meaning of inner-worldly asceticism — provides us with an example of very sophisticated use of historical materials. Although Weber never used this term, he selected a theoretical sample, a sample deliberately chosen because it possessed certain qualities. His two non-Western societies had a trading group with money, technical expertise, commercial know-how, but no Protestant ethic and no capitalism.

Indian religion, for example, stressed magic, mystery, unknowable gods. Puritans knew what God wanted: good men should work hard to please Him. Indians would not presume to know what kind of worldly activity might be pleasing to the gods. For them, the path to holiness lay in a life of passive meditation, not a life of active enterprise. Furthermore, Indians feared that foreigners would disturb the unknowable, magical spirits. Consequently, most Indians preferred to avoid trade and other contaminating contacts with outsiders (1916-7:329-43).

The Chinese world view also inhibited the growth of capitalism even though Confucian teachings stressed wealth as a supreme good. In China, wealth could free men from further work and enable them to live in dignity, to learn literature, scripture, and philosophy. By contrast, Puritans disdained such studies as an idle waste of time better spent in hard work. For the Chinese man, the world was a good place, which he should accept with self-control and dignity. For the Puritan, the world was an evil place, which he should change through active service (1915:226-47).

In sum, Weber argued that, given certain conditions, certain idealtypes will encourage the development of certain institutional forms; given a credit economy, bookkeeping, and other efficient commercial practices, inner-worldly asceticism will encourage the growth of capitalism. "Why?" is another question. Did the new religious ethic actively promote capitalism? Or did it operate indirectly by destroying the old cultural system, thus permitting all manner of innovations? Whatever the reason, this ideal-type value appeared in the same societies that harbored the new economic style.

CONCLUSION

Weber's example shows a sophisticated approach to very difficult research problems. His method of *Verstehen* probes the subjective elements of social life. His use of the ideal type shows us how to select a portion of reality, to cut out an understandable area of life instead of trying to see everything at once. His isolation of variables in historical comparisons — the experiment — provides an example of fruitful cross-cultural study. Taken as a whole, his work demonstrates the need for such comparison of social meanings. We cannot assume that serving God in Muncie, Indiana, is the same as serving God in Bombay.

When he moved from theoretical definitions of social action to research practice, Weber shifted his subject matter from individual subjective meanings to cultural values. He realized that he could not get information about subjective orientations of all the people in a society. Furthermore, even if this information were available, it would be meaningless because many men simply act without conscious thought and follow the lead of others. In the end, Weber gathered evidence to support his hypotheses by assessing the recorded ideals of community leaders, the cultural ideals that may or may not be cherished by the mass of men. However, as Weber demonstrated, these ideals can shape the course of everyday human action.

In sum, Weber worked with a major substantive problem, conducted an ingenious search for the proper data, and got as close to his subject matter as he could, given the materials at hand. Although he did not fulfill his original intentions, his work stands as a fine example of research on very complex topics. But more than that, since he provides clues about how sociologists can directly assess the substance of social life, his example continues to lead those who prefer interpretive, humane sociology to rigorous positivism.

Bibliography

Weber, Max

1896 "The social causes of the decay of ancient civilization."
Journal of General Education 5 (October, 1950) : 75-90.

1904 " 'Objectivity' in social science and social policy." Pp. 49-112 in
The Methodology of the Social Sciences. Glencoe, Ill.: Free Press,
1949.

1904-5 *The Protestant Ethic and the Spirit of Capitalism.* New York:
Charles Scribner's Sons (1958).

1905 "Critical studies in the logic of the cultural sciences." Pp. 113-88
in *The Methodology. . . .*

1906 "Capitalism and rural society in German." Pp. 363-85 in *From
Max Weber: Essays in Sociology.* New York: Oxford University
Press, 1946.

1915 *The Religion of China: Confucianism and Taoism.* Glencoe, Ill.:
Free Press (1951).

1916-7 *The Religion of India: The Sociology of Hinduism and Buddhism.*
Glencoe, Ill.: Free Press (1958).

1917 "The meaning of 'ethical neutrality' in sociology and economics."
Pp. 1-47 in *The Methodology. . . .*

1917-9 *Ancient Judaism.* Glencoe, Ill.: Free Press (1952).

1918 "Science as a vocation." Pp. 129-56 in *From Max Weber. . . .*

1922 *Economy and Society: An Outline of Interpretive Sociology.*
New York: Bedminster Press (1968).
Includes material previously published other English books.
The material used here can also be found in:
The City. Glencoe, Ill.: Free Press (1958).
From Max Weber: Essays in Sociology. New York: Oxford University Press, 1946.
The Sociology of Religion. Boston: Beacon Press (1963).
The Theory of Social and Economic Organization. New York: Free Press (1964).

Secondary sources

Aron, Raymond

1957 "The logic of the social sciences." Pp. 77-89 in Dennis Wrong (ed),
Max Weber. Englewood Cliffs, N.J.: Prentice-Hall.

Bendix, Reinhard

1960 *Max Weber: An Intellectual Portrait.* Garden City, N.Y.: Doubleday.

Blau, Peter M.
  1963 "Critical Remarks on Weber's Theory of Authority."
       Pp. 147-65 in *Max Weber.*
Coser, Lewis A.
  1971 "Max Weber, 1864-1920." Pp. 217-60 in *Masters of Sociological Thought.* New York: Harcourt Brace Jovanovich.
Gerth, H. H., and Mills, C. Wright
  1946 "Introduction." Pp. 3-74 in *From Max Weber: Essays in Sociology.* New York: Oxford University Press.
Parsons, Talcott
  1947 "Introduction." Pp. 3-86 in Max Weber *The Theory of Social and Economic Organization.* New York: Free Press (1964).

Vilfredo Pareto

Vilfredo Pareto (1848-1923) analyzed society as an abstract "system." This concept, which replaced the older analogies of society as a mechanism or as an organism, eventually became an orienting framework in the theories of many modern sociologists. Like the other analogies, the conceptualization of the social system requires its own explanation of continuity and change. In this view, society is not a clock-like machine powered by impersonal forces. Nor is it an animal growing naturally in response to an inherent sequence of development. Pareto explained movement within his system in terms of *non-logical forces* — the true but often well-disguised reasons for human behavior. He probed beyond the excuses and master plans for social behavior to the real, unspoken, sometimes unspeakable, reasons. Like Freud he summarized current ideas about the non-rational and disseminated them to a wide audience. Since Freud, since Pareto, all social science must recognize the non-logical motivations in human affairs.

From his examination of non-rational motives, Pareto developed his explanations of elites, stratification, and social mobility, specifically the social mobility of climbers who manage to push into elite circles and of incompetents who get pushed out. This circulation of personnel is a response to both the exigencies of the situation and the non-logical tendencies of the people involved. For Pareto, society is a delicate balance of such forces maintaining a relatively stable equilibrium: elites rise and fall; individuals suffer, but society survives.

Although the system we study may be non-rational, Pareto insisted on a rational methodology for sociology. Specifically he recommended his *logico-experimental* method, progressing from observation to sound reasoning to a deductive framework and, ultimately, to empirical research testing deduced propositions. Unfortunately, Pareto preferred writing about his theoretical ideas to conducting systematic empirical research and, therefore, he failed to provide instruction by example when he himself studied various social phenomena.

INTELLECTUAL BACKGROUND

Never overeager about acknowledging the sources of his ideas, Pareto did, nevertheless, borrow heavily from other writers. In developing his idea of social system, for example, he combined the organic analogy of Comte and Spencer with the physical-system ideas he had acquired from his own training in mathematics and engineering to build his conception of society as a *system* tending toward *equilibrium* — a whole with interdependent parts that manages to maintain integrity as a whole even though drastic changes occur in the parts, in the relationships among the parts, and in the relationship between the parts and the whole.

However, Pareto did not share the Comte-Spencer faith in progress for the system. Judging from his theory of social change and stability, we may suppose that his spiritual brother was Machiavelli, not Adam Smith, and not Rousseau. Pareto did not trust the common man to create a good society but suggested instead that a capable elite must impose order. The problem for him was explaining how elites manage to rule, or more generally, locating the mechanism that holds the social system together. For his explanation of societal change and equilibrium he borrowed heavily (often without citing his sources) from numerous nineteenth-century writers when he began examining sentiments, beliefs, rationalizations, hopes, fears, instincts, and other sides of human nature that did not conform to the eighteenth-century ideal of reason (1916-23: #1477n by editor). Furthermore, for his specific ideas about how these sentiments and other mental-emotional states affect elites and the rest of the class structure, Pareto elaborated on the theories of Gaetano Mosca and Karl Marx.

DEFINITION OF SOCIOLOGY

Oddly enough, Pareto did not define sociology in terms of his specific interests, but chose, instead, to call it simply the study of "human society in general":

Human society is the subject of many researches. Some of them constitute specialized disciplines: law, political economy, political history, the history of religions, and the like. Others have not been distinguished by special names. To the synthesis of them all, which aims at studying human society in general, we may give the name of *sociology*. (1916-23:#1)

Pareto, who must have considered this definition much too vague, dismissed it as "very inadequate" but added that none of the other sciences had formulated good definitions either. Instead of wasting time defining a science, he said, we should proceed to work in the field, to examine empirical data (1916-23:#2).

SUBJECT FOCUS

Considering Pareto's ideas about subject matter — ideas he elaborated with hundreds of pages of detail — we can see that his interest was, indeed, much more specific than a vaguely articulated concern for some amorphous entity called "society." With his heavy emphasis on a systems analogy, he naturally centered attention on the mechanism that holds this type of system together. Thus, his non-logical forces, which he called *residues* and *derivations,* serve as the focal point in his explanations of both order and upheaval. He argued that society is not a well-planned machine and sociology cannot be reduced to the study of a set of laws defining the rational actions of men. Sociologists, he insisted, must observe human behavior, listen to the reasons men offer for what they do, and, finally, judge the states of mind that lie behind both the actions and the excuses (1916-23:#862-68). To understand Pareto's reasoning, we should consider: 1) his conception of the social system; 2) his definition of non-logical action; and 3) his description of the general categories of non-logical thought (*residues*) along with the types of rationalizations (*derivations*) men use to dress their actions with a rational disguise.

First, like any system, society is an interdependent network of parts consisting of both change and stability. Although every society changes from year to year, it maintains its integrity and, at any given moment, it appears to be a coherent unit (1916-23:#2067-78).

Since Pareto did not equate social systems with biological ones, he did not believe that society could be progressing toward some ideal state or disintegrating in death. On the other hand, since his conceptualization of system was not purely physical, he could not describe society as a perpetual-motion machine. A clock runs as the clockmaker designed it to run until it is overpowered by some outside force such as friction or rust or a little boy with a hammer. Pareto noted that social systems respond both to outside pressures like climate and warring neighbors and to internal elements that regulate order (1916-23: #2060). These internal non-logical forces, the residues and derivations, are the main causal variables of Pareto's sociology; with these forces he accounts for change and stability in the social system.

What did Pareto mean by "non-logical" action? When we desire a particular goal and deliberately choose the best means to achieve this goal, then our action is logical. In all other situations, we perform *non-logical action*. Although he recognized many occasions when logical thought and action is appropriate, for example when we choose the ultimate goals in our lives or express deep emotions, Pareto's scientific concern centered on misguided non-logical behavior, that is, on the actions we perform under the mistaken assumption they will further our goals. Of course, we usually think that we are proceeding toward our goals in a sensible fashion regardless of reality. To illustrate this improper perception, Pareto compared different kinds of people trying to accomplish the same goals. A modern chemist and an ancient alchemist may have both believed that they could combine two substances to produce a third, quite different substance. A modern arsonist burning a grain field and an ancient Roman casting a spell on a harvest may have both intended to destroy a crop. The distinction between these activities lies in objective truth about the results. Applied chemistry changes more substances than magical alchemy. Fire really destroys a crop and spells do not (1909:143-49; 1916-23: #145-248). Even so, when the crop did not wither before his eyes, the sorcerer could explain why his spell failed " . . . this time, it usually works. Perhaps there was already another spell on the field counteracting mine." In other words, we can always explain why we act as we do. But in the case of non-logical action, our verbal pretenses often remain in the face of overwhelming objective evidence that we may be wrong.

Essentially Pareto's sociology is a study of our explanations for such non-rational behavior. First he reviewed the special excuses we create for concrete situations (the *derivatives*). Then, moving to a more abstract level, he analyzed types or categories of rationalizations (the *derivations*). Finally, he concluded that these various derivations spring from six persistent human tendencies (*residues*: *class* 1 — "combinations," a need to innovate, to link solutions with problems, to link omens with events; *class* 2 — "persistences," a need to preserve the *status quo,* to retain old customs, to keep in touch with dead ancestors; and four less important residues). In other words, these constant enduring mental states (residues) inspire numerous elaborations (derivations), which, in turn, appear in the concrete form (derivatives) when someone tries to explain some specific human action. These explanations provide a rational camouflage for deep-seated, enduring, non-logical human feelings. For example, Christians baptize their children explaining that the sacrament removes original sin. By itself this derivative would not interest us. But pagans also use water for purification. In fact, numerous religious groups use some material substance to remove sin, to atone for the violation of tabooes, to cleanse away all forms of spiritual pollution. These various derivatives spring from the same constant type of mental state — a propensity to combine problems and solutions, in this instance a tendency to combine spiritual impurity with a ritual cleansing (1916-23:#842-88). Once members of a society have formed such a combination, class-2 residues encourage them to preserve the custom. Indeed, over a long period of time these persistence residues will cause people to perform the same action even though they have changed the derivation as well as the derivative. Thus, as Christianity spread, many groups retained their pagan rites and beliefs under the guise of Christian ceremonies and dogmas (1916-23:#991-1088). The ritual cleansing for evil doers became baptism; the local god became the local patron saint.

It is the residues (and the psychological sentiments underlying them) that determine social equilibrium. Each person in society contains some combinations of residues just as each chemical compound contains some mixture of elements. The balance of a social system depends on the kinds of people in a group (really the kinds of residue mixtures), much as the stability of a compound depends on the chemical elements within it (1916-23:#2080).

In sum, Pareto used residues, derivations, and derivatives to explain man's behavior in society — or more explicitly to label the psychological source of man's action. Thus, his "science of society" is really a science of residues, derivations, and derivatives as they occur within a social system.

SCIENCE — THE PLAN

According to Pareto the purpose of science is the discovery of truth, a purpose best served by the *logico-experimental* method. Here logical thought reigns supreme. (We might even call Pareto's sociology "logical thought about non-logical thought.") In science, if nowhere else, rationalizations built on residues must give way to a clear-sighted explanation of the real relationships between different objects in the empirical world. In sociology we must observe the derivations and, eventually, draw inferences about the residues behind this verbal behavior and about the other effects of these residues in society. In his *Treatise*. . . . Pareto outlined the assumptions of this logico-experimental approach: the connection between objective data and scientific theory, the use of his equilibrium analogy, and the principle mistakes made by non-logical scientists.

In essence, the *logico-experimental* method requires us to observe the real world and record empirical uniformities or *laws* (1916-23: #1-144). We begin with a description of objective facts: when X goes up, Y comes up, down, or remains the same. In physics we can manipulate Y and X to discover the relationship, but in sociology relationships are so complex and so intractable that we must simply observe them a few at a time when they occur naturally. Then after observing specific social relationships we can abstract the common patterns. We can observe the Smith baptism (along with countless others) and eventually notice the recurring elements. People explain the ceremony as a ritual of purification, as a way to cleanse the baby of his sinful inheritance. Observing further, we notice other purification rituals accompanied by other explanations about why such rituals are necessary. Abstracting the common element in all of these derivations, we can find evidence of a residue, specifically the combination residue that unites a problem with a solution.

But what if our inferences lead to other explanations? What if we conclude that the Smith baptism is a ritual reinforcing group loyalty, that the ceremony really labels a child as a member of some group, that group persistence is the underlying residue? Perhaps both explanations are correct; perhaps both combination and persistence residues inspire an individual baptism. In these ambiguous situations, Pareto told us, we can make an arbitrary decision to select one explanation or both. Further observations may confirm one explanation, but until the relevant facts are known, we have no scientific reason to prefer either interpretation over the other (1916-23: #52-53).

Once we establish a collection of compatable law-like interpretations, we can combine them, build more general statements, and deduce new laws. However, the new laws must reflect empirical fact. No matter how beautifully they fit within a deductive framework, they are worthless unless they describe the objective world. Pareto concluded that scientific logic begins with induction from observed fact and ends with deductive statements describing other facts (1916-23#58-65, 2396-2411).

Strictly following this strategy, Pareto could have begun by listing a series of pedestrian, unconnected statements about residues and derivations — four hundred "laws" telling which residue X seems to inspire derivation Y and explain situation Z. However, he wanted a more coherent framework, a synthesizing explanation. For this, he suggested the *equilibrium-system* analogy. He reasoned that regardless of what the real essence of society may be (as scientists we do not consider essences), we can think about society as a network of interdependent conditions. Some conditions (called *forces*) encourage change; others (the *ties* or *restraints*) encourage stability. When one set of forces produces an extreme change in society, the end point of this change is equilibrium. Of course, the system is not likely to reach equilibrium because restraining conditions impede the extreme change. However, the lack of real equilibrium need not concern us because the system is just a theoretical framework, an analogy. When we think of interdependent forces and restraints, we should consider how a change in one condition could produce a corresponding shift in some other condition or even a new balance for an entire system. For example, if one type of residues predominates in the ruling classes of a society, what would happen if international alliances changed requiring a different type of elite personality? In his research Pareto raised such questions about adjustments in the social equilibrium system (1916-23: #121-40).

But without strict attention to the logico-experimental method, scientific research about this system breaks down into two critical conceptual errors: 1) non-logical inductive leaps from the right data to the wrong conclusions; and 2) abstractions beyond the subject matter of the science in question.

First, Pareto warned, we must not move from direct experience to sweeping statements about the essence of man and society. Physical scientists exercise caution when explaining their data. Astronomers can calculate celestial motion without defining gravitation and chemists can mix elements without defining matter. With similar scholarly restraint, sociologists can observe abstract social patterns without speculating about the reality of freedom, the origin of the family, or other interesting but non-scientific problems. Science, in other words, develops through the slow accumulation of laws about empirical uniformities, not through careless speculation about the wider meanings of data (1916-23: #91-99). But even the cautious scientist can make mistakes. Since different scientists abstracting the same empirical uniformities can create different explanations (1916-23: #53, 64), we may suspect that some of these inductions are false. Induction is a risky enterprise at best, always a creative leap that may end in error.

Discussing abstraction, Pareto reviewed another perennial scientific issue: Should we explain social life in terms of the group or in terms of the individual? When does abstraction end? A chemist, for example, abstracts physical properties — heat, electricity, and light — from chemical substances. Later he can abstract force and motion from the physical properties and produce a statement about pure mechanics (1896:98). In similar fashion sociologists must abstract the residues and derivations from knowledge of derivatives (1916-23: #862-68). However, we must not take our abstractions too far. By the time he finished, the chemist had turned into a mechanic. Pareto wanted to preserve the integrity of sociology; specifically, he warned sociologists not to abstract psychological types from residues and thus change sociology into psychology:

> And lo, another prodigious genius, who holds that because many economic phenomena depend on the human will, economics must be replaced by psychology. But why stop at psychology? Why not geography, or even astronomy? For after all the economic factor is in-

fluenced by seas, continents, rivers, and above all by the Sun . . . .
(1916-23: #37)

Perhaps this sense of scientific boundaries explains why Pareto studied the residues, used them to explain the circulation of the elites, but did not analyze the psychological origins of these non-rational tendencies.

In sum, Pareto has left us with two basic instructions about methodology: first observe empirical social reality and then abstract concrete details into general statements about certain types of uniformities. Although not a sophisticated legacy in itself, this approach, combined with Pareto's use of the system analogy, could inspire a series of provocative statements suggesting how one aspect of society links with another.

RESEARCH — THE PRACTICE

Basically a theorizer, Pareto appears to have devoted more energy to constructing a typology of residues than to researching their empirical manifestations. However, since he wrote about the logico-experimental method as the only real basis of scientific knowledge, we are justified in judging his work by the way he used, and failed to use, this method. To render our judgment we must consider two aspects of his work, namely the quality of empirical evidence he presented and the kinds of reasoning he employed to connect his theoretical statements with research data.

Like his contemporary Max Weber, Pareto recounted historical events and cited documents as data for his studies. Both men used these events and statements as indices of human mental states. The chief difference between them lies in their use of reasoning (the "logico" aspect of Pareto's method) — and it is a great difference. Weber had constructed artificial types based on social meanings, predicted how these types would affect social life, and then examined the empirical world for situations that contained some typical elements. Pareto, in contrast, often observed a social situation and used his types of residues to label forces within the situation. Weber and Pareto also differed in their conceptualization of causality. Although Weber recognized mutual causality, he clearly differentiated between parts of a causal sequence. Pareto did not always delineate his sequences carefully; sometimes he defined elements as inseparable parts of the same entity and then analyzed "causality" between these inseparable parts.

Fortunately, Pareto did not use such faulty reasoning in all of his work, and, even when he did, he often made telling observations that must be acknowledged regardless of the reasoning he used to explain them. Here we will examine both the strengths and weaknesses in Pareto's research approach as he used it to analyze two important empirical problem; first the relationship between social utility for an entire group and benefits for individuals within the group, then the relationship between elite classes and the rest of society.

In his analysis of *social utility,* Pareto challenged the social reformers of his day. How, he asked, can anyone decide what is "best" for a community? There is no one "best" way. Rather, we must ask: "Best for whom — for people who want to use the community, for the community as a whole, for certain groups within the community, or for the majority of the citizenry?" A great increase in population, for example, might please a dictator who plans military conquest using the excess population to occupy new territories. However, the average citizen might prefer to live with smaller families safe at home (1916-23: #2111-45).

Pareto's analysis of utility also illustrates several important points about his concept of the social system. First, since social systems have interdependent parts, utility for the military elite must affect other groups as well. Second, given this interdependence, we must assume that any action has many consequences, the intended one (if plans go well) along with a host of others. Third, we can examine social systems as a network of alternative activities with alternative utilities. If population increases, for example, we may find that economic structures can absorb this increased labor through expanded industrialization or, alternately, that the surplus labor forms a pool of unemployed. If population remains stable, on the other hand, we may find great economic expansion as resources that formerly went for food and shelter shift to factory construction or, alternately, great decline in gross national product due to decreased consumer demand. Although social utility *per se* was not Pareto's main research interest, this conception of utility or benefit — in modern terms, social function and dysfunction — became an integral aspect of his systems analysis and recurs throughout his research.

Pareto's explanation of the circulation of elites further illustrates this interest in functional relationships, particularly during political change. Like Marx he recognized class conflict, that is, the inevitable clash between socio-economic groups with irreconcilable interests, but unlike Marx, he did not predict the eventual triumph of the proletariat. Rather, he stated, talented members of the non-elites regularly join or overthrow the upper classes to form a new elite. Furthermore, when revolution does occur, it is not because a new economic class overthrows the political regime of old exploiters but because there has been a shift in the social distribution of talent and needed residues. Depending on the situation, elites contain a predominance of people with residues for either combinations or group-persistences. During eras of political change, the "foxes" — those who are shrewd, innovative, unscrupulous — plan new tax schemes, create new administrative tools, and plot the downfall of political enemies. During eras of retrenchment, the "lions" — loyal plodders — build up the army and police force, serve in the bureaucracy, and love the old ways even when new ones would serve better (1916-23:#2227-78). A clever ruling elite retains its position by recruiting capable, ambitious people from other classes who also exhibit whichever kind of residues are needed to meet current emergencies. However, when the aristocracy does not recruit a supply of people with needed mental tendencies, it invites revolution. As such a moribund elite declines, its members become more humane and less likely to use force against other classes in the society, but at the same time, remain greedy and unjust — a tempting target for revolutionary plotters (1901:59-71). Thus, class circulation, whether peaceful or revolutionary, does not destroy a social system; indeed, if incompetents are in charge of the government, a social system may need the saving force of revolution:

> Revolutions come about through accumulations in the higher strata of society — either because of a slowing-down in class-circulation, or for other causes — of decadent elements no longer possessing the residues suitable for keeping them in power, and shrinking from the use of force; while meantime in the lower strata of society elements of superior quality are coming to the fore, possessing residues suitable for exercising the functions of government and willing enough to use force. (1916-23:#2057)

In abstract terms, Pareto portrayed the inner workings of a very complex system. He detailed how changes in one social area function to affect other parts of the system. His portrayal is marred, however, by his use of illustrations instead of systematic research and by his tendency to observe an effect and designate it as the result of an unobserved cause — problems that persist throughout his work.

To begin, he built his typology of derivations and residues from a collection of observations that did not include a fair sampling of relevant possibilities. He simply observed life and decided on a set of labels for it. For example, Pareto researched political events like an historian, gathering concrete details about the backgrounds, people, and events of the situation in question and analyzing it as a unique occurrence. In the "Epilogue" of *Fatti e Teorie* (1920) he described prominent derivations during and after World War I. He wrote an account of diplomatic reasoning (the remarks, speeches, and memoranda of diplomats) and linked these statements to derivations. But, after detailing the jesuitical arguments of those statesmen who would do anything to further a government goal, he simply concluded: "the reader will have little difficulty in recognizing in these remarks that derivation which asserts that the end justifies the means" (1920:290). After noticing how people continue to believe in war-crime trials as a deterrent to war in spite of great evidence to the contrary, he declared: "Only derivations by accord of sentiments can blind people to this" (1920:297). Thus, he described a series of situations and named them as examples of derivations. Unfortunately, since there seems to be no logical limit to the possible derivations that could be created as labels for various circumstances, each can be unique, not a proper object for scientific study of general tendencies. Worse, we can attach a wide range of explanations to each situation thus rendering all explanation futile.

Pareto hoped to solve this problem by building a framework from these explanations and then deducing new statements which could be verified in empirical research. However, he never constructed such a framework. Furthermore, his deductive work contains its own errors in the use of evidence and reasoning. For example, when he discussed the effete, impotent, declining elites, he pointed to Louis XVI, a monarch so indecisive that he could not make crucial decisions or use force even to save his own life (1901:59-71). That may be. But what about Charles I, executed after his army was defeated by Parliament's army? Granted Charles used his military force ineffectively, but he did use it. This leads us to ask how Pareto would describe the defeated elite in any civil war. There appears to be a crucial variable Pareto did not examine, something besides the use of force. Considering this question, we may conclude that Pareto chose convenient examples to demonstrate his points but ignored the inconvenient paradoxes that challenged his ideas. A systematic cross-cultural examination of declining elites in a few specified situations (perhaps something on the order of Crane Brinton's *Anatomy of Revolution*) would have provided a sounder empirical basis for Pareto's theory of circulating elites.

But the problem in Pareto's arguments may lie elsewhere, for one, in his definition of elites: "I use the word elite (It. *aristocrazia*) in its etymological sense, meaning the strongest, the most energetic, and the most capable — for good as well as evil" (1901:36). According to this definition, "elite" means "strongest." So when a group of people ceases to be strongest, they cease to be elite. In another work, *Les systèmes socialistes* (1902:136), Pareto states, "Any elite which is not prepared to join battle to defend its position is in full decadence, and all that is left to it is to give way to another elite having the virile qualities it lacks." In translation: any strong group that no longer uses its strength may be defeated by a strong group that does use its strength. These circles illustrate a conceptual problem marring Pareto's work. Often his logico-experimental method involved defining an object and naming part of the object as a cause for the other part — elites are strong; loss of strength causes them to lose their elite position. Naturally empirical research (or a series of well-chosen examples) can verify this type of statement.

Similar reasoning reappears in Pareto's more general explanation of social change. In his discussion of social equilibrium (1916-23: #2412-612), for example, he cited such diverse political events as the success of Philip of Macedon and the failure of Napoleon III, explaining them in terms of the residues and derivations prominent in these men and their societies (1916-23:#2415-20). However, since Pareto assumed that each society and each class within the society contains individuals who possess a predominance of either combination or group-persistence residues, he could always find examples of whichever residues might be needed to explain a situation. This analysis lead Pareto to another circular set of propositions. First, social change occurs when there is an improper distribution of residues (relative to the situation) in the elite and lower classes. Then, one knows that there is an improper distribution of residues in the elite and lower classes because this situation of imbalance is followed by social change.

The residues themselves exacerbate this problem because they do not form a coherent typology of the reality Pareto tried to describe. According to Pareto the six residues: 1) combinations and innovation; 2) persistences and stability; 3) expressiveness; 4) sociability; 5) personal integrity; and 6) sexual expression form an empirical typology of all enduring mental states that affect human modes of non-logical thought (1916-23: #888-1396). Even assuming these six residues do exhaust the sources of non-rational thought, we may question the logic of the categories: the first two residues explain the change and stability in thought; the "need of expressing sentiments by external acts" tells why and how men express themselves; and the last three residues detail the situations and subject matter inspiring some derivations. This arrangement resembles a typology of eating habits that includes: 1) the physiological and social need for food; 2) table manners; and 3) meats, bread, and vegetables. One suspects that categories should be ordered differently — although, of course, empirical forms do not always conform to logical ideals. Moreover, since these residues fall in overlapping categories, any given derivation could easily represent thought inspired by two or more residues. Weber solved this problem by using ideal types and assessing reality as part of a continuum that approaches, but never matches the types. Pareto, however, could not proceed that way because he intended to label a real empirical phenomenon rather than an abstract concept. But whether he used ideal types or empirical ones, Pareto should have enumerated a check list of discriminating empirical symptoms to designate, among other things, when a derivation represents innovation (class 1) and at what time the innovation becomes a group staple supported by persistence residues (class 2).

In other words, using the typology as it exists now, we could observe situations and type them in quite arbitrary fashion. Under these empirical rubrics, any explanation will prove true — simply review a few speeches, name a residue that "fits" the context, explain how the residue caused the thought represented in the speeches, and conclude by noting that the "wrong" residues harmed a situation that turned out badly or the "right" residues helped a situation that turned out well.

Furthermore, despite Pareto's strictures against "psychological abstraction," explanation-by-residue often proved to be psychological explanation. By definition, residues are persistent categories of thought that reflect underlying psychological sentiments. So, when we explain behavior by referring to the residues that inspire it, we are, in effect, referring to the psychological predispositions of individual people. Thus Pareto joined the reductionists, who explain social behavior by reducing it to the sum of individual behavior. Durkheim, a key exponent of the opposite strategy, had provided sociological explanations of individual behavior by showing how personal deviance varies from group to group. Pareto, in contrast, showed how a group situation could change depending on the types of individuals (or residues) within the group.

In sum, Pareto's research exhibits weaknesses in reasoning. He often defined elements in a situation and then explained some essential elements as causes of other essential elements: elites are strong and strength produces elites; an imbalance in residues precipitates class mobility and class mobility is an indication of imbalance in the residues. Nevertheless, the data he used to illustrate these statements convincingly demonstrates two of Pareto's basic points: there are non-logical forces in social life and these forces power a functionally interdependent network within the social system.

CONCLUSION

Pareto studied equilibrium in the social system by analyzing various forms and combinations of non-logical motivations as they appeared in the derivations and derivatives and as they reflected the underlying residues. Abandoning the old organic view of social system (the one used by Comte and Spencer), Pareto suggested other explanations for cohesion in the system. His stress on non-logical forces, his explanation of balance in the social system, his conception of social utility, and his hypotheses about the role of elites in society remain as significant contributions to sociology. His logico-experimental method contains sound policies in embryo (making generalizations from observation, explaining group life solely on the sociological level), but unfortunately, his actual research provides many bad examples with the good.

Pareto also made less obvious contributions to sociology. Sprinkled throughout his comments about elites and other forms of social wildlife, are a number of interesting, testable hypotheses. For example, his remark about the humane, soft, forceless tendencies of declining elites contains a statement we could test (in addition to the redundant one criticized earlier) : as elites decline they become more humane. Is this true? Does a rising interest in the arts, perhaps, signal the decline of a political aristocracy? Although Pareto did not devise such an independent measurement of humaneness in order to verify this hypotheses or to specify just when humaneness becomes a political handicap, he has suggested the possibilities for us to pursue.

Bibliography

Pareto, Vilfredo

　1896 "Excerpts from *Cours d'economie politique.*" Pp. 97-122 in S. E. Finer (ed.) , *Vilfredo Pareto: Sociological Writings.* New York: Frederick A. Praeger, 1966.

　1901 *The Rise and Fall of the Elites: An Application of Theoretical Sociology.* Totowa, N.J.: Bedminster Press (1968) .

　1902 "Excerpts from *Les systèmes socialistes.*" Pp. 123-42 in *Vilfredo . . .*

　1909 "Excerpts from *Manuel d'economie politique.*" Pp. 143-64 in *Vilfredo. . . .*

　1916-23 *The Mind and Society: A Treatise on General Sociology.* New York: Dover Publications (1963) .

　1920 "Excerpts from the Epilogue of *Fatti e teorie.*" Pp. 287-98 in *Vilfredo. . . .*

Secondary sources

Aron, Raymond

　1967 "Vilfredo Pareto." Pp. 101-76 in *Main Currents in Sociological Thought: II Durkheim, Pareto, Weber.* New York: Basic Books.

Coser, Lewis A.

　1971 "Vilfredo Pareto, 1848-1923." Pp. 387-426 in *Masters of Sociological Thought.* New York: Harcourt Brace Jovanovich.

Finer, S. E.

　1966 "Introduction." Pp. 3-91 in Finer (ed.) , *Vilfredo Pareto: Sociological Writings.* New York: Frederick A. Praeger.

Lopreato, Joseph

　1965 "Introduction: a reappraisal of Pareto's sociology." Pp. 1-35 in Lopreato (ed.) , *Vilfredo Pareto.* New York: Thomas Y. Crowell.

Parsons, Talcott
  1936 "Pareto's central analytic scheme." Pp. 71-88 in James H. Meisel
       (ed.), *Pareto and Mosca*. Englewood Cliffs, N.J.: Prentice-Hall,
       1965.
  1937 "Vilfredo Pareto." Pp. 178-300 in *The Structure of Social Action*.
       New York: Free Press (1968).
Timasheff, Nicholas S.
  1967 "Vilfredo Pareto." Pp. 160-68 in *Sociological Theory: Its Nature
       and Growth*. 3rd ed. New York: Random House.
Zetterberg, Hans L.
  1968 "Introduction." Pp. 1-22 in Vilfredo Pareto *The Rise and Fall of
       the Elites: An Application of Theoretical Sociology*. Totowa, N.J..
       Bedminster Press.

Charles Horton Cooley

Like most sociologists before him, Charles Horton Cooley (1864-1929) tried to explain the mechanisms of social cohesion. For him, the specific problem was locating the moral basis of society. His discovery: the *primary group,* the intimate, face-to-face group that socializes the individual and thus provides a common nature and sense of morality among members of a society and, to a great degree, among all humans. Human interaction — more explicitly human communication — is the mechanism that gives the primary group its power. First, we learn through our communication exchanges with others. Then, we build a complex of mental states that reflects the one held by our fellows. Through these states, through our thoughts, our sentiments, and our emotions we share social life. In effect, we become part of a *social-mental complex,* an *organic whole* composed of the mental processes that occur between the individual and his society. Finally, this continuous mental process coalesces into the mental underpinnings of our political structures, social classes, and other features of group life.

Cooley researched his ideas using a very simple methodology. For him the method had to suit the problem, and the problem was gaining insight into the social-mental process that ties the person to society. Quite sensibly Cooley developed his methodology around his two principle assumptions about social life. First, since he assumed that social proces is an organic whole which can only be understood as a whole, he did not try to dissect it for analysis. Instead, he relied on description, data-pictures of an entire process situation, not systematic comparisons of one variable against another. Second, since he believed that interior mental processes were the basic subject of sociology and that he could not observe these mental activities directly, he relied on imaginative insight, or *sympathetic understanding,* to carry him from observed behavior to his real concern, the inside of someone else's thought system — really the inside of everyone else's thought system, the source of human nature and morality.

INTELLECTUAL BACKGROUND

Like many Americans of his era, Cooley first learned sociology by reading Herbert Spencer. His Spencerian period did not last long, however. Cooley's own experience as a government researcher coupled with his reading of Charles Darwin's work, taught him the necessity for a new methodology, a strategy for replacing Spencer's use of data to prove preconceptions with the careful scientist's use of data to develop and test propositions. For his ideas about the specific subject matter he preferred to study, he also drifted away from Spencer's global concerns and borrowed instead from the social-psychology of James Mark Baldwin and William James. Baldwin had discussed child development as a product of the interaction between a child and other people. James had defined the *social self,* a man's image of himself as he imagines that others think of him (1922:125). These social-psychological ideas reappeared in Cooley's theories about socialization and other mental-social processes. But in spite of his growing interest in research methods and social psychology, Cooley retained one of Spencer's key precepts, the conviction that society must be studied with "an evolutionary outlook" (1926:309). Combining these insights, Cooley produced his unique ideas about evolutionary process, not about the sweeping change of history but about the evolutionary development of the self as a social being.

DEFINITION OF SOCIOLOGY

In *Human Nature and the Social Order,* Cooley defined sociology as the study of society or the study of "life regarded from the point of view of personal intercourse" (1922:135). In this work, he discussed the links between an individual and his social surroundings: the development of a child's personality as he relates to other family members; the growth of a leader's power as other members of the group decide to accept his leadership; in general, the course of any mental communication as one person interacts with the others in a group. Cooley designed his sociology to study this communication and its effects:

> And personal intercourse may be considered either in its primary aspects, such as are treated in this book, or in secondary aspects, such as groups, institutions, or processes. Sociology, I suppose, is the science of these things. (1922:135)

Using Spencer's biological analogy, Cooley naturally observed "personal intercourse" as an evolving process. Just as biology studies slow change in a physical organism, so, he decided, sociology must study rapid alterations in social life. In other words, "Any real study of society must be first, last, and nearly all the time a study of process" (1918:396). But although he retained Spencer's organic analogy, Cooley chose to research different topics. Spencer had outlined societal change from primitive times to the industrial age. Cooley examined human personal growth that occurs in socialization, changes in a class system that are encouraged by communication, moral cohesion that develops within a primary group. Thus, for Cooley evolutionary sociology became the study of continuous mental communication process, not the delineation of global change.

SUBJECT FOCUS

According to Cooley, this mental communication process is both the subject of sociology and the means through which we learn of social life. Cooley explained that we contact the material world — the province of natural science — solely through our senses, but we discover the social world through our communication with other men and our observation of them combined with our imagination of their mental process. Each person, whether he is a child first examining his social milieu or a scientist probing for specialized knowledge of societal ways, develops a *mental-social complex* an "individual human mind, including all . . . socially developed sentiments and understandings" (1926:295). Without the mind, without this mental-social complex, there would be no social life and no society. In other words, we simply cannot observe social behavior as if it were no more than physical action. We cannot speak, for example, of charity, or homicide, or social status without considering the social attitudes that define charitable, homicidal, or status-maintaining acts. These mental states are the subjects that sociologists should investigate (1922:120-22).

The complex of mental states incorporates individual and social elements as an organic whole, as a dramatic process of interaction between the person and society. Psychic mechanisms of communication, that is, speech and writing, bind men together in a unit just as a network of streets links the far corners of a city (1928a:7-8). Thus, any movement in one part of the network has repercussions somewhere else. Within each network, there are a series of smaller ones: neighbors within the city, institutions within society, persons within the family. We may choose to study the giants or the smaller units, but whether we examine a race, a nation, a political party, a community, or a family, we should view it as a whole — as a complete network of reciprocal activities, as a total communication complex (1918:26-29).

Cooley did not fight the border war between sociologists and the other social scientists. For him, distinguishing the natural from the social sciences seemed more critical than defining some peculiar subject matter to separate sociologists from historians, economists, and their relatives. Indeed, his interest in mental-social processes as a subject merges sociology with psychology, especially social psychology. He himself did not see a firm distinction between the two disciplines and often wrote about the social activities that form human outlooks, indicating that he included both social and individual mental processes within the purview of his sociology (1926: 305-07). Indeed his discussion of the relationship between person and group — particularly during child development — is his most enduring contribution to sociology.

SCIENCE — THE PLAN

Like Max Weber, Cooley explicitly considered the interplay between social life and the meaning structure in the mind of an individual. Neither of them could simply name the desire motivating some form of action as Tarde did. Nor could they simply follow Pareto's lead and explain social activity by naming the dominant psychological predisposition held by the people involved. Instead of assuming that man's inherent nature controlled social life, Weber and Cooley assumed that social life shaped and directed an individual's mental outlook. Therefore each of them had to develop a methodology that could explore the source and direction of personal meanings instead of just determining an appropriate label for them. However, since Weber also assumed that cultural differences would distinguish the world view of Calvinists and Chinese, he looked for ways to measure this difference. Cooley, on the other hand, assumed that all people are basically alike, that all are developing a common human nature, and so he observed the process through which we develop this common nature and then communicate it to others.

Naturally, these rather divergent assumptions about subject matter accompanied different methodologies: a different relationship between theory and research, a different technique for gathering and evaluating data, and a different strategy of analysis.

To begin, these divergent assumptions required different modes of reasoning. From the outset Weber used his theory to predict the consequences of "rational" and "non-rational" meanings and used research to verify these deductions. Cooley, in contrast, predicted the existence of a universal process and used research to trace the natural sequences occuring as the process unfolds. From this perspective Cooley could argue that deductive reasoning leads straight to error. For example, he criticized Spencer by saying " . . . Spencer spun a theory from any material he happened to have and collected facts to illustrate it"; moreover his " . . . light which seems so clear is not daylight but the artificial illuminations of a theory . . . the assertions do not stand the test of real life" (1920:270).

Rather than use data to illustrate statements as Spencer had done, Cooley wanted to present facts that would reveal their own story. Following his own advice, he simply described social life as he saw it, as an interdependent communication network linking primary groups, social classes, and other group phenomena. This meant, of course, that he did not formulate hypotheses to predict the occurrence of these phenomena under specified structural conditions. Instead he relied on *post hoc* explanation, although we must admit, a talented analyst like Cooley could provide some very plausible *post hoc* explanations.

To collect the data necessary for such inductive reasoning, Cooley developed a method called *sympathetic understanding*. He suggested that we can observe and measure physical things, including the behavior of humans, with the senses, but we acquire knowledge of human mental processes through observation of a person followed by "flashes of vision as to what he would do in particular situations" and "inner sentiments which you yourself feel in some degree when you think of him in these situations, ascribing them to him" (1926: 294). In other words, we observe human behavior, and, with sympathetic understanding, we interpret many social acts; we learn to imagine how pride, anger, fear, loneliness, and other mental-social phenomena affect human action.

In essence, Cooley understood scientific knowledge of the social world as a normal extension of the knowledge system creating human nature. When they are young, he said, people learn the mentality of others in their social world through words, gestures, expressions, and other acts of communication (1926:293). Since all infants learn to be human through this social process, men in different societies form rather similar mental-social complexes. For these reasons Cooley could suppose that twentieth-century Americans would understand the mentality of ancient Carthaginians (1926:301). This assumption — that people throughout the world share both a common nature and a common understanding — lead to a second major methodological differences between Weber and Cooley, the distinction between *Verstehen* and sympathetic understanding. Using *Verstehen,* Weber first defined an objective set of criteria (for example, his description of how "rational" man operates in economic matters), and then compared the actions of real men with these defined traits to detail far-reaching dissimilarities between the motives of Indians, Chinese, and Western Europeans. Cooley, in contrast, assumed his motives would be similar to those of the people he "understood" in a research study. So for assessing Cooley's technique this is the critical question: Does sympathetic understanding produce valid results when we study the mental complexes of those in other cultures? Given his assumption about a universal human nature (with a corresponding universal mentality), Cooley did not see a need to defend this method. Those who share Weber's perspective might judge differently. To them, sympathetic understanding may seem to be a better technique for developing insights about one situation than for testing their validity in a variety of settings.

As we would expect, considering his substantive assumptions and inductive reasoning, Cooley differed from Weber on one other important aspect of methodology. Instead of analyzing intergroup differences or tracing the long-term change in one setting, as Weber often did, Cooley recommended that we summarize our insights in descriptive reports about a total setting. Indeed, he believed that all science is, by nature, primarily descriptive. Sociology differs only by being more complex and difficult than most fields (1928b). He hoped sociologists would eventually use descriptions to build a set of theories which could be verified or refuted by further study of social data, but he failed to offer workable suggestions for those who would create and test these theories. Although he noted that social situations are very complex, hence very unpredictable, at the same time he insisted that men should observe this complex organic whole rather than isolated features of a social situation. Further, he allowed that introspective observation would vary with the observer but suggested precise communication between researchers as the only practical way to make observations more reliable and insights more valid.

Someday, Cooley hoped, working sociologists will solve these problems in specific research projects, but they will never enumerate a general check-list for would-be methodologists: "I am not sure but that methodology is a little like religion. . . Each one, if he is clever, works out something adequate for his own use, but the more general principles remain unsettled" (1928c:326). If we would learn methodology, then, it is through the example set by those who actually solve an empirical problem, not through the declarations of those who pronounce methodological dogma.

In the end, sympathetic insight into a total interaction situation remained Cooley's chief research approach both for developing theories and for verifying them. Therefore, although he was able to observe and describe socialization processes, primary-group relations, and other forms of mental social activity, he did not measure the relative effects of different child-rearing techniques, different types of primary groups, and other conditions affecting human behavior. For example, he could have asked if there was a difference in the behavior of a child socialized by an isolated nuclear family and a child trained by village neighbors — even if both groups are trying to teach the same basic values and norms. While this quesion may interest us, it was not Cooley's main concern. Since he preferred viewing life as an interdependent whole, he would not isolate small pieces of the world or specify the conditions making the whole in Nigeria differ from the whole in Ontario. However, as we shall see in the next section, an alert sociologist like Cooley could produce testable hypotheses in spite of his desire to explain everything at once.

RESEARCH — THE PRACTICE

Cooley's writings often appear to be more art than science, displaying flashes of insight without a detailed theoretical structure, telling a series of colorful stories that show how a perceptive observer viewed his world. Typically he gathered data by watching the scene around him and by reading about less familiar settings. From this he built his theoretical ideas. Consistent with his own scientific ideals, he generally researched the mental-social process by examining some process situation as an organic whole, by recording the influence of communication in one area that spreads through the mental-social network to far-distant places and far-different institutions. Every so often, however, Cooley collected a more comparative set of data to demonstrate the limited effects of a specific physical or structural variable. We will consider both types of research here: descriptions of social processes that begin in small groups and spread to the larger society and analyses of variables that cause certain processes to begin in the first place.

Cooley's most famous works, *Human Nature and the Social Order* (1922) and *Social Organization* (1909), belong to the first group. In these books he recorded his inductive insights about the relationship between the social person and his group. *Human Nature. . . .* described the process that transforms a human animal into a social being. The child acts, watches others react, and uses his impressions of other people's reactions to form an idea of who and what he is. In the process he creates a *looking-glass self*, a social picture that reflects himself through his perceptions of these outside judgments (1922:168-210). *Social Organization* focused on the group instead of the individual and identified a group so intimately identified with each of us that "the simplest way of describing this wholeness is by saying that it is a 'we'; it involves the sort of sympathy and mutual identification for which 'we' is the natural expression" (1909:23). This, of course, is our *primary group*.

In a separate study Cooley verified his chief hypotheses from *Human Nature. . . .* by observing three children as they learned to identify themselves through their interaction in a group. First they imitated others: when a mother pointed to an object and said "cat" or "you" or "me," each child would do the same. Eventually, however, the children began to distinguish other people from themselves, to learn that their own point of view was not the same as everyone else's. As they perceived this difference, they began to use words like "you," "me," and "I" in proper context. Obviously these children were acquiring a looking-glass self based on interaction with others in their primary group. How else, Cooley wondered, could they grasp the concept of "I" — except by putting themselves in the place of those who used the term (1908)? Hence their own use of "I" evidenced their understanding of this subtle concept. In other words, to verify his hypothesis about the formation of human nature, Cooley observed behavior (children learning to speak) and imagined what was occurring in the minds of these persons as they stuggled with a concept in the social mental complex.

Unfortunately, however, his holistic conceptualization of social process encouraged circular thought on the socialization problem. He reasoned:

1) Children learn social skills through interaction with parents and other family (primary group) members.

2) These children are learning social skills.

3) Therefore they are learning skills through the primary group.

In this analysis he assumed what he set out to prove. First he defined speech as a skill learned through primary-group interaction. Then, after he observed children learning to talk, he explained this learning as a product of primary-group interaction; that is, he presented his basic assumption as a conclusion.

When Cooley moved his analysis from the small group to the total society, he once again suggested how the mental-social complex acts as cause and effect in social life. He defined social class, for example, as "any persistent social group, other than the family, existing within a larger group" (1909:209), and explained how these groups persist by virtue of interaction and a common mentality. If the mentality or social mind defining the class is based on a biological principle, the group becomes a caste; if members insist on a system of free training so that promising careers become accessable to all youngsters who are naturally fit for them, the group becomes a class in an open-class society like the United States. Inherited positions still exist even here, of course, because family training and attitudes tend to educate a child for the position of his father no matter what his personal ambitions might be. The sons of professional men learn how to judge the best opportunities for a brilliant professional career; the sons of farmers simply do not have access to this subtle advantage brought by home training any more than a lawyer's son learns when and where to get the best prices for a wheat crop. To counter-balance the initial advantages of upper-class groups, Cooley recommended a high-quality public-school education available to all so that talented and ambitious lower-class sons would acquire the knowledge they needed to find their proper upper-class positions. Popular suffrage provides another important form of communication, from the lower-class as a group to the upper-class as a group, and thus helps protect the freedom of lower-class members as well as guaranteeing them the right and opportunity to live in comfort regardless of their ambitions (1909:209-35).

Cooley's analysis of the relationship between class and power demonstrates the effects of the mental-social complex even more vividly. In his conceptualization, power is not the use of economic advantage to force others into compliance; instead it is "control over the human spirit," most notably control that "one mind exercises over another by virtue of what it is, without any means but the ordinary symbols of communication" (1909:264). Marx to the contrary, Cooley claimed, upper-class power does not rest on the ability to exploit the less fortunate by controlling their economic lives, but rather on the ability to control their thinking through influence over the press and other sources of public opinion. However, in a society like ours, where popular suffrage, unionization, and other structures provide channels of communication for the lower classes, public opinion becomes an open forum — an opportunity for all class groups to demonstrate their common humanity and common interests — not a vehicle for one group to force its ideology on the rest of society (1909:256-309).

On the other hand, those less optimistic than Cooley could use his analysis to show that even with universal education, voting rights, and related lower-class opportunities, upper-class groups can still use public opinion to secure their own interests. For example, Cooley noted that in the United States public opinion had fostered the belief in open-class mobility: "Given hard work and decent luck, anyone can get to the top." As a result, ambitious young people worked to join the American elite. Why, he wondered, should a farmer's son organize a protest against railroad monopolies and exorbitant freight charges if he can go to law school and join the company (1909:273-74)? A sociologist like Pareto would have explained this as part of the mechanism through which a clever elite incorporates talented would-be revolutionaries. Cooley optimistically suggested that the "naturally talented" would find their proper class position in the open-class system. In such a system, there is no need for conflict because everyone knows he will get his just share eventually. Both, however, could have concluded that an open-opportunity system like the American one, coupled with belief in the system and wide-spread communication of that belief functions to reduce class conflict.

This is a functional analysis — although Cooley did not use that term. A certain set of economic opportunities coupled with a certain set of beliefs encourage a certain set of behavior patterns. Communication, that distinctly human activity, forms a network of coordinated parts and assures that one section of society will coordinate with another. In sum, the functional sequence is: a socially defined situation, the social-mental complex defining the situation, and the consequences of that definition, which, in turn, redefines the situation. Here is another circle — as long as Cooley researched the whole network of a mental-social process, he could not escape these circles.

Occasionally Cooley did introduce an outside variable and then describe a straight-foreward causal sequence. In "The theory of transportation" (1894), he analyzed transportation as a physical form of communication, a means of distributing foods and services, a way of bringing silks to queens and transporting armies to battlefields. Since such physical needs shape social life, he hypothesized, it is no accident that cities often rise on sites where there is a break in transportation, especially if the break is a change between water and land. London, for example, was built along the Thames and New Orleans along the Mississippi (1894:75-83).

After writing this article (which also served as his Ph.D. dissertation), Cooley abandoned his research on the physical aspects of communication to concentrate on mental-social phenomena. But over twenty years later, sociologists like Robert Park used similar ideas about how physical environments affect social life to create the ecological school of research.

In another research article, "Genius, fame and the comparison of races" (1897), Cooley used structural variables (or group properties), as the first variables in a causal sequence. Instead of "understanding" a social situation, he assembled objective data — biographies, autobiographies, statistics — to support his point, a refutation of Francis Galton's work on *Hereditary Genius*. Galton had argued that race produces genius which, in turn, produces fame. After reviewing the evidence of his data, Cooley made other claims: society assigns the label of "genius" to prominent, talented people. If you choose the right historical period, (Elizabethan England, ancient Athens), you can find many geniuses in your group (particularly in its upper classes) and very few in other contemporary groups. Assuming racial capabilities remain constant, Cooley concluded that societies choose to recognize and appreciate different qualities, perhaps in a response to social needs of the era. Furthermore, a society is more apt to notice "superiority" among nobles than among serfs. Thus, to be a famous person, one should be born with talent and born into the upper classes of a society that is currently appreciating this type of talent! Socrates might not have been famous as a peasant in fifteenth-century Greece. Although this article citing the social correlates of fame (and anticipating modern labeling theory) is certainly not typical of Cooley's work, it does demonstrate one of his basic research principles: suit the techniques to the problem at hand. It also illustrates his ability to marshal comparative data about some limited set of variables. But, most important, it describes a mental-social process fimly tied to a structural situation: it describes how men came to be considered famous because they provided for societal needs and belonged to the upper classes.

In sum, Cooley normally used sympathetic introspection to produce descriptive insights. Building on the data of personal experience (supplemented by historical examples), he analyzed child behavior in the primary group, the growth of the social self, and other mental-social phenomena. But, although he used an inductive strategy to detect general tendencies, he did not build a deductive system with hypotheses about the conditions that could alter these trends. Furthermore, it was only on rare occasions that he abandoned holistic studies to examine specific structural conditions that could deflect, delimit, or define the course of the mental-social process.

CONCLUSION

Clearly, Cooley preferred to create concepts and hypotheses rather than test them. He presented fruitful ideas — especially ideas about the growth of the social self within the primary group — but he seldom verified them with anything more objective than his own insight. In his opinion, the method must suit the subject, and sympathetic understanding is the best method for studying mental-social complexes. Unfortunately this method leads to reliability problems; no two scientists produce the same insights. Cross-cultural studies exacerbate this problem further and highlight the question of validity. How can we understand men who are different from ourselves? In spite of this problem (which Cooley acknowledged), he preferred to use his methodology because it provided a description of his subject matter, mental-social process. We may fault him for failing to test his hypotheses in a rigorous manner, but within the limits of his definition of sociology, Cooley conducted more then adequate research. To criticize his methods we must also criticize his definition of the field and its subject matter.

Here lies the deeper problem in Cooley's research work: he was content to observe the organic whole of process in social life without isolating the specific elements of structure that affect the course of a given process. He observed the action between a family and a child without accounting for the effects of different family types, different child-rearing techniques, or even different cultural settings for the family. In more general terms, Cooley defined a situation and illustrated his definition. Human nature, he stated, is a product of social influences. Child-socialization studies show the growth of individual human personalities. Therefore, child-socialization studies show social influence on human nature.

Although we may not admire Cooley's basic line of reasoning, we must not ignore his great contributions: his stress on social interaction as the process that shapes human personality, his emphasis on the primary group as an enduring feature of social life. These facets of social life provide Cooley's answer to that old sociological question: What is the mechanism binding people together in society? Comte had said, "Consensus produces a commonly held world view." Spencer and Durkheim had claimed, "Social integration and feelings of solidarity are based on the division of labor." Cooley examined the problem from the perspective of the person instead of the group and discussed the person's mental framework as a product of his society, an orientation first learned within the primary group and later carried to the diverse secondary groups that compose the social organization of society. Thus, instead of emphasizing the group structural elements that accompany social cohesion, Cooley discussed the person-group process through which this structure operates.

Bibliography

Cooley, Charles Horton
    1894 "The theory of transportation." Pp. 17-118 in *Sociological Theory and Social Research*. New York: Henry Holt and Co., 1930.
    1897 "Genius, fame and the comparison of races." Pp. 121-59 in *Sociological Theory*. . . .
    1908 "A study of the early use of self words." Pp. 229-47 in *Sociological Theory*. . . .
    1909 *Social Organization: A Study of the Larger Mind*. New York: Schocken Books (1962).
    1918 *Social Process*. New York: Charles Scribner's Sons (1922).
    1920 "Reflections upon the sociology of Herbert Spencer." Pp. 263-79 in *Sociological Theory*. . . .
    1922 *Human Nature and the Social Order*. 2d ed. (1st ed. 1903) New York: Schocken Books (1964).
    1926 "The roots of social knowledge." Pp. 289-309 in *Sociological Theory*. . . .
    1927 *Life and the Student: Roadside Notes on Human Nature, Society and Letters*. New York: Alfred A. Knopf.
    1928a "The development of sociology at Michigan." Pp. 3-14 in *Sociological Theory*. . . .
    1928b "The life-study method as applied to rural social research." Pp. 331-39 in *Sociological Theory*. . . .
    1928c "Sumner and methodology." Pp. 321-27 in *Sociological Theory*. . . .
Cooley, Charles Horton, Angell, Robert Cooley, and Carr, Lowell Juillard
    1933 *Introductory Sociology*. New York: Charles Scribner's Sons.
Secondary sources
Angell, Robert Cooley
    1968 "Introduction." Pp. 1-12 in Albert J. Reiss, Jr. (ed.), *Cooley and Sociological Analysis*. Ann Arbor: University of Michigan Press.
Coser, Lewis A.
    1971 "Charles Horton Cooley, 1864-1929." Pp. 305-30 in *Masters in Sociological Thought*. New York: Harcourt Brace Jovanovich.
Jandy, Edward C.
    1942 *Charles Horton Cooley: His Life and His Sociological Theory*. New York: Octagon Books (1969).

Robert Ezra Park

Robert Ezra Park (1864-1944) has made a lasting impression on American sociology for three reasons: he helped to pioneer important substantive research areas; he coauthored the introductory text that became the sociological bible for twenty years; and he inspired a generation of creative graduate students. Using a viewpoint quite different from Cooley's, Park studied the social processes as they occur in objective behavior. Both men examined the social control mechanisms that regulate group activity despite the inherently uncooperative tendencies of individual members. But, where Cooley had observed how children internalize moral rules through socialization in the primary group, Park pointed to the external forces, especially competition in the community, that compel men to cooperate with each other; where Cooley had discussed normal, expected activity, Park highlighted tensions that break normal patterns; and where Cooley analyzed the functionally interrelated whole of social life, Park traced the causal sequences of social change.

For his studies of *social control,* Park recommended experimental research on social processes. But he did not practice sociology as he preached it. Instead of becoming an experimental scientist, he remained, in his terms, a "super reporter," observing life and recording patterns of interaction. It was Park's choice of subject matter that influenced him to neglect his theoretical preference for experimental science in favor of a more purely descriptive technique. When he studied the social process he looked for regular sequences of behavior binding people together in social groups. To trace this course of events he chose a technique called natural history; he reported types of social control patterns much as a natural historian records steps in the development of a species.

However, Park's real contribution to sociology is not based on his personal research. Once settled into an academic chair at the University of Chicago, he himself seldom ventured into the field. Instead he urged his students to research social control problems by observing the evil and good in city life. Through these students he established a solid empirical tradition in American sociology, a tradition that still guides the field in its research studies of social behavior patterns.

INTELLECTUAL BACKGROUND

Toward the end of his life, Park wrote "An autobiographical note" (1944), outlining his intellectual adventures. Reading it, one imagines an academic sitting at his desk while his mind wanders to a scene of life on the streets; then, alternately, a man standing on a street whose mind has already begun to compile the notes he will eventually record at his desk. Park began his work career as a sedentary academic but soon left teaching for the "real" world of newspaper reporting. Later he decided that newsmen are a special breed of social benefactor, that truth disseminated through the paper would further social progress (1944:v-vi). In effect, he defined his search for truth as a moral virtue and decided to practice this virtue by learning the facts about important social issues and situations. Pursuing this goal, he returned to school, traveled and studied in Europe, worked with Booker T. Washington, and, finally, at age fifty, returned to his career in reporting: he became a sociologist.

In his terms, he became a "kind of super-reporter," someone who described the process of interaction and delineated long-term trends "a little more accurately, and in a manner a little more detached than the average" (1944:ix).

Given this orientation, Park naturally chose a research model that would depict change in everyday life. Clearly the evolutionary perspective of Comte and Spencer would not do. Nor would the functional analysis of Pareto or the psychological reductionism of Tarde. While studying in Berlin, Park found a model in the work of Georg Simmel, who analyzed social process by tracing the sequences of development that can occur within the limits of a specified situation. However, although Simmel considered the limits imposed by a psychological motive like animosity or a structural circumstance like intergroup conflict, Park chose, instead, to examine the limits imposed by the physical environment and the moral order groups create to regulate activity within that environment. In other words, he applied Simmel's analytic method to problems suggested by contemporary theories in biology and social psychology: for example, he studied how the exigencies of interpersonal cooperation regulate human competition in a city neighborhood just as symbiosis limits plant growth within a prairie ravine.

DEFINITION OF SOCIOLOGY

Park singled out social control as the central problem of sociology (1924b: 27-43). He not only wanted to describe and explain the natural control processes of present-day society, but also hoped to provide information for city planners and others who would direct the course of future social life (1929a: 73-75).

But his sociology is first a "science of collective behavior" and only indirectly a vehicle for social reform (1924b:42). Before planning social change, he insisted, we must first consider the regular patterns of daily living. As individuals compete for the same scarce resources, they develop a division of labor. As they participate in the common enterprise of survival, they communicate and form some consensus about their mutual concerns (1939:244). This group consensus defines norms that exert control over individual behavior and molds this behavior into institutional patterns (1924b:39). Thus, if sociology is the science of collective behavior (planned or unplanned), then it is also the science of institutions:

> Sociology, as ordinarily conceived, is primarily concerned with the nature and natural history of institutions; with the processes by which institutions develop and eventually evolve the specific and stable forms in which we know them. But customary cultural and moral relations are notoriously dependent on, and responsive to, political, economic, and, ultimately, those more elementary associations brought about by the sheer struggle for existence. (1939:244)

In sum, Park defined sociology as a scientific study of regular group behavior rooted in biological-economic needs and controlled by common norms that develop as a group learns to cooperate in order to meet these needs — or as the science of collective behavior.

SUBJECT FOCUS

Park defined *collective behavior* as "the behavior of individuals under the influence of an impulse that is common and collective,

an impulse, in other words, that is the result of social interaction"
(1924b:865). After giving this definition in their *Introduction* . . . ,
Park and his coauthor, Ernest Burgess, analyzed collective behavior
as it appears in revolutions and similar upheavals associated with
rapid social change. Clearly, however, Park also intended something
else. More typically he stressed the quieter forms of "corporate
action" — child rearing, gang activity, and other daily interaction
promoting some group end. Taken as a whole, this human action
"directed to a common end" is the "touchstone" of Park's sociology
(1924b:42).

Society is born of this corporate action. At first, the "common
end" of a group is survival. Left on his own, each individual person would compete with all his neighbors for land, food, and other
basic needs. This competition forms the *biotic* (or *symbiotic*) level
of society. The results of this competition — social communication
and consensus about the need for some coordination to assure group
survival — form the *cultural* (*social* or *moral*) level. The cultural
order, in turn, imposes *social control* over the unbridled economic
jousting that occurs on the biotic level: I've-got-mine changes to
we're-in-this-together (and here are the rules we must follow if we
are all to get a share) (1936:155-58). Finally, the social-cultural-
moral order gives each individual a *personality*, a self-conception
that corresponds to his social status within this order (1925d:177).

Using Cooley's ideas about personality, Park explicitly considered
the link between the individual and society (1924b:67-68;708-12).
However, where Cooley examined the interdependence and mutual
causality between person and group, Park posited the group as one
of the conditions circumscribing individual expression: "Sociology,"
he said," is not concerned with individuals as such, but with a special type of relation, not fundamentally physical, existing between
individuals, and which constitutes them as persons." Furthermore,
he noted, sociologists should examine societies as "things with a
natural history and with characteristics which are determined by
the interaction and mutual relations of the persons who compose
them" (1929b:179).

In other words, Park's primary concern centers on group interaction, not on the mental framework of individuals, nor even on the
shared culture of the group. Park's sociology studies the types of
regular cooperative relationships existing between members of a

society, in his words, collective behavior that forms the institutional patterns of social control and enables a society to continue despite the inherently non-social tendencies of individual members.

SCIENCE — THE PLAN

To study the growth of institutions — the spread of social control — Park tried to combine the data of social history with the conceptual framework of natural science. He explained that both history and sociology comment on the social milieu, but they use this data differently. History records and interprets facts, unique events, concrete situations. Sociology, like all "natural sciences," formulates laws about the behavior of abstract types or classes of objects. Portraying events is the aim of history. Science, on the other hand, states facts and formulates hypotheses as a prelude to further observation, experiment, and theory verification. Natural history (as it applies to social science) lies between these two, a sort of scientific halfway point we reach when we begin to study institutions instead of eras (1924b:1-24). In other words, an historian might investigate the marital piccadilloes of Henry VIII; a natural-social historian would trace the growth of modern divorce practices; and a sociologist could hypothesize that legislators in industrial areas tend to favor women when formulating divorce laws.

Tracing the growth of sociology (up to 1921), Park believed that it was just leaving the natural history stage and "becoming an experimental science." In the future, he predicted, sociologists would no longer define problems in terms of common sense and collect facts to support doctrines; rather they would state theories, formulate hypotheses, and devise tests to disprove or verify their ideas (1924b:24-45). Park even suggested a few experimental strategies for sociologists to use in their studies of social control.

To begin, Park maintained that social-control studies should be conducted where the social-control problems originate — in the city (1929a:75). This may be the bias of a country boy, but nevertheless it provided Park with a rationale for his pioneering research on urban life. He looked for *natural areas* in the city, neighborhoods where people with similar backgrounds congregate to enjoy a similar life style: ghettoes, immigrant colonies, bohemias, and other identifiable communities. Each of these geographical regions contains a distinctive moral order: one area enjoys a low divorce rate;

another features juvenile delinquency; a third, low in suicides, witnesses many murders. Park hoped to use these natural areas as the source of initial data for hypotheses linking the various moral orders to patterns of social control. Then comparing similar areas in different cities, he could use these natural experiments to verify his ideas (1929b:196-99). Going further, he even suggested controlled experiments using legislation: generalizing from scientific data about the present situation, planners could propose appropriate legal reforms and then evaluate the results (1929a:73-74).

However, Park himself did not develop such experiments. To the end, he remained a natural historian, or perhaps an anthropologist, who told his students to research a city neighborhood by observing as much as possible — street layouts, occupational opportunities, red-light districts, family patterns (1915) — just as an anthropologist would observe the hunting technique and fertility rites of an isolated tribe. He also suggested a comprehensive data-gathering approach to students who were researching the growth of a single institution. For example, he recommended histories of specific newspapers and the biographies of newsmen as good sources for a natural history of the newspaper (1927). These suggestions, one written several years before the *Introduction. . . .* , one several years after, represent a continuous practice in Park's methodology that he did not advise in his textbook discussion of sociology as a natural science. Although the descriptive case study often provides numerous insights and reveals important sociological facts, it does not resemble an experiment and it does not compare the various different contingencies that comprise the common variants of a basic situation. Anthropology, like natural history, lies somewhere on Park's continuum between history and natural science (1924b:43). Perhaps his life-long practice of working in the urban laboratory with the methods of anthropology and natural history represents his effort to be as scientific as possible given the state of the discipline when he wrote.

RESEARCH — THE PRACTICE

Park examined social control processes in both the biotic and cultural orders of society. His strategy for exposing control mechanisms provides an alternative to the example set by Emile Durkheim: Durkheim had described the stable relations of normalcy, but Park traced the sequences of social change. For biotic-order studies (that is, studies in *human ecology*), Park instructed numerous young sociologists to map the spatial distribution of juvenile delinquency, urban blight, and other community attractions and to document how the behavior of various groups conformed to the prevailing norms of their area, even when these norms had been established before they themselves arrived. His work on the social order produced some of those glimpses into life-as-it-is, insights about phenomena like natural areas, social distance, and marginal man, that make the rest of us envy his interpretive instinct and flair. Nevertheless, by his own standards, he did not conduct a real sociological study. According to his typology of social science techniques, he engaged in two types of research; history and natural history. Sometimes he described a situation; sometimes he described types of situations; but he never compared the effects of independent variables in experimental studies. Like a good reporter, he used whatever data suited the purpose at hand: census statistics about immigrants, old clippings from the foreign-language press, newspaper circulation figures, personal experience, historical reports, and, quite often, the research of fellow professors and graduate students from the University of Chicago. But he used this data to outline sequences of social processes, to point out trends, not to systematically investigate the various conditions under which these trends usually occur. Here we will review a few of his studies; first some ventures into human ecology, then his work on the moral order as it can be observed in institutions and in roles.

At the beginning of his Chicago career, Park wrote an article summarizing trends he had observed and suggesting new research possibilities in urban ecology. He linked land values to residential patterns: rich New Yorkers tend to settle in mid-Manhattan rather than mid-Harlem. He located ethnic neighborhoods: Chinatown in San Francisco, Little Sicily in Chicago. And he urged his readers to discover the sources of stability and change in these residential patterns (1915).

In his own work, he used a natural history approach to document the existence of different spatial patterns, or more precisely to notice patterns and label them. For example, in his article on "Urbanization as measured by newspaper circulation" (1929c), Park used statistics showing the growth of city paper circulation in farm areas outside of metropolitan regions (or in human ecology terms, the growth of dominance by the major city). Then he argued that spreading circulation meant spreading urbanization without testing this against other indices. He did mention other possible measures of urbanization — audience size for city radio programs and number of area residents making regular visits to the city — but he did not compare these with readership to see if all were really measuring the same urbanization phenomena. Nor did he delineate sources of stability and change in this pattern of spreading urbanization.

However, in spite of the limited scope of his own research Park contributed greatly to human ecology by pioneering the field and urging others to research the terrain more thoroughly. In fact, he and two former students collected several of their urban ecology articles — pieces on juvenile delinquency, urban growth, and other patterns — into a volume titled *The City* (1925a), which provides an early sample of work inspired by Park on the natural history of urban areas.

Even here we can appreciate Park's deep concern with problems of social control. He considered the ecological order, not as a determinant of interaction, but as one of the outer limits that circumscribe the mechanisms of social control. For example, several articles examine juvenile delinquency and other forms of disorganization that persist in an area despite the identity of various groups successively occupying the neighborhood. In the first article, Ernest Burgess (1925) presented a cognitive map of Chicago's natural areas: economic zones circling out from the Loop and ethnic areas located within the zones. As immigrants moved to Chicago they settled with compatriots in the zone adjacent to the Loop, the zone with the poorest housing and the highest rates of juvenile delinquency and other forms of social depravity. As they became more affluent and more Americanized, they migrated; first to "better class" ethnic areas in a more expensive residential zone, then to the American sectors even further from their first slum settlement.

Park, however, was not primarily interested in mapping zones. In two of his own more theoretical articles, also in the same volume, he considered social control or moral order as exerted within various zones and as exerted by various ethnic groups. Juvenile delinquency, he decided, is predominantly social, not individual. As each person becomes self-conscious or socially alert, he also becomes aware of family rules, and later, community rules. In stable community areas, a child learns proper behavior through primary relations supplemented in large communities by formal agencies like courts, churches, and the like. But when the community itself is changing rapidly or when the individual has moved from one community to a radically different one, controls break down (1925b). So naturally, we should expect that a city like Chicago, which was experiencing rapid social change at the time, would have more disorganization than a small, stable village of farmers in northern Maine. We should also expect that a zone where new immigrants huddle together in rooming houses would have more street gangs than an outer zone of affluent third-generation families. However, juvenile delinquency and other disturbances vary even within zones because each zone contains several distinct natural-area communities. Oddly enough, the areas with the most talented people are not necessarily the most orderly and organized. These people often direct their talents toward occupational advancement and ignore the social control problems of their local community. In contrast, the relatively undistinguished members of a rural European village may resettle in an impoverished natural area of Chicago bringing their old-world patterns of stability with them. Or members of an unpopular racial or ethnic group may form a cohesive, orderly unit as part of their united front against American prejudice (1925c). In either event, the natural areas peopled by these groups would become the more orderly areas within their zone.

Park's articles, really informed essays based primarily on the history of Chicago, literary accounts of related conditions in other places, and contemporary research by other sociologists outline some relationships between human ecology and social behavior. Nevertheless, those of us who can review over half a century of additional history that has passed since Park wrote, may wonder if sequences suggested in his outline are the inevitable ones or merely one set of possibilities out of several. When members of two rural villages resettle in some large American city, does it matter that one group came from Sicily and the other from Sweden? If the ethnic minority in a natural area must unite against American prejudice, does this common action differ among blacks or American Indians or Jews? Clearly both answers must be "yes." Many of the Chicago immigrants arrived from rural American or rural Europe and settled in

Little Sicily, the black belt, Maxwell Street (Jew town), and other distinct natural areas. But even before they arrived these diverse groups held differing cultural values that set limits on their inter-action with each other as well as with members of other groups. The Sicilian peasant and the black tenant farmer did not migrate to the same neighborhood or create identical natural areas even when they moved to similar jobs and earned comparable pay. With our his-torical hindsight we can also appreciate that the process of migra-tion through ecological zones does not describe a universal sequence of city growth but rather the migratory results of a very peculiar local situation: between 1920 and 1930, Chicago's population in-creased by over half-a-million, an extraordinary expansion for any city at any time, and, even more extraordinary, an expansion based largely on immigration from foreign countries. It was this unusual immigration that created the Park-Burgess "zones of transition."

In other words, the natural-history approach, so well suited to Park's theory, also reinforced a basic problem inherent in that theory. Descriptions of common sequences are important but they do not explain social life. For explanation we must learn both the conditions that accompany action patterns and the group character-istics that could shape alternative patterns. Why did certain types of people choose to move in and out of certain ecological zones? Economic level alone does not answer this question. When we simply describe a sequence of process steps, as Park often did, we tend to assume we have described the Master Sequence. When we look for conditions that affect the sequence, we also discover conditions that could change it. Park, an acute observer, understood this problem, but he left the solution for his students to seek.

Turning to Park's work on urban institutions, we find, among other things, his continuing interest in the press, especially such phenomena as the growth of the foreign-language press in the United States and the functions of daily papers in modern life. For example, in *The Immigrant Press and Its Control* (1922), he wrote about foreign-language papers using census and press statistics to document the spread of foreign-speaking communities and the growing circula-tion of newspapers speaking to these communities. Then referring to letters, press stories, and other literary material, he discussed the effect of the press — the Americanization of immigrants — and sug-gested how the press would have a differential impact on immigrants with various types of attitudinal dispositions. However, he did not explain the rationale behind these types. (He had borrowed three from the six types depicted in *Old World Traits Transplanted*, a book written by W. I. Thomas but published in 1921 under the names of Park and Herbert A. Miller.) More important, Park did not clearly demonstrate that the press really was an Americanizing force. He did not compare readers with non-readers to determine which group was more acculturated, nor did he define the conditions which make some immigrants more interested than others in the local foreign-language paper. Nevertheless, we cannot simply dismiss Park's basic contention about the relationship between the press and the immigrant. Although he did not compare readers with non-readers in the United States, he did document the shift in readership between the old country and America. Many immigrants arrived as unlettered peasants, often from areas where their own language was forbidden or when papers were written for the literary elite. After arriving in the U.S., they began reading the local paper written in their own vernacular about the sort of topics that would interest the ordinary person. Many of the stories were translations from those in the English-language press — and certainly had some influence in teaching the immigrant about American ways (1920; 1922).

Park's work in "The natural history of the newspaper" (1923) exhibits a similar methodology. He recounted the growth of a mass reading audience, community papers, party papers, big-city presses, and yellow journalism. Doing this he told a pleasant, anecdotal story about the development of today's newspaper and its growing influence on the common man. In both of these works, he reported an interaction situation without making any attempt to create an experimental framework. Instead he emphasized one variable, the institutionalization of the press, and told its story against a background of many other undifferentiated variables.

Using a related strategy (borrowed from Simmel), Park analyzed the activity of role players in unusual situations. He had a gift for summarizing the process that defines a role or relationship with a special concept — like *marginal man* (1928) or *social distance* (1924a). In both instances he observed types of activity much as Simmel would, noting the forms of action that grow within the limits of some social setting: the way a man comes to be "marginal" between two cultures and how this marginality affects his behavior; the ways people manage to prevent undesired social intimacy and how these techniques enable very dissimilar people to interact harmoniously.

But where Simmel would exhaust the logical possibilities of a situation, Park highlighted the most probable or most general chain of events. Simmel, for example, had discussed the "poor"; first, as persons with a just claim on a share of our material possessions; then, as objects of whatever charity we might care to dispense; and finally, as threats to the social order who must be appeased lest they harm the rest of us. Park, in contrast, wrote of the main cause and principle activity of personages like the *marginal man* — a potential wanderer: someone who lives in a community, shares in the local division of labor, but does not participate in more intimate social life; someone like the Eurasian, the mulatto, or the Christian convert in Africa who may serve a vital function promoting exchange of goods and services between two social groups without belonging to either. On the biotic level marginal man lives along the periphery of two cultures: perhaps he emigrated from his homeland; in any event he is no longer part of his old group but will never be fully accepted in a new one. On the social level, he has freed himself from the parochial norms and values of his childhood but, because of his rearing, will never completely accept the customs of any other group either. On the personal level, he possesses a detached personality; emancipated from any one set of standards, he creates his own. The ways of marginal men are clues about future social control, Park concluded, because large numbers of such people can change a civilization by introducing their fresh perspectives on old cultural ways (1928).

Very intriguing so far — Park has defined a situation and suggested the generic circumstances that produced it along with the generic consequences. However, marginality must have very different effects if the person involved is a member of a colonizing group who chooses to live among the natives or if he is an unlettered economic refugee who has emigrated to a more prosperous, more sophisticated land; marginality must also differ for the refugee scientist whose unique skills prove invaluable to his adopted country and the common laborer who, along with hundreds of nameless others, helps dig a canal or lay a railroad track. Simmel would have considered such differences; Park did not.

If he had systematically addressed this problem of variability, Park might have transformed his natural-history method into an experimental one, a special experimental method that examines changing events instead of stable relationships. Normally we think of experiments as a device to test whether a relationship exists: we examine a control group and a treated group to see if the treatment produces some change. In essence, this is the procedure Durkheim followed in his analysis of egoistic suicide. He looked for a "control" group with low social cohesion and a "treated" group with high cohesion to see if their suicide rates differed. Using similar logic, Weber compared the "control" groups of India and China (where there was no Protestant ethic) with the "treated" group of Calvinists to see if their economic practices differed. Park could have begun with some condition like marginality and then examined natural situations "treated" with different kinds of intervening variables. As it exists, his natural-history method simply labels the steps in an observed sequence: a man leaves his childhood home, experiences marginality, frees himself from parochial views, and develops a new personality; groups of immigrants move into a poor neighborhood, experience disorganization, gain economic security, move to a better neighborhood, and become integrated into their adopted society. With a more experimental strategy — with more analysis of intervening variables — Park might have distinguished between such marginal men as Al Capone and Benjamin Disraeli or explained the different migration patterns in such immigrant cities as Chicago and Calcutta. In the end, he could have created experiments like those used by Durkheim and Weber but with one key difference — Park could have examined alternative process steps instead of alternative stable relationships.

However, Park's basis theoretical assumptions elicited other methodological strategies. His primary independent variable was the biotic order. Although Park was certainly not a crude physical or economic determinist, he did generally explain process sequences in terms of these variables. Thus, he looked at the basic migratory-economic circumstances of marginal man, not at the cultural differences that mark the various groups marginal man moves between. In similar fashion, Park looked at immigrant groups suffering prejudice or at immigrant groups migrating en masse from stable villages, without seriously considering the cultural values that differentiated these groups long before they began to share a comman economic and physical plight. When comparing the biotic and social orders, Park generally used the social order as a dependent variable. If he had used the present social order as a dependent variable, and the variety of pre-existing social orders (for example, the variety of old-country cultures) as an intervening variable, he could have developed a methodology that combined natural history with experimental comparisons.

CONCLUSION

For Park, research served as a source of inspiration, data for insights, not a testing ground for theory. He preferred generalizing from small amounts of data and highlighting the broad trends to executing the detailed comparisons needed to support his ideas thoroughly. Park's use of natural history did support his theoretical ideas, however. With this approach he could describe processes like the growth of natural areas housing various immigrant groups, the development of ecological dominance exerted by urban culture over the surrounding hinderlands, and the patterns of the relationship between marginal man and society. He could describe types of areas, types of dominance, types of relations — types of special patterns and forms of competition occurring in these spaces.

However, Park's real contribution may lie elsewhere: as we have already noted, his *Introduction. . .* stood as *the* sociology text for many years. This book spread his brand of sociology to the American student community beyond the Chicago Midway and it described a science quite different from the one in older classroom texts like Spencer's *The Study of Sociology* (used by Sumner) or Small and Vincent's *An Introduction to the Study of Society* (the first official text). Instead of relying on biological models, Park and Burgess adopted an analytic framework: instead of referring to "social physiology," they stressed the social origins of human nature, the relationship between the person and the group, and the types of human interaction. Instead of identifying the biological deficient individual, they pointed to impoverished community areas that produce deviants regardless of genetic background. Park was only one of many scholars rejecting the biological model, but his textbook guaranteed that a new model of sociology would be adopted by the next generation of sociologists.

Park's residence at Chicago also insured that the new generation would conduct field studies into the problems and prospects of city ways. They would map the incidence of gang activity and develop theories about how environmental conditions affect the course of social life. They would examine urban occupational roles (like the jackroller and the professional thief) and develop theories about how cultural surroundings encourage deviance. They would, in the end, develop a tradition of field research that marks sociology to this day.

Bibliography

Burgess, Ernest
   1925 "The growth of the city: an introduction to a research project."
      Pp. 47-62 in Robert E. Park, Ernest W. Burgess, and Roderick D.
      McKenzie, *The City*. Chicago· University of Chicago Press (1967).
Park, Robert E.
   1915 "The city: suggestions for the investigation of human behavior in
      the urban environment." Pp. 13-51 in Everett C. Hughes, *et al.*
      (eds.), *Human Communities*. Glencoe, Ill.: Free Press, 1952. Also
      Pp. 1-46 in *The City*.
   1920 "Foreign language press and social progress." Pp. 133-44 in Ralph
      H. Turner (ed.), *Robert E. Park on Social Control and Collective
      Behavior*. Chicago: University of Chicago Press, 1967.
Thomas, W. I. (published under the names of Robert E. Park and Herbert
A. Miller)
   1921 *Old World Traits Transplanted*. New York: Harper.
Park, Robert E.
   1922 *The Immigrant Press and Its Control*. New York: Harper.
   1923 "The natural history of the newspaper." Pp. 80-98 in *The City*.
   1924a "The concept of social distance." Pp. 256-60 in Everett C. Hughes,
      et al. (eds.), *Race and Culture*. Glencoe, Ill.: Free Press, 1950.
Park, Robert E. and Burgess, Ernest W.
   1924b *Introduction to the Science of Sociology*. 2d ed. rev. Chicago:
      University of Chicago Press (1969).
Park, Robert E., Burgess, Ernest W., and McKenzie, Roderick D.
   1925a *The City*.
Park, Robert E.
   1925b "Community organization and juvenile delinquency." Pp. 99-112
      in *The City*.

1925c "Community organization and the romantic temper." Pp. 113-22 in *The City*.

1925d "The urban community as a spatial pattern and a moral order." Pp. 165-77 in *Human*. . . .

1926 "Behind our masks." Pp. 244-55 in *Race*. . . .

1927 "American newspaper literature." Pp. 176-84 in Everett C. Hughes, *et al.* (eds.) , *Society*. Glencoe, Ill.: Free Press, 1955.

1928 "Human migration and the marginal man." Pp. 345-56 in *Race*. . . .

1929a "The city as a social laboratory." Pp. 73-87 in *Human*. . . .

1929b "Sociology, community and society." Pp. 178-209 in *Human*. . . .

1929c "Urbanization as measured by newspaper circulation." *American Journal of Sociology* 35 (July) : 60-79.

1936 "Human ecology." Pp. 145-58 in *Human*. . . .

1939 "Symbiosis and socialization: a frame of reference for the study of society." Pp. 240-62 in *Human*. . . .

1944 "An autobiographical note." Pp. v-ix in *Race*. . . .

Secondary Sources

Boskoff, Alvin

1969 "Robert Park: processes in the community." Pp. 94-111 in *Theory in American Sociology: Major Sources and Applications*. New York: Thomas Y. Crowell.

Coser, Lewis A.

1971 "Robert Ezra Park, 1864-1944." Pp. 357-84 in *Masters of Sociological Thought*. New York: Harcourt Brace Jovanovich.

Faris, Robert E. L.

1967 *Chicago Sociology, 1920-1932*. San Francisco: Chandler Publishing.

Reissman, Leonard

1964 "The ecologists: analysts of urban patterns." Pp. 93-121 in *The Urban Process: Cities in Industrial Societies*. New York: The Free Press.

Stein, Maurice R.

1960 "Robert Park and urbanization in Chicago: an interpretation of American studies." Pp. 13-46 in *The Eclipse of Community*. New York: Harper and Row.

Suttles, Gerald D.

1972 "The natural community: its followers and revisionists." Pp. 3-18 in *The Social Construction of Communities*. Chicago: University of Chicago Press.

Turner, Ralph H.

1967 "Introduction." Pp. ix-xlvi in Turner (ed.) , *Robert E. Park on Social Control and Collective Behavior*. Chicago: Phoenix Books, University of Chicago Press.

George Andrew Lundberg

During the 1920's, while Park was sending his students into Chicago's back alleys to observe taxi dancers and count rooming houses, George A. Lundberg (1895-1966) was learning a different brand of social science. Both men stressed the empirical aspects of sociology. However, where Park had recorded the colorful facets of city life, Lundberg measured the common attitudes of people. And, although Park had inspired a school of journalistic, gut-level sociology, Lundberg examined the philosophical assumptions behind research tools. In colorful moments, he penned bits of methodological nonsense, like his remark equating the action of a paper flying before the wind the action of a man "flying" from a crowd. More typically, he questioned the epistemological basis of sociological research by asking how we link our theoretical concepts with reliable data-gathering techniques.

Lundberg began his scientific career during an era when American sociologists were becoming more and more concerned with the details of research methodology. Cooley's dictum, " . . . work out something . . . , " would no longer suffice. Lundberg adopted a rigorous stance: he insisted on *operational definitions* (explicit statements of our research operations) and quantitative measures. His methodological position lead, in turn, to his definition of a subject matter that could be measured with accuracy — even if reliable indices did not always tap those elements that many would consider the most essential features of the topic in question. For Lundberg what we measure is no more important than how well we measure it.

Some sociologists consider this pronouncement a bit extreme. But even those who disagree with Lundberg admit that his insistence on rigorous technique inspired fruitful controversy among contemporary American sociologists at a time when they were debating the alternative research strategies for a young science on the make.

197

INTELLECTUAL BACKGROUND

Lundberg, probably the most articulate member of the group, became the spokesman for *neo-positivists* in American sociology. This school of thought did not start with him, however. In *The Grammar of Science,* Karl Pearson had stressed the numerical aspects of scientific method and limited scientific knowledge to things we can observe directly with our senses. This approach fit naturally with the work of Gabriel Tarde, who had measured human beliefs and desires by observing repetitious bits of overt behavior and compiling statistical tabulations of those acts. In the United States, Franklin H. Giddings incorporated this perspective on measurement into his sociological framework which was *the* sociology taught at Columbia during his tenure as chairman. Lundberg eventually joined this tradition: his dissertation director had studied under Giddings; he himself had read and admired Pearson's work. Elaborating on the ideas of these men, Lundberg developed his own position on sociology stressing its nature as an empirical science with operational and quantitative measures (1968).

Aside from the theoretical debate over neo-positivism, Lundberg was, no doubt, affected by trends in American social science. During the 1920's sociologists refined the attitudinal questionnaire, a tool for getting quantitative statements about subjective states: survey researchers asked thousands of people for opinions about sex, war, and the church and then correlated the answers with the socio-economic traits of these respondents. During the thirties and forties, the federal government recognized the value of such surveys and hired sociologists to conduct research projects measuring public attitudes toward work programs, military discipline, *ad infinitum.* Both of these techniques — the use of verbal response as indices of probable behavior and the collection of large masses of data — required serious thought about operational definitions and the proper use of statistics in research. Lundberg not only used these techniques but, more than any other contemporary sociologist, he examined the underlying implications of research measures and the use of quantitative methodologies.

DEFINITION OF SOCIOLOGY

Lundberg' definition of sociology reveals his peculiar research strategy as well as his conceptualization of the subject field:

"Sociology," "the science of society," *etc.*, arose when men became interested in certain phenomena of group behavior as objects of scientific study. . . . All languages have words designating numbers-of-individuals-in-interaction as behaving entities about which generalizations can be made. (1939b:155)

The scientific study of individuals-in-interaction seems familiar enough, but Lundberg added one qualification, "Sociology is concerned, as we have seen, with (primarily) human interaction by means of symbols" (1939b:311). Lundberg's sociology became the study of what we say when we express ourselves. And sociological research for Lundberg became the study of these expressive symbols, particularly as they occur in answer to a field worker's questionnaire.

SUBJECT FOCUS

Naturally, Lundberg defined his subject matter in terms of social expressions. He did not look for gods or policemen but rather the symbols people use to communicate their reactions to these objects:

Symbols representing these meanings of societal behavior as inferred from behavior are what sociological science deals with. Other sciences may deal with the symbols representing height, weight, and metabolism of policemen and priests. (1939a:49)

In other words, people act in social situations — let us say they interact — and we can describe this interaction in words. These words or verbal symbols representing interaction form the subject matter of sociology just as other kinds of symbols stand for subjects in other sciences. Biologists study something called "metabolism" in alley cats; sociologists study something called "discrimination" in banking practices.

Lundberg's definition of interaction also illustrates his emphasis on sociology-the-science. Interaction, he wrote, "is a word employed to denote reciprocal or interdependent behavior between or among any number of components in a situation" (1939b:217). The situation is some part of the universe which we have chosen to study, a closed-off section of reality. Within this situation, each human responds to the stimulus presented by other parts of the environment and the total of these responses is "interaction" (1939b:217, 234).

Since the responses must be "interdependent" or "reciprocal," they must occur between organisms that can react to each other. A man shouting after a thief who has just stolen his wallet is interacting. The same man shaking his fist at the rain which has just spoiled his picnic is not interacting with the rain. On the other hand, he may be interacting with God who plans to respond by striking him with lightening. . . .

As scientists, we may ignore such atypical possibilities and define Lundberg's subject matter as the stimulus-response action of interdependent humans in the same (arbitrarily defined) situation — or the verbal interaction between humans. Why didn't Lundberg just say, "we study interaction"? Because throughout his work he explored and discussed the relationship between symbols and reality. His definition of science as a study of the symbols of reality stressed a central tenet of his philosophy of science: we study what we can observe and measure, not the inner essence of a phenomenon.

SCIENCE — THE PLAN

If Lundberg had to name the most important aspect of sociology, he would probably tell us, "Sociology is a science, therefore. . . ." Therefore, we must define our concepts in strictly empirical terms so that many other sociologists can test our theories by working on the same problems. Because of his great interest in the link between data and concept, he addressed some major research concerns — validity, reliability, and their relationship to theory testing — throughout his work. We will consider these in the following paragraphs, but first, the basis of Lundberg's research strategy, his definition of science.

According to Lundberg, a field is not a science because it stresses a particular subject matter but rather because it adheres to a rigorous fact-gathering method:

> Science, then, is fundamentally a technique of delivering reliable knowledge about any type of phenomena in the universe and then applying this derived knowledge for the purposes of prediction and control. (1942b:5)

Science, in other words, is a way of looking at the world; with the proper use of symbols, even a subject like human interaction can be studied as a science. And, of course, this proper method must include provisions for validity and reliability.

Validity means that our research technique "measures that which it professes to measure or which we want it to measure" (1942b: 300). If we want to assess homosexual tendencies (perhaps with the question "Do you kiss other men?"), we should develop a measure that carefully separates sexuality from the non-sexual customs of certain ethnic groups. Lundberg discussed this problem in terms of: 1) symbols; 2) the links we perceive between symbols and reality; and 3) the special types of symbols we construct for social science research.

Following the tenets of behavioral psychology, Lundberg viewed science as a symbolic response to the stimulus of data. He recommended that sociologists should first describe all behavior as stimulus followed by "the responses of the organisms-in-environment." Then, as scientists, we should observe responses and label them with some symbol (our response to the response) (1939b:9-22). To take a modern example, if we have seen college students protesting against war, we may study the protest (their response) and take their feelings about war (their stimulus) for granted. Of course the word "protest," (our response) symbolizes the marching, placard carrying, letter writing, and other behavior of organisms-against-war. But, we may wonder, what sort of situations provoke anti-war protest? As scientists we can ignore the answer to this question: we observe response behavior — the protest activities — but we do not consider the reality causing such behavior.

For empirical research, we must symbolize the response behavior with *operational definitions,* a set of directions delimiting how we observe some phenomenon:

> Operational definitions, then, are merely definitions which consist as far as possible of words *clearly designating performable and observable operations subject to corroboration.* Thus, they may consist of (1) physical manipulations, such as baking a cake or reading a thermometer; (2) objective verbal designations of these manipulations; or (3) verbal designations of symbolic or mental operations, such as the definition of cube root or other mathematical operations. 1942b:89)

With operational definitions we enumerate a limited set of a crucial features that distinguish some item as it exists in the observable world. On the crude level, we can point to a cat and define it as "the thing we are pointing at." More precisely, we can define water as "H_2O" even though we never see any pure H_2O running in ditches or through faucets (1942a:730-35). But whatever definition we formulate, it prescribes what we study in our research — or, as Lundberg remarked, "Intelligence is what the intelligence tests test" (1955:193). His unsettling comment makes an important point: as scientists we examine the results of well defined types of behavior — the combination of three molecules, the scores on an IQ test — we do not study water, intelligence, and other popularly defined objects.

Behavior can mislead us, however, as Lundberg discovered, when his behavioral definition of flying precipitated a famous controversy. Robert M. MacIver (a contemporary of Lundberg's) had distinguished the essential differences in causality between when a paper is "flying before the wind" and a man is "flying from a pursuing crowd." But Lundberg disagreed about this distinction because "the principle of parsimony requires that we seek to bring into the same framework the explanation of all flying objects" (1939b:12-13). Like the tax collector at the railroad station, he argued "pigs is pigs" — and flying is flying. Years later Lundberg recanted with his admission that human "flying" is shaped by cultural background and mental states (1955:199). Guinea pigs are not Poland China boars and fleeing from a crowd is not floating with the wind.

Although Lundberg resolved this one, his flying-man controversy returns us to the basic validity question: How do we know we are really measuring intelligence, fear, and other intangible states? To answer this question sociologists rely on corroborating evidence — expert opinion, the educated hunch, non-verbal behavior, or even common sense — as rough tests for validity. But these checks only suggest whether our measures may be valid; they provide no guarantee that what we observe reflects the essence of a phenomenon. Recognizing these difficulties, Lundberg recommended that we ignore the problem of tapping the true meaning of a situation and concentrate on analyzing whatever we can measure. To do this we should evaluate data-gathering tools according to how well they help us solve "some adjustment problem other than the mere confirmation of common-sense." This means that if our scale, pointer reading, or other test works in scientific research, then, for our purposes, it is valid (1942b:300-01). If the IQ test enables us to predict school grades, then we need not worry about how it corresponds to the theoretically-defined essence of intelligence. In other words, *reliability* — "the ability of a scale to measure *consistently,* i.e., repeatedly and in the hands of different investigators, whatever it purports to measure" — is the most important criteria for assessing the validity of an operational definition.

If we need reliable measures to judge validity, then we also need quantitative studies to judge reliability. Although a single case or example can inspire us to generalize about social life, we need to evaluate many cases of the same type to determine if our concepts can be used "repeatedly and in the hands of different investigators." This, in turn, suggests that we should retain the same operational definitions for numerous research studies of a particular phenomenon. A physicist who develops his own weight system and temperature scale cannot compare his work with anyone else's. But sociologists commit this fault whenever they insist on redefining social class, juvenile delinquency, or any other variable for each new study (1940:360).

Unfortunately, sociological researchers often prefer to pioneer a large, new area of research (complete with newly-minded definitions for each concept) than perform the background work of retesting hypotheses in an established field (1942b:18). For mature development, sociology must outgrow the concept-definition phase. Using commonly defined variables, sociologists must begin to examine the same relationships in numerous settings.

RESEARCH — THE PRACTICE

Lundberg tested his ideas about methodology in his research. Although he studied a series of substantive problems, he concentrated on formulating proper operational definitions and developing numerical summaries for various forms of interaction. His early work illustrates his interest in how numerical measures can be used to compare variables. Later (after a flirtation with less quantitative descriptive research) Lundberg progressed to the numerical measurement of elusive literary concepts like ethnocentrism. Naturally, throughout his work he searched for masses of repetitious data —

census counts, questionnaire answers, budget records, voting tallies, and other quantitative information.

In his early research, he developed simple operational definitions that could measure the relationship between two variables. To judge the effects of wealth on political campaigns, he compared campaign expenditures with the win-loss record of candidates. His conclusion should not surprise us: those who pay more win more fourteen times out of fifteen (1928). In another article, he used census data to compare socio-economic characteristics with voting patterns in the five most radical and five most conservative counties of two midwestern states. Using the percentage of a county's voters who had favored the Non-Partisan League as his operational definition of radicalism, he noted that the newer, poorer communities tended to be the more radical ones (1927).

In his next major project, a study of leisure and its attendant social problems in Westchester County during the early thirties (1934), Lundberg (and some co-workers) faced the challenges of defining a rather subtle concept and collecting masses of descriptive data from numerous individuals. Not surprisingly, this study displays some major strengths and weaknesses. The researchers used ingenious methods (by the standards of their day) to secure information about the spare-time activities of their respondents. They distributed questionnaires, collected diaries, conducted interviews, and observed activities that would disclose the leisure life of their respondents. However, they never presented an operational definition of their topic! Their most precise definition — "time during which we are not actively engaged in making a living" (1934:3) — depicts a "leisure" that could include all non-economic activities from eating to taking a bath to running a household. Moreover, they used biased sampling, most notably when they based their conclusions about housewives on the activity of club women (apparently only white clubwomen) who formed a minority of the Westchester County females (1934:129, 136, 374). Lundberg recognized the inadequacy of his housewife sample. But when we consider his rationale for quantitative studies, even this admission does not excuse his fault. He favored quantitative work because a large number of examples can reveal the common trends that persist despite the idiosyncratic features of a single situation. The single example, on the other hand, can only provide insight from which we can guess about the general tendencies (1960). In effect, he introduced this very bias in *Leisure* . . . by selecting a group of similar, but atypical, respondents and neglecting the rest.

Fortunately we can find better illustrations of Lundberg's scientific principles in his later *sociometry* research. In these projects, he tried to measure subtle forms of interaction, like love and friendship, which normally appear in novels and other art forms. He hoped to measure these intangibles by asking people about "attraction" and "repulsion" — "Who is your best friend?" and "Who do you like least?" With a set of such choices for an entire group, he could test hypotheses by comparing friendship choices with social class, ethnic group, and other characteristics of his respondents (1937b).

For his first sociometry project, Lundberg (and a new group of associates) interviewed most of the housewives in a small Vermont village, asking each to name a friend. The authors tabulated the results in an elaborate schema showing friendship clusters, social isolates, sociometric stars (everybody's friend), and other choice patterns. They also tested an hypothesis about friendship and social class by looking at the percentage of women who chose friends outside their own class. Their results suggest that people tend to choose, or at least name, friends from their own social class or a higher one (1937a; 1938). Now, if housewives in rural Vermont seek equal or higher-class friends, then many of them must suffer a mild version of unrequited love. Is this friendship? Certainly, one-sided attraction is not the way a Semitic storyteller described the friendship of David and Jonathan. We must remember, however, that Lundberg stressed reliability rather than validity. Another sociologist asking about friendship choices could tabulate similar results even though another narrator watching David and Jonathan might judge them quite differently. As Lundberg remarked, the sociometrist develops measurements for "more objective description and communication, so that verification can become more definite and reliable" (1941:13).

Later Lundberg used his attraction-repulsion measures to investigate in-group feelings — consciousness of kind (a concept developed by Giddings) and ethnocentrism (as developed by Sumner). To examine consciousness of kind, Lundberg (and another group of co-workers) asked college women to make a series of choices designating their three "most wanted" roommates, three "least wanted" roommates, and more. Using a statistical test (Chi-square), the authors concluded that these women preferred to choose roommates and friends from the same residence house, school class, academic field, and social class. In Giddings' literary terms, they preferred their own "kind" (1948; 1949). To study Sumner's ethnocentrism, Lundberg elaborated this same technique; he asked high-school students from five ethnic-racial groups to choose the fellow students they would prefer as leaders, co-workers, dates, and friends. As expected, the "non-Jewish white" majority displayed the most ethnocentrism in their selection of leaders; that is, of all the groups surveyed, they were the least willing to accept a leader from outside their own group. But, for the other three choices, the majority group was least ethnocentric (1952a; 1952b).

To examine the validity of Lundberg's work, however, we should consider another conclusion from that last study. When Lundberg analyzed the ethnocentric tendencies within the majority, he discovered deep antagonisms. The Irish-Yankee split was sharper than some of the majority-minority differences. To understand, we must evaluate the operational definition of majority: "non-Jewish white." One important consideration is the social situation of these respondents. The authors conducted this study in the late 1940's, long before John Kennedy made Irish Catholicism fashionable in the United States. Perhaps parents and grandparents of these students could remember unpleasantries that had occurred when another Irish Catholic ran for president in 1928. Perhaps some could also remember employment signs: "Help wanted — no Irish need apply." Given this history, Lundberg might have guessed that Irish Catholics and Yankees would not share the same in-group — even though he could lump them together in his operational definition of "non-Jewish white" majority.

In sum, Lundberg applied his principles to develop objective-reliable measures of subjective states like friendship and ethnocentrism. However, as he defined it, sociology did not evaluate historical background. Because he stressed verbal responses that occur in reaction to the stimulus of the immediate situation, he ignored cultural values, institutional practices, and numerous other variables that limit the possibilities for these responses.

CONCLUSION

The whole thrust of Lundberg's work shows his concern with operational definitions and numerical data gathering as ways to achieve reliability and allow replication studies. With the single exceptions of his work on leisure, he defined his measures in such a way that others could understand what he had observed and count the same noses in new situations.

Some of us may quarrel with him because his operational definitions lack validity. Lundberg himself would tell us that validity is a less important research concern than reliability, that we can never be sure of validity in any situation, that we deal with symbols instead of other reality. However, Lundberg's problems with validity teach us one more lesson. If we rely on reliability as our sole criterion, we may end up with impressive frequency tables and other statistical apparatus describing a symbol that exists only in relation to our research. If IQ scores are only what the IQ tests test, if the majority group is just a collection of people designated by the researcher, then why do we care to know about them?

There may be a middle ground. For example, if Lundberg had continued his study of ethnocentrism, he might have decided that the numerical majority is not necessarily an interacting group. Perhaps he would have redefined his concept in terms of power or discrimination and then compared members of more powerful groups with members of less powerful ones. In any event, when reliable research produces anomalous findings, we should search further: we should redefine the concepts or re-examine the relationships or introduce additional variables. This is one route to the validity that eluded George Lundberg.

Bibliography

Lundberg, George A.
  1927 "The demographic and economic basis of political radicalism and conservatism." *American Journal of Sociology* 32 (March) :719-32.
  1928 "Campaign expenditures and election results." *Social Forces* 6 (March) : 452-57.
Lundberg, George A., Komarovsky, Mirra, and McInerny, Mary Alice
  1934 *Leisure: A Suburban Study*. New York: Agathon Press (1969).
Lundberg, George A.
  1937a "Social attraction patterns in a rural village: a preliminary report." *Sociometry* 1 (July-October) : 77-80.
Lundberg, George A., and Lawsing, Margaret
  1937b "The sociography of some community relations." *American Socio-*

logical Review 2 (June) : 318-35.

Lundberg, George A., and Steele, Mary

1938 "Social attraction patterns in a village." *Sociometry* 1 (January-April) : 375-419.

Lundberg, George A.

1939a "Contemporary positivism in sociology." *American Sociological Review* 4 (February) : 42-55.

1939b *Foundations of Sociology.* New York: Macmillan (1953) .

1940 "Some problems of group classification and measurement." *American Sociological Review* 5 (June) : 351-60.

1941 "Editorial." *Sociometry* 4 (February) : 10-14.

1942a "Operational definitions in the social sciences." *American Journal of Sociology* 47 (March) : 727-43.

1942b *Social Research: A Study in Methods of Gathering Data.* 2d ed. New York: Longmans, Green and Company.

Lundberg, George A., and Beazley, Virginia

1948 " 'Consciousness of kind' in a college population." *Sociometry* 11 (February-May) : 59-74) .

Lundberg, George A., Hertzler, Virginia Beazley, and Dickson, Lenore

1949 "Attraction patterns in a university." *Sociometry* 12 (February-August) : 158-69.

Lundberg, George A., and Dickson, Lenore

1952a "Selective association among ethnic groups in a high school population." *American Sociological Review* 17 (February) : 23-35.

1952b "Interethnic relations in a high-school population." *American Journal of Sociology* 58 (July) : 1-10.

Lundberg, George A.

1955 "The natural science trend in sociology." *American Journal of Sociology* 61 (November) : 191-202.

1960 "Quantitative methods in sociology: 1920-1960." *Social Forces* 39 (October) : 19-24.

Larsen, Otto N.

1968 "Lundberg's encounters with sociology and vice versa" (with autobiographical notes by Lundberg) . Pp. 1-22 in Alfred de Grazia, *et al.* (eds.) , *The Behavioral Sciences: Essays in Honor of George A. Lundberg.* Great Barrington, Mass.: The .Behavioral Research. Council.

Secondary sources

Adler, Franz

1968 "Comments on Lundberg's sociological theories." Pp. 34-47 in Alfred de Grazia, *et al.* (eds·) , *Behavioral Sciences: Essays in Honor of*

George A. Lundberg. Great Barrington, Mass.: The Behavioral Research Council.

Alpert, Harry
1968 "George Lundberg's social philosophy: a continuing dialogue." Pp. 48-62 in *The Behavioral Sciences.* . . .

Butler, Ellis Parker
1905 "Pigs is pigs." Pp. 96-107 in Robert W. Linscott (ed.), *Best American Humorous Short Stories.*

Catton, William R., Jr.
1968 "An assessment of Lundberg's substantive inquiries." Pp. 23-33 in *The Behavioral Sciences.* . . .

Timasheff, Nicholas S.
1967 "Neo-positivism and mathematical sociology." Pp. 193-211 in *Sociological Theory: Its Nature and Growth.* 3rd ed. New York: Random House.

Talcott Parsons

Talcott Parsons (1902-   ) is probably the most widely read — and most fiercely debated — sociological theorist of our day. A pioneer in medical sociology, he has also written about kinship structures, socialization, stratification, right-wing movements, deviance, small-group leadership, bureaucracy, professionalization, and a variety of other special concerns. For his analysis he prefers a broad sweep: a general theory of action, an explanation of social life so comprehensive that it can account for the love between mother and child, the doctor's detached treatment of his patient, and the adaptive capacity of post-Reformation England.

Like many earlier sociologists, Parsons considers the problem of freedom *versus* order: How do we manage to achieve personal goals without destroying the other members of our group? Instead of focusing on specific control mechanisms — mental unity, social facts, biotic restraints, and the like — Parsons envisions great action systems of individuals within groups, each part affecting the total, the whole system adjusting to a constant tension exerted by interacting parts. Parsons hopes to account for all social action in his theory.

What an ambitious task! Whether anyone can accomplish such a program, whether anyone can build a theory general enough to encompass all of social life, specific enough to guide research, and simple enough to promote easy understanding is the question sociologists have debated since Parsons first articulated the basics of his theory.

Here we are particularly interested in the research utility of this theory. Parsons himself has conducted very little empirical research. He has introduced an approach to the study of social life rather than a series of these studies. Throughout his writings, he considers theoretical problems: 1) the nature and subject matter of sociology; 2) the methodological approach best suited for this subject; and 3) the relationship between sociology and other sciences of human action. Reviewing his perspective, I will mention some of the research he has actually conducted and how he has used it to formulate methodological suggestions for other sociologists.

INTELLECTUAL BACKGROUND

In his first major work, *The Structure of Social Action,* Parsons critiqued his intellectual ancestors for some seven hundred-plus pages. Doing this, he noted two major trends of European thought — utilitarian positivism and idealism — converging in action theory. The utilitarians (the classical economic writers) had described man as a goal-seeking animal. They had conceived a social world peopled by rational beings who actively chose pleasure over pain. For example, they would tell us, we work to earn money for pleasantries like food and shelter and to avoid poverty with its attendant unpleasantries. But why work? Why not beg, borrow, steal, or promote a new Mississippi Bubble? Later positivists (especially Pareto and Durkheim) added the missing dimension to this analysis: social values and norms defining good and bad. Society commends honest employment over thievery, trickery, and other dishonest means of earning money. In *The Elementary Forms of the Religious Life,* Durkheim had hinted about the individual's role in the creation of these social norms. As a rule, however, positivists described what they could see: the objective behavior of people trying to achieve some good, not their subjective desires, not their role in creating these goods, not even what good may lie beyond the immediate object of the observed behavior (1937:87-125, 451-70). Thus the positivists started with a search for common principles of human behavior. Eventually some of them, like Pareto and Durkheim, probed the culturally defined meanings that influence social interaction. The idealists, a second major influence on Parson's thought, started by explaining behavior in terms of cultural meanings; our personal action, they said, reflects the *geist* of our culture. Viewed in terms of the *geist,* social actions must be interpreted separately for each culture. We may detail the history of the Roman way or the Sicilian *mafiosi,* but we cannot outline the common features of all societies. Max Weber had transcended this parochialism and analyzed the social world in terms of rational cultural values and norms (1937:473-87; 714-19). He observed that rational activity, the choice of efficient means to achieve goals, exists under some guise in each society. His thought reflected the old utilitarian idea — seek pleasure and avoid pain — but he had elaborated the idea by discussing the different ways we choose to define and seek this pleasure. Seizing the convergent strands in these positivistic and idealistic theories, Parsons extended and combined them into a new comprehensive explanation, his theory of *volunteeristic social action* — a theory about the social behavior of people who perceive, who judge who choose their course of action.

Parsons has continued to develop his theory, expanding from the limits he first set in *The Structure of Social Action* and rearranging his thoughts to accept fresh insights including some from other fields (1968b). From Pareto he first acquired the idea that social life operates somewhat as a mechanistic system; later he turned to biology and anthropology for a different conceptualization of system. Durkheim's work on social solidarity had shown Parsons how certain normative patterns integrate society. Using this idea and the example set by English anthropologists, he developed *structural-functional analysis* (his own brand of functionalism). From Freudian psychology, he learned where the personality system relates to the social system; from Weber, the links between culture and social structure. . . . The list is much too long for detailing here. And there is good reason for the number and variety of Parsons' intellectual ancestors: building a framework that purports to explain all social action, Parsons has tried to include a wide range of valid insights about his topic.

However, glancing at this list of inspirations cited by Parsons, we may suspect that he relied on early thinkers and ignored his contemporaries. He even appears to have ignored Pitrim A. Sorokin who chaired the department at Harvard when Parsons joined the faculty and anticipated many "Parsonian" ideas. Indeed, Parsons may have ignored most of his contemporaries within sociology. Aside from those he worked with or consulted during the course of writing, he has seldom mentioned living sociologists. This omission may indicate an unfortunate ignorance of modern sociology — or it may be the natural result of Parsons' interests: he has tried to build a general theory of cultural-psychological-social action, not a detailed account of the modern specialities within sociology itself.

DEFINITION OF SOCIOLOGY

Criticizing both the positivists and idealists, Parsons tried to define sociology in a way that would incorporate only the best from these traditions. He wanted one science to account for man's freedom in seeking goals and for order within a society of goal-seeking humans. He wanted a science with concepts broad enough to describe the ideals of Ibos and Canadians, but specific enough to distinguish between the two. He wanted a science to encompass norms and values in social life: to explain what they are, how men create them, and how men use them to guide later action. He developed a science of social-action systems based on the concept of volunteeristic action.

In his first major work, *The Structure of Social Action,* Parsons defined the key elements of this volunteeristic social action: 1) actors who choose to orient their activity toward other persons; 2) a common set of related values and norms (ideas about goals and the means to these goals) held by social actors; 3) a system containing these actors and values. These elements occur in everyday life as we interact with others and evolve a related set of mutual ideals, that is, a *common-value integration.* Over time, our actions and our common-value integrations coalesce into a system. Sociology is the study of this system with its sources, its operations, and its effects:

> If this property is designated the sociological, sociology may then be defined as "the science which attempts to develop an analytical theory of social action systems insofar as these systems can be understood in terms of the property of common-value integration." (1937: 768)

This focus on shared norms and values in a social-action system persists in Parsons' later statements. In his next major synthesis, *The Social System,* he wrote that sociological theory explains "the phenomena of the institutionalization of patterns of value-orientations in the social system" (1951a:552). More recently he has described sociology as a science that studies systems of human interaction from the "action frame of reference." This action focus treats behavior as "goal-directed," "motivated," or otherwise guided by human ideals (1961a:32-33). These systems include the personality, social, and cultural systems, all of which depend ultimately on the biological systems of the individual personalities (1970:28-48). Systems within systems within systems . . . a great seamless web, all interrelated with each other because of volunteeristic action of individuals, because of social action based on common-value integration.

Parsons' task, of course, is to peer into the system of systems, to stop the action, analytically at least, and to tell us how one part affects the others. He constructed his theory as a framework for research. In the next few sections, we will review how he proposed to move from interlocking systems to the real world: to the doctor's office, the market, the small group.

SUBJECT FOCUS

The subject matter of Parsons' action theory shows, once again, that he tried to incorporate the positivistic-utilitarian tradition and the idealistic one in a single framework. The social act, his basic unit of analysis, includes both a personal desire for a goal and a social norm regulating that desire. As his career progressed (through four stages, no less) he broadened his focus from the basic social act to the action of men in social systems to the relations between parts of a system to the actions of the systems themselves (1968b). But behind his later formulations lies the groundwork set in stage one — the action frame of reference and its basic elements: the unit act and analytic or emergent properties.

In *The Structure of Social Action,* Parsons presented his *action frame of reference,* a way of looking at goal-seeking human behavior modeled on Pareto's mechanistic idea of systems. Using this viewpoint, Parsons proposed that we examine social life as a system with concrete parts and analytic properties. A part can (and sometimes does) exist separately from the total system. Pistons exist without engines and cells without bodies, even though neither can act or live apart from its system. Of course, each of these parts has a much fuller meaning within some frame of reference than outside of it. In a machine, the piston provides power; by itself, it is just a piece of shaped metal. The analytic properties, on the other hand, exist only as part of the relationships between parts and, therefore, have no meaning by themselves.

In a system of *action* (that is, subjectively meaningful action), the smallest part that can exist intact outside of the system is the *unit act.* This act (or part) contains three elements: 1) an end; 2) a situation (which includes means and conditions); and 3) at least one norm relating the end to the situation. For example, an American may want to kill himself and decide to do it by jumping out of a twentieth-story window after he writes a suicide note justifying his action. In this example, the man's suicide is the unit. His desire to kill himself, his choice of a twenty-story drop, and his need to explain himself in a parting note are all aspects of this unit. Others matters, like the velocity of his fall, are not part of the action frame of reference.

The group-centered elements in an action system (the *emergent* or *analytic properties*) cannot be seen or touched or heard. Rather, they are analytic constructs (abstract terms) defining the relations of units — they are constructs like "power" or "rationality" (1937: 27-42, 43-51, 77-78, 731-48). Piston-power or political-power, both tell us something about how pieces of a machine relate to each other. And, compared with the alternatives possible in a given system, suicide can be judged as more or less rational then declaring bankruptcy or moving to Tahiti.

These emergent or relational properties exist in all action systems. In *social action* (goal-seeking behavior that involves a relationship between two or more actors) the emergent property is *common-value integration,* that is, the property that holds the group together by reminding members of their common goals. To understand this element, let us consider the problem of power. Power exists only when there is a relatively forceful person or group of persons who can exert influence over the relatively helpless. Once we acknowledge an unequal distribution of this ability to influence others we return to the old value question of freedom versus order, of who defines the order and whose rights are curtailed in the process. We can settle this dispute with brute force, incessant warfare terminating only when one side seizes absolute control, at least for the moment. But, looking around we can see that most groups do not act this way most of the time. Rather, the people in these groups obey norms, cherish values, perform rituals, and express ideas that indicate the existence of a type of mind set which encourages some people to accept the power of others even when no one is "forcing" them to do so. In Parsons' terms, group members share a set of social meanings; the group has common-value integration (1937: 767-68).

Therefore sociologists should look at systems of interaction to discern the integrated network of mutually held values and the activities related to these values. Within a social system we find values that define *roles* (for example, the expected actions of a father or a priest or a rebel). A complex of related role definitions describe an *institution* (like parenthood or religion or opposition politics). During phase two of his career, Parsons named these value-informed institutional patterns as the subject matter of his sociology (1951a:36-45, 545-55).

In phase three, Parsons continued to analyze social action but shifted his focus from interaction of role players within an institution to the relations between institutions within larger social systems. In *Economy and Society* (1956), for example, he traced the effects of common values on the operation of economic structures. Economic costs and profits, he maintained, cannot be measured solely in dollars or pounds or kroner, but also include social ideas about the meaning of wealth and the steps one may legitimately take to obtain it.

In phase four Parsons has continued to define the *social system* as a complex of interaction based on shared norms and values (1968a; 1968c). But he expanded his discussion to include the relationship between the social system and its environment (1970:28-36). Now he argues that social systems, like cybernetic ones, constantly engage in feedback between themselves and the environment. During this (the current) phase, Parsons has chosen to observe how a social system adapts to its environment, how, to cite one of his examples, northern Europe first separated religious, economic, and political institutions during the era when a new international credit economy made old religious-economic rules obsolete. This cybernetic conception of the social system raises, once again, the problem of freedom opposed to order. As social beings we must somehow choose new ways that will simultaneously buttress and remodel old structures. Always Parsons tries to explain this by uniting creative latitude for innovators with stability for the shifting system of creative individuals. We choose our actions, but society guides our choice.

In sum, starting with volunteeristic social action, Parsons broadened his theory to include, first, systems of such action (*institutions*), then, systems of institutions (*societies*) and finally, systems of societies (the international community). A whole system and its parts — two constants in Parsons' conceptualizations — and, as we shall soon see, he used a methodology peculiarly suited to analyze the relationships between parts and wholes.

SCIENCE — THE PLAN

To build a scientific theory, Parsons recommends that we select or construct a frame of reference, describe the empirical world in terms of that framework, articulate a set of propositions summarizing some of the relationships in the empirical world, and, finally, combine the propositions in a logically closed theoretical system (1937: 28-34; 1945:212-13). Using his action frame of reference, Parsons has described important forms of social action and explained the functions that exist between parts of his system. Indeed, he has devoted over fifty years of scholarship to the second stage of theory building, the background work of searching for these functional relationships. For an appreciation of his contribution, we must review what his approach — *structural-functionalism* — entails, how he has used it to describe social life, and what we may criticize about it.

The *structural-functional* approach begins with the idea of living systems and their external and internal survival problems. In their external relations, all living systems (from the amoeba to society) face one critical functional problem: they must establish a mechanism to maintain some distinction between themselves and their environments (1970:29-30). Without distinct boundaries, there is no system. The amoeba decays and its chemicals disappear into the soil or woodwork. The society disintegrates and loses its identity as a more successful society overpowers it. Furthermore, in order to maintain its distinctive boundary vis-a-vis the environment, a system must also coordinate and integrate its internal states. If the digestive and elimination subsystems do not provide complimentary operations, the amoeba will starve or poison itself. If the society does not coordinate its political and economic activities, it will collapse in internal chaos.

To examine how a system meets these survival needs, we must consider functions, structures, and processes within the system. *Function* presupposes the existence of a whole with interdependent parts all within a larger environment. Studying functions requires examining social-action systems — institutions made up of roles, societies made up of institutions, or civilizations made of of societies — to determine how change in one part affects the others, how change in the parts affects the whole. (Of course, the parts are always changing unless the system is dead.) When reviewing a functional drama, we should ask, "What would be the differential consequences for the system of two or more alternative outcome of a dynamic process?" (1951a:21-22). If the part changes, what are the different ways this change could rearrange the whole? These parts are *structures,* "any describable arrangement of a system's elements which are distinguishable from each other, and the properties and relations of which can be presumed to remain constant for purposes of a particular analysis" (1070:35). Like motherhood. Mothers have changed since grandpa was a boy but, at a special time, in a particular place, most people know the accepted minimum standards of behavior for the role of mother. For the purposes of analysis, we can assume that most structures, most roles and most institutions, mothers and motherhood, will be stable for the moment. If this convenient assumption were empirically true over long periods of time, if American society in 1776 were much like American society in 1976, we could describe a system once and consider our research complete. But as we know, the parts change. And we examine these changes a few at a time by assuming that most of the structure is stationary and looking at some selected *process,* that is at "the theoretically significant aspects of a system which undergo 'change of state' within the time period of significance for a given investigatory purpose" (1970:36). When industrialization occurred in the United States, when Americans moved off the farm into the city, what happened to motherhood? Structural-functional theory (or more correctly structural-process-functional theory) can describe the interdependence between an urbanizing economy and family life (1970:28-36).

In other words structural-functionalism is a tool for examining systems of unit acts — roles, institutions, societies — which explains both the regularity and the change in these structures. In adopting this method, Parsons had to shift his emphasis from the unit act to the system. (How can we explain functional interdependence between one act and itself?) Parsons also abandoned his old mechanistic model of a system in favor of a model comparing social systems to organic beings. As biology examines the organism's stability (the "physico-chemical interchange" between an organism and the environment), so action sciences based on an organic analogy analyze the stability of interaction relations in a situation or social environment (1951a:541-45).

Using functional analysis Parsons has explained human behavior in terms of his three basic action "systems": personality, social, and cultural. We do not simply react like Pavlov's dog. Rather we act within the limits set by these systems, limits defining what we want to do, what we can do, and what we should do. As *personality systems,* we each have desires and needs. Given these psychological predispositions, we appraise our situations in cognitive, cathetic, and evaluative terms — we think; we feel; we judge. But not by ourselves. Our interaction with others functions to shape a *cultural system,* a set of shared expectations (expressed in symbols) telling us how to behave and how we can anticipate that others will behave. The cultural tradition we create contains cognitive, appreciative, and moral standards corresponding to the thoughts, feelings, and judgments made on the personal level. In other words, through social interaction we produce the norms that regulate further activities. The organized, integrated system of action based on these shared normative expectations is the *social system.* Within this system there are *roles* or patterns of behavior that most of society expects from people who perform certain functions. Mothers, for example, must discipline their children, although the permissible limits of that discipline will vary with the group. Sets of these expected activities, that is, clusters of roles providing for some basic societal need, form the *institutions* of society, such as the family or the church or the economy. However, there is no society where all roles are performed identically, for example, where everyone shares the same expectations about how a mother should behave. So, it is the task of sociology to determine what functions must be met for the society's survival and to delineate the various structures that can serve those needs in at least a minimal way (1951a:3-67).

Parsons has developed two famous typologies to assist researchers interested in these problems. His *pattern-variables* define the types of decisions that must be made as actors negotiate their ways through some situation. His four-functions table (the *AGIL scheme*) defines the needs of a social system. These typologies (which will be considered in more detail in the research section) describe analytic elements (the intangibles in Parsons' theory) and summarize the fit between a specific set of personality-social-cultural systems.

Parsons' structural-functionalism clearly provides a descriptive framework for sociological research. But can his theory do more than describe and explain *post hoc?* He assures us, "Yes . . . eventually." At present, however, sociologists must describe what exists, particularly what functions exist, before outlining the specific areas of interdependence between different types of action in a particular social system (1950:364; 1970:32-33). For example, political institutions function to help a society obtain its goals. But, if a system continues to exist, then, surely, it must be obtaining some of its goals. (One of these is survival!) And we can assume that the system's behavior somehow contributes to that goal-attainment. In other words, this descriptive-analytic type of theory provides pictures of the obvious in social life — pictures a perceptive observer might paint without the use of theory. It does not provide any statements predicting how changes in one structure might effect changes in another. We know that each surviving system maintains integration and obtains goals. But what sort of political structure should we expect in a society integrated by totemistic religion? And do bureaucratic rationality and "rational" religion tend to appear together in society? Durkheim and Weber tried to specify the types of structures that appear together. Parsons suggests that "functional alternatives" can fill the same societal needs, that political rule can differ to suit various types of societies. Certainly, Charlemagne — who could not read, who commanded distant subjects by sending messengers hundreds of miles over semi-passable roads — did not expect the type of orderly, centralized rule possible in a modern society with computers, air travel, and telephones (1951a:167). But this suggestion does not hint at the forces in society that direct changes from a traditional to a technological society. Parsons recognizes this deficiency, the low yield of his type of theory. Scientists, he believes, must eventually move beyond his descriptions to construct and test specific hypotheses based on the implications of his general frame of reference (1950:354; 1961b:318-19).

RESEARCH — THE PRACTICE

Throughout his career, Parsons has displayed greater concern about the assumptions and strategy of empirical research than about the details of the actual data-gathering and measuring, a concern well illustrated by his nuanced considerations of the nature and subject matter of sociology. Nonetheless, he has used empirical work (both his own and the work of others) to develop his theory — surely a fruitful use for research. Aside from his informed, essay-analyses of topical issues like race relations and the radical right (which we will not consider here), he has been actively involved in four empirical

areas that contributed significantly to his theory: 1) a content analysis of social theories; 2) a review of medical practice in the Boston area; 3) a study of leadership styles in small groups; and 4) an
analysis of secondary material describing the institutional history of
several societies. We will review these, phase by phase, as Parsons
used them in the stages of his theory-building.

Parsons has described his first book, *The Structure of Social Action*,
as an empirical monograph, a study of European social thought
based on original documents. In two volumes of exhaustive and
exhausting analysis, he reviewed the works of Alfred Marshall, Vilfredo Pareto, Emile Durkheim, Max Weber, and others as a prelude
to articulating his own theoretical synthesis of positivism and idealism. For his analysis (which remains an important secondary source
on the theorists discussed), Parsons had deliberately chosen these
writers because they represented quite different intellectual traditions. His conclusion: starting with apparently divergent basic ideas,
these social thinkers independently developed parts of a single theoretical system, the volunteeristic theory of action. Since this theoretical convergence cannot be explained as the result of common European ideas held by these authors (Parsons did not tell us why!), we
must conclude that the volunteeristic theory of action contains sound
concepts and precepts (1937:719-26). Many sociologists have questioned both this conclusion and Parsons' interpretation of Durkheim
et al., but those controversies need not concern us here. The point
for us to consider is this: Parsons developed his theory of action by
using the works of sociological pioneers as original documents sus-
ceptible to empirical research. Noting similarities (or what he perceived as similarities) within each theory system, he treated the systems as multiple indicators of one phenomenon. As Durkheim had
used religion, family structure, community, and education to measure
social cohesion, Parsons used the works of different men to show
the existence of one basic thought system growing in the works of
sociological pioneers. And, as we have seen in the "Intellectual background" section, he used these ideas to build his theory of social
action.

In phase two, Parsons applied his action frame of reference to
some empirical-research data and developed his *pattern-variables*.
This typology lists a set of dichotomous choices made by role players
in social situations, or from the other side of the action, a set of
alternative cultural standards guiding such choices.

First, the theoretical background. Weber's types of social action (important inspirations for Parsons's theory) had been developed from Ferdinand Töennies' dichotomy of social orientations, the *Gemeinschaft* and *Gesellschaft*. Going back to these concepts, Parsons distinguished between *Gesellschaft* relations defining specific, limited obligations and *Gemeinschaft* action encompassing unspecified and unlimited duties. Normally, an employer expects to pay an employee who, in turn, performs certain acts (anything beyond that is outside of the *Gesellschaft,* employer-employee relationship). But in the name of friendship (a *Gemeinschaft* relationship), a person may do many things: eat lunch with someone, loan him money, listen to him, and in some situations, die for a friend (1937:686-94).

With these concepts in mind, Parsons applied the action frame of reference to a field study of medical practice. After observing the actors, the situation, and the common values growing from the interaction, Parsons refined his ideas about how values affect social roles through the motivating personal orientations. Specifically he delineated the common value integration that defines motive orientations and role expectations in medical practice where the doctor's role require extreme *Gesellschaft* elements:

	Technical-modern orientations	*Traditional orientations*
1)	Specificity	Diffuseness
2)	Affective neutrality	Affectivity
3)	Universalism	Particularism
4)	Achievement	Ascription
5)	Collective-orientation	Self-orientation

To put the matter in terms of concrete choices, a physician:

1) treats a specific illness like the flu instead of trying to solve all of the problems in a patient's life;
2) judges illness in affectively neutral scientific terms instead of expressing his or her own emotional reaction to a patient's personal problems with the disease;
3) applies the same standards universally when accepting patients (only treats skin disease) instead of choosing relatives, neighbors, or others with some particularistic, personal claim to his or her attention;

4) relies on achieved technical competence instead of asserting that family status, sex, or other ascribed traits affect his or her ability as a doctor;

5) stresses the welfare of the group — both the group of fellow professionals and the group of patients — instead of practicing medicine for personal profit.

These are the choices — not necessarily as an individual physican makes them, but as we think he should. Society has defined these choices as part of the doctor's institutionalized situation and a physician who chooses differently may be called "deviant" (1939; 1942: 142-63; 1951a:433-36; 1951b).

Parsons used his data about medical practice for two purposes. In two articles, he analyzed information and built concepts. Later he selected the same data to illustrate his developed typology. But these pieces on the pattern variables used by physicians are all written the same way, as insightful essays punctuated with tales from the doctor's office. What kind of data did Parsons collect? Observations in the examining room? Unstructured interviews on the subject of how a doctor reacts to patients? Parsons did not explain this in his work, leaving us the impression that he just applied his frame of reference to medical situations (1951a:428-29n2). As far as we can tell, his data are sets of unstructured observations made by an intelligent, perceptive commentator.

Nevertheless, the pattern-variables typology stands as an ingenious conceptual tool that locates a point of interaction between the personal, social, and cultural system. Therefore, although Parsons developed this tool during phase two while he was concentrating on social roles, he naturally refined it to interpret organizational and institutional activity during his phase-three work. In fact, his chief phase-three accomplishment, a typology of systems functions, combines the pattern variables with another typology from small-group research.

This new typology began with a collaboration between Parsons and Robert F. Bales. First, in a series of laboratory experiments, Bales required small groups of subjects, who had been assembled expressively for the purpose of the experiment, to complete some specific task. Bales then observed patterns of interaction within these groups. He noted which member organized the group for work, which member helped the group release tension, and so on. Finally he developed a typology defining group needs and the styles of leadership that meet these needs: the task or job leader directs the group as it accomplishes its stated purpose while the expressive leader provides for release of emotional tension, encouragement, and other personal needs. Then Parsons rephrased this dichotomy of leadership styles in terms of what each leader does for his group. The task leader manages relations with the external environment, the relations needed for accomplishing group goals and, in the process, acquiring the necessary resources. Meanwhile the expressive leader manages internal relations, that is, promoting group unity and, along the way, motivating each member to cooperate in the group. Both leaders, of course, are working for the good of the group or displaying collectively orientation. However, in other pattern-variable orientations, the no-nonsense task leader, who wants to get the job done with impartial efficiency, tends to stress specificity, affective neutrality, universalistic judgments, and a preference for achievement standards. The expressive leader, on the other hand, balances the group with the opposite perspectives (1953a; 1953b:179-90).

In other words, Parsons used the pattern variables to describe the orientations of certain types of group leaders, in effect, to describe the orientations that meet certain kinds of group needs. Reworking these ideas from the perspective of the group rather than the actor, Parsons defined group needs in a four-fold schema of functional problem areas: adaptation, goal-attainment, pattern-maintenance, and integration (1953a; 1959a:4-16). Group systems, like individual actors, must be orientated toward some goals and seek these goals through some means. Moreover, the whole must obtain its needs from the external environment, while, at the same time, maintaining some internal balance.

	Instrumental (Means)	Consummatory (Goals)
External	A Adaptive Function	G Goal-Attainment Function
Internal	L Latent Pattern-Maintenance Function	I Integrative Function

(1959a:7)

All of these functions serve the need for "boundary maintenance." Unless a system solves each of the functional problems (adapts to new environments, obtain goals, integrates activities, and maintains useful behavior patterns), it disintegrates, looses its boundaries — or, in biological terms, it dies (1953a:91-92).

The functional or systems needs of a society can be served by institutional patterns. The class structure, for example, helps pattern-maintenance by motivating people to remain in their proper (and useful) places. Religion, at least in a homogeneous society, integrates people by reminding them of their common values. Successful political activities assure the society of safety, prestige, and other long-term goals. And economic aggression provides the technical and financial base for successful diplomacy (1971:10-18). Each institution and each organization can, in turn, be analyzed as a system. Within the economic sphere, for instance, there are four functional areas: 1) capitalism and investment adapt the economy to the larger society; 2) production is the goal; 3) entrepreneurship integrates the economic group with changing economic conditions; and 4) the given economic base (resources and commitments) assure pattern-maintenance (1956).

In his subsequent analysis Parsons has ignored the pattern-variables in favor of the AGIL framework because, in his opinion, "the new scheme is a more generalized one from which the scheme of pattern-variables can be derived" (1959a:7). Some sociologists quarrel with that opinion. However, we must realize that Parsons has retained his original outlook and continues to study social action, or human interaction informed by values. In his AGIL scheme he is attempting to locate the meeting point between personal orientations, group values, group needs, and social roles.

For example, in "A revised analytical approach to the theory of social stratification" (1953c), Parsons used AGIL to demonstrate how these social properties meet in the operation of social stratification. He argued that stratification is grounded in cognition and evaluation: we recognize a quality, possession, or performance and we judge its value. If we are recognizing and judging a personal role performance we must do this by assessing its relationship to the social system in question, specifically by assessing its contribution in one of the AGIL categories. The value of the performance (and the stratification ranking it earns for the role actor) depends on the socially defined importance of the category itself and the importance within the category. In other words, the AGIL categories represent cultural orientations as well as system needs. If a culture (like that of the United States) places premium value on efficiency, competence, universalism, and related traits, its basic orientation is adaptive. Those who share such a culture would admire people who excel at acquiring and manipulating resources. So naturally most Americans consider the head of General Motors more important than the president of the D.A.R. Nineteenth-century England, in contrast, still retained an orientation based on pattern-maintenance and judged noble and gentry families to be more prestigous than the *nouveau riche,* however talented and capable. Of course, we could enumerate criticisms of this analysis. Empirically, Parsons provided no criteria for us to determine just when an orientation fits a particular category. For example, how are we to determine if a church leader, seeking converts, is acting on behalf of a goal-oriented group that must spread the good word or a pattern-maintenance orientated group that must keep a membership base? Worse, he provides no clear criteria for determining which orientation is more valued by a particular culture or how to rank those whose roles contribute to several categories. Theoretically, Parsons ignores the problem of power struggles within a system, struggles that enable some people to gain high position despite majority values. Indeed, he assumes that stratification arises from necessary evaluation of necessary role performances. However, these criticisms aside, we must recognize this essay as an important attempt to summarize the personal, cultural, and social elements of stratification in one analytic framework.

During phase four, Parsons has continued to explore the implications of social-action theory by studying "post-linear evolution." In his article on "evolutionary universals," he argued that social systems, like biological ones, increase their *adaptive capacity* (their ability to use resources) by developing specialized structures. Species can change suddenly through mutations that enable them to survive in new environments. Man can plan housing and clothing that enables him to survive within a wide range of climate conditions that would kill less adaptive animals. In society, man can also develop special structures to handle problems of government (goal-attainment), community loyalty or religion (integration), and economics (adaptation) instead of retaining the primitive forms with the same tribal structure serving all of these functions. For example, the society with a distinct stratification hierarchy that includes specialized governing or administrative officials can mobilize for war faster than a large, but unorganized, federation of families or clans (1964).

In two recent books (1966; 1971), Parsons has researched his idea of societal adaptation by reviewing the literature on a wide range of societies: primitive societies (like the Australian Arunta), archaic societies (Egypt, Mesopotamian groups), intermediate groups (China, India, Islam, Rome), special types (ancient Greece and Israel), and the modern development in post-reformation Europe (chiefly England). Throughout, he viewed each society as an adaptive system. Successful systems have accurate cybernetic communications with the border-cultural milieu and develop separate specialized social structures to handle the changing environment. Seventeenth-century England, he suggested, continued its separation of church, state, and economy, at least to the point where each institution could deal with problems independently and, thus, efficiently. Businessmen no longer depended on semi-religious, craft-guild restrictions established to handle a medieval economy. It was no longer a national embarassment if king and cardinal differed over foreign policy. Overall, he argued, spurts of social evolution occur when a society like post-Reformation England develops such an increase in adaptive capacity.

Parsons defined this *adaptive upgrading* as "the process by which a wider range of resources is made available to social units, so that their functioning can be freed from some of the restrictions on its predecessors" (1971:27). As it stands, "adaptive upgrading" is a process by which a social unit gets new resources to make it more adaptable. Working with such a tautology Parsons was bound to find what he sought. A society that adapts must have gone through the process of adaptive ungrading — by definition: successful groups have had success.

Parsons' use of adaptation illustrates another basic problem with his methods: since he has paid more attention to strategy than to technique, he indicates what general areas should be explored but he does not limit the research boundaries. Just what is an adaptive mechanism — the economic institutions, the specialization of all institutions? Parsons shifts his meaning between the two, leaving us with a concept that can be applied whenever "adaptation" seems to occur. Worse, adaptation of some sort must occur in any surviving society. Therefore, if we observe a society, we are bound to notice adaptive functions — back to the tautology. One way out of this circle entails specifying the elements of an adaptive capacity. If we could define and measure specific traits, we could develop ordinal or interval comparisons. Then, at least, we could speak of relative degrees of adaptation — we could ask if seventeenth-century France was more or less adaptive than Germany. Parsons has laid the initial groundwork for such analysis but has not formulated the necessary operational definitions.

In other words, Parsons does not advise us to pursue circular paths by observing a situation and attaching one of his descriptive labels. Rather he hopes that his definitions will provide tools for measuring the empirical world, perhaps so that they will form the basis for limited, testable theoretical hypotheses like those Robert Merton has recommended specifically as an antidote for Parsonian generalities (1959b). We might hypothesize, for example, that the more rational (adaptive) the system, the more likely that integrating functions and goal-attainment ones will be performed by distinctly different subsystems. In more vernacular terms, if efficiency is important, the people who direct activities will concentrate on their main goal leaving the public relations and personnel work to others. Trying to phrase this idea in operational terms, we might suggest that work groups are more likely than social groups to develop clearly recognized task leaders and expressive leaders.

Parsons himself has not followed such empirical leads but has developed a framework he hopes will be used by others. He has limited amount of his empirical work by choice (1961b:318-19), a choice that may have also limited his theoretical clarity. He has recommended, for example, that we determine the functional significance of a structure by looking at the dysfunctional consequences that occur when the structure fails. We know that oxygen intake is empirically important to an animal because, when an animal is deprived of oxygen, it dies (1968c:460). But there are many ways to bring oxygen into a living system. In similar fashion, we can discover that some political order is empirically important to a society. But there are many forms of political order, and we wonder, among other possibilities, if democracy is the best arrangement for a developing nation. Parsons has not listed the specific research hypotheses implied here much less tested them. Perhaps if he had tried to test his ideas — tried to find situations where they do and do not hold true — he might have paid more attention to the operational definitions of his concepts. This in turn would have forced him to eliminate tautologies, ambiguities, and other fuzzy edges on his theory.

CONCLUSION

Parsons has accomplished two of his major scientific goals. First, he has constructed an answer to the extreme empiricist view popular at the start of his career, the tenet (advocated by researchers like Lundberg) that all scientific knowledge can be measured directly. To refute this position Parsons has travelled far in the other direction and built a theory about intangibles, about common-value integrations. These integrated sets of goals and directions also answer Parsons's main substantive question: How can we explain order in society while still allowing for human choice? In his formulations he assumes that men act in a socially acceptable fashion because they believe in society's values and accept social norms. But there are societies where men behave because they are afraid of being shot. While stressing our value orientations to a situation, Parsons sometimes ignores the impact of the situation itself. Comparative studies — like those of Max Weber — could show how common value-integration grows out of social interaction in some particular group at some special time and how the exigencies of a situation can force people to adopt new ways in spite of old rules.

The problem, of course, is that Parsons has not conducted many of the research studies needed to substantiate his theory and to explore its limitations. Therefore, his theoretical structure remains incomplete. He had hoped to create a "logically related" theory system. Has he actually built such a construct? By his own admission, no; "my approach is not yet a logico-deductive system, but rather a temporal and historical series of contributions toward the development of such a system" (1961b:321). In other words, Parsons has told us where to look even if he has not developed a tightly related set of testable hypotheses for us to use while we are looking. He has elaborated a complex scheme of definitions, not a simple set of related propositions. Even though he recognizes the incomplete nature of his work, he risks an inherent danger that threatens all scientists who build theories from illuminating examples without later testing them in systematic research. His theoretical concepts may prove to be so vague or so esoteric or so tautological that they cannot be used in research without major alterations, and it is unlikely that Parsons himself will live to direct the necessary rearrangements of his theory.

Although in terms of research utility Parson's failures have been great, we cannot limit our criticism to these failings. His ambitions have also been great. A theorist who tries to explain how the modern U.S. could evolve from tribal society may not clearly distinguish integration from pattern maintenance in feudal dukedoms. And a theorist who tries to find common traits in a biological organism and a set of cultural symbols may well have trouble defining function in a way that applies to both systems. Perhaps he has tried too much. Perhaps his final contribution will be a set of limited propositions that we manage to draw from his vaulting ideas. Or maybe the vision of a general theory — any general theory — will be his lasting contribution. Parsons has recalled sociology from the trivial (though testable) concerns of extreme positivists back to the wider interests of early sociologists.

Bibliography

Parsons, Talcott
  1937 *The Structure of Social Action: A Study in Social Theory with Special Reference to a Group of Recent European Writers.* New York: Free Press (1968).
  1939 "The professions and social structure." Pp. 34-49 in *Essays in Sociological Theory.* Rev. ed. New York: Free Press, 1954.
  1942 "Propaganda and social control." Pp. 142-76 in *Essays. . . .*
  1945 "The present position and prospects of systematic theory in sociology." Pp. 212-37 in *Essays. . . .*
  1950 "The prospects of sociological theory." Pp. 348-69 in *Essays. . . .*
  1951a *The Social System.* New York: Free Press (1964).
Parsons, Talcott, Shils, Edward A., and Olds, James
  1951b "Values, motives, and systems of action." Pp. 47-275 in Talcott Parsons and Edward A. Shils (eds.), *Toward a General Theory of Action: Theoretical Foundations for the Social Sciences.* New York: Harper and Row (1962).
Parsons, Talcott, and Bales, Robert F.

1953a "The dimensions of action-space." Pp. 63-109 in Talcott Parsons, Robert F. Bales, and Edward A. Shils, *Working Papers in the Theory of Action*. New York: Free Press.

Parsons, Talcott, Bales, Robert F., and Shils, Edward A.

1953b "Phase movement in relation to motivation, symbol formation, and role structure." Pp. 163-269 in *Working Papers*. . . .

Parsons, Talcott

1953c "A revised analytical approach to the theory of social stratification." Pp. 386-439 in *Essays*. . . .

Parsons, Talcott, and Smelser, Neil J.

1956 *Economy and Society: A Study in the Integration of Economic and Social Theory*. New York: Free Press (1964).

Parsons, Talcott

1959a "General theory in sociology." Pp. 3-38 in Robert K. Merton, Leonard Broom and Leonard S. Cottrell, Jr. (eds.), *Sociology Today: Problems and Prospects*. New York: Basic Books.

1959b "The role of general theory in sociological analysis: some case material." *Alpha Kappa Deltan* 29 (Winter): 12-38.

1961a "An outline of the social system." Pp. 30-79 in Parsons *et al.* (eds.), *Theories of Society*. New York: Free Press.

1961b "The point of view of the author." Pp. 311-63 in Max Black (ed.), *The Social Theories of Talcott Parsons: A Critical Examination*. Englewood Cliffs, N.J.: Prentice-Hall.

1964 "Evolutionary universals in society." Pp. 490-520 in *Sociological Theory and Modern Society*. New York: Free Press, 1967.

1966 *Societies: Evolutionary and Comparative Perspectives*. Englewood Cliffs, N.J.: Prentice-Hall.

1968a "Interaction: social interaction." In David L. Sills (ed.), *International Encyclopedia of the Social Sciences* New York: Macmillan and Free Press.

1968b "Introduction to the paperback edition." Pp. v-xiv in *The Structure of Social Action*. . . .

1968c "Systems analysis: social systems." In *International*. . . .

1970 "Some problems of general theory in sociology." Pp. 27-68 in John C. McKinney and Edward A. Tiryakian (eds.), *Theoretical Sociology: Perspectives and Developments*. New York: Appleton-Century-Crofts.

1971 *The System of Modern Societies.* Englewood Cliffs, N.J.:
  Prentice-Hall:
1965 "Unity and diversity in the modern intellectual disciplines: the
  role of the social sciences." Pp. 166-69 in *Sociological Theory.*

Secondary sources

Black, Max
  1961 "Some questions about Parsons' theories." Pp. 268-88 in Max
    Black (ed.), *The Social Theories of Talcott Parsons: A Critical
    Examination.* Englewood Cliffs, N.J.: Prentice-Hall.

Boskoff, Alvin
  1969 "Talcott Parsons: the quest for a dynamic formalism." Pp. 182-211
    in *Theory in American Sociology.* New York: Thomas Y. Crowell.

Buckley, Walter
  1967 "Social systems models." Pp. 7-40 in *Sociology and Modern Systems
    Theory.* Englewood Cliffs, N.J.: Prentice-Hall.

Devereux, Edward C., Jr.
  1961 "Parsons' sociological theory." Pp. 1-63 in *The Social Theories.*

Heydebrand, Wolf
  1972 "Review symposium." *Contemporary Sociology* 1 (September) :387-95.

Toby, Jackson
  1972 "Review symposium." *Contemporary Sociology* 1 (September) :395-
    401.

Williams, Robin M., Jr.
  1961 "The sociological theory of Talcott Parsons." Pp. 64-99 in *The
    Social Theories.*

Robert King Merton

Robert K. Merton (1910-) obtained his Ph.D. during the 1930's when large-scale survey research (occasionally collecting masses of data without relating it to substantive theory) became fashionable in sociology. This practice stood in contrast to the Parsonian approach of illuminating critical scientific problems with a few crucial examples. Merton has developed a strategy for reconciling these two trends. His *middle-range* theorizing requires a set of propositions concrete enough to suggest empirical research procedures, but abstract enough to apply beyond the interests of the moment. Typically Merton used these middle-range statements to describe some *functional* sequence. He has argued that a particular situation functions to produce (or at least encourage) a particular result: our belief that some people are untrustworthy funtions to elicit untrustworthy behavior from them (or to make us interpret their behavior as untrustworthy) : our cultural stress on rational religious and economic forms functions to encourage rational-experimental science; our beliefs and behaviors in one area of social life function to produce wide-ranging effects in other areas.

Using this format, Merton has generated ideas about scientific institutions and knowledge structures in general, about deviant behavior and broader aspects of social control, about medical-school training and other social processes. Expanding the work of earlier theorists, he defined or redefined several concepts that have become part of the common currency of sociology, concepts like the *self-fulfilling prophecy* (people tend to do what you expect them to do) and his famous reformulation of Durkheim's *anomie*.

To date he has left a large number of ideas — both substantive and methodological — that continue to inspire other sociological researchers in the search for a middle way between abstract theory and atheoretical empiricism.

INTELLECTUAL BACKGROUND

Reading Merton's work and glancing through his copious foot-notes, we can learn some of the numerous sources of his thought. Indeed, he often overwhelms a reader with parenthetical comments and notes detailing the history of each idea. But fortunately, he has singled out those few men who had the greatest influence in shaping his approach to sociology, chiefly academics from Harvard, where he got his Ph.D., and Columbia, where he has taught for many years (1949a:ix-x).

At Harvard, studying under Pitirim A. Sorokin and Talcott Parsons, Merton learned to analyze patterns of social life and to construct theories about these patterns, instead of just gathering data about divorce, juvenile delinquency, and other popular-interest topics. He also studied under George Sarton, a history-of-science writer, who encouraged Merton's career-long interest in the institution of science and his close attention to the historical background of sociological problems. Merton left Harvard with a proper respect for general, abstract explanations.

He was hired at Columbia to be an idea man, to theorize. There he met Paul F. Lazarsfeld, who had been hired at the same time as an empirical researcher, a technician. The two men became complete friends: colleagues, challengers, collaborators, critics. In the process, Lazarsfeld questioned many of Merton's theoretical ideas and thus inspired him to explicate these ideas in detail — to specify the conditions under which a relationship exists, to formulate a theory that can be tested empirically.

DEFINITION OF SOCIOLOGY

Merton has not devoted much attention to an original definition of sociology. He has left only a few clues; causal references to the "science of society" (1967b:2) and the study of "social behavior, organization, and change" (1967a:45). Instead of phrasing his own definition of sociology, complete with an elaboration of its scope, Merton has pointed to Durkheim and Weber as the masters whom the rest of us should follow:

> We are all residuary legatees of Durkheim and Weber, whose works furnish ideas to be followed up, exemplify tactics of theorizing, provide for the exercise of taste in the selection of problems, and instruct us in raising theoretical questions that develop out of theirs. (1967a:68)

In essence, he assumed that we already know what sociology is about; that sociology does exist whatever its exact boundaries may be.

Reviewing how Merton himself engaged in the business of sociology, we may speculate about his private definition of the field. He began working in the social-action tradition of Weber and Parsons. Although his mature work does not explore cultural meanings with a *Verstehen* methodology, Merton did retain an interest in cultural values and their implications, particularly as these values informed particular structural situations. When he developed his strategy for *functional analysis* (that is, the study of the observable sources and objective results of social behavior), he often analyzed cultural values as the "observable sources." Merton eventually named his approach the "most promising," in sociology even though it was but one possibility among many (1949d:19). So if we had to suggest a definition for Merton's sociology, we could call it "the scientific study of cultural values and their functions."

SUBJECT FOCUS

Since Merton assumes that the boundaries of sociology have already been drawn, he believes that the current challenge is not defining the substance of the field, but learning to define the proper research questions, preferably questions "so formulated that the answers to them will confirm, amplify, or variously revise some part of what is currently taken as knowledge in the field" (1959:x). Toward this end, he has outlined three steps for "problem-finding in sociology": originating a question, developing a rationale for interest in the problem, and specifying the particular empirical inquiries that answer the main question in terms of the rationale (1959:xiii-xix).

To do this, we must begin the first step by deciding what it is we want to know. Does the object of our interest really exist? Before analyzing why mental illness has risen in modern society we should ascertain that, in fact, it has risen. Before explaining cultural differences we should demonstrate that "culture" is more than just a sociological label. We must also ask about relationships between classes of objects that have attracted our interest. Does the cultural value of legitimacy change during times of conflict? Do changes in the social structure accompany changes in rates and types of mental illness? Then we must determine what specific empirical areas we will examine and whether our findings can be applied more broadly. If we study how a fundamentalist religion defends scripture against liberal interpretation, are we studying a peculiar problem in the sociology of religion or are we addressing the broader issue of how any organization maintains legitimacy in the face of environmental change?

Answering a question like that is also part of Merton's second stage of problem-finding. When we decide on a rationale for our study, we should be alert to both practical and theoretical reasons for pursuing a topic. The study of defensive fundamentalism could have great practical importance for religious groups trying to "hold the line" on some moral or dogmatic issue, and at the same time could tell us a great deal about the nature and correlates of social legitimacy. Merton clearly implies that the best questions usually have both practical and theoretical implications and the worst questions often have neither. Idle curiosity, in other words, is a way to waste time, money, and energy on trivia; worse it can encourage sloppy, unfocused fact-fishing. It is better that we specify a rationale for our studies as one step to finding and delineating our research problem.

Having found a question and a rationale, we need only take the third step in problem-finding and look for the particular empirical circumstances likely to illuminate the issue. When Park wanted to examine Simmel's "stranger," to see how living on the border of two cultures could affect a person's social behavior, he looked at the European immigrant in America. His "marginal man" provided some insights into how a person lives with foreign norms and values.

In sum, Merton considers defining a sociological research problem one of the very important steps in scientific work. He has pursued this interest in his research, not only by defining problems for his own investigations, but also by reviewing other people's research within the framework of his own original questions.

SCIENCE — THE PLAN

Working on these sociological problems, Merton developed a comprehensive methodological strategy. In a series of seminal essays, he highlighted key aspects of the scientific approach to the study of social life: the nature of sociological theory, the relationship between theory and research, the usefulness of middle-range statements, and functional analysis as a research tool. Reviewing his ideas we can understand his emphasis on a new mode of functionalism based on middle-range propositions about immediate structural situation instead of abstract hypotheses about societal needs.

To begin, Merton defined sociological theory in terms of its utility for research: " . . . the term *sociological theory* refers to logically interconnected sets of propositions from which empirical uniformities can be derived" (1967b:39). He also provided a setting for middle-range theory somewhere between "general sociological orientations" and "empirical generalization." The general orientations point up important variables like the institution of religion. Empirical generalizations describe the trends indicated by data, like the differential suicide rates of Protestants and Catholics. Theory encompasses both in a set of logically connected statements (1949c: 87-96). To illustrate this relationship between data and theory Merton restated the assumptions and predictions from Durkheim's study of suicide:

1) Social cohesion provides psychic support to group members subject to acute stresses and anxieties.
2) Suicide rates are functions of *unrelieved* anxieties and stresses to which persons are subjected.
3) Catholics have greater social cohesion than Protestants.
4) Therefore, lower suicide rates should be anticipated among Catholics than among Protestants (1949c:97).

Clearly these statements belong to the same logical sequence. If the first three hold true, the fourth must follow: if suicide results from unrelieved anxieties, and if Catholics do not have such anxieties because of the support of group cohesion, then the group-based cause of suicide is not present among Catholics and their suicide rate must be low. If the rate is high, one of the other statements must be false. Of course logicians know that the reverse is not necessarily true: even if Catholics do have lower suicide rates, this does not necessarily mean that they have great social cohesion, that unrelieved stress produces suicide, or that social cohesion provides psychic support.

In other words, we can falsify a logical theory by demonstrating that the conclusion is not empirically true and, thereby, implying that the assumptions behind this conclusion cannot all be true either. However, we cannot verify a theory because, even if the conclusions prove true empirically, they may be the right results for the wrong reasons. Scientists have not found an empirical solution for this logical problem. Merton suggests that we create a partial solution by making our empirical predictions (our research hypotheses) as precise as possible. At least that practice will eliminate some of the possible alternative explanations (1949c:97-99).

For example, Durkheim could have refined his theory about social cohesion and deviance by first determining how strongly various groups censure a particular type of deviance. If he discovered that Catholics prohibited church burials for suicides, but Protestants often conducted normal services, then he might conclude that suicide is slightly less abhorent to Protestants even though both groups clearly prohibit it. Group cohesion aside, this difference in attitudes could affect suicide rates. On the other hand, perhaps some Catholic groups prohibit church burial while others permit it (disobeying canon law in the process). Perhaps some Protestant groups reject suicide even more firmly than most Catholics. If this were the situation, Durkheim could compare four groups — Catholics completely against suicide; Catholics less firmly against suicide; Protestants completely against suicide; and Protestants less firmly against suicide. Assuming that group cohesion is more important than these slight variations in group attitude, Durkheim could predict a greater difference in suicide rates between all Protestants and all Catholics than that within either religious group. Thus, with this more precise prediction, Durkheim could strenghten his original conclusion by eliminating attitude differences within groups as an alternative explanation.

Looking at the opposite side of the theory-research process, Merton also examined how research affects theory. As theory produces discriminating hypotheses for research, so empirical facts modify theoretical ideas. Obviously we need data to confirm or reject hypotheses But beyond this, Merton identified four other contributions that research makes to theory (1949b):

1) Research initiates theory — the serendipity factor: research often produces anomalous findings that require new explanations. For instance, when Lundberg discovered the Irish-Yankee hostility within his "majority" in-group, he could have used this finding to formulate new statements about power groups — suggesting, perhaps, that economic position is more important than religion or ethnicity or numerical strength in defining the dominant and subordinant groups in a community.

2) Research reformulates theory — sociologists often reconsider common-place facts, social patterns which did not seem important when they were first observed. Many nineteenth-century observers must have noticed the Protestant flair for business, for example, but Weber was the one who reformulated ideas about cultural community into a theory describing the relationship between religion and economic rationality.

3) Research deflects theory — new data-gathering tools enable researchers to examine new problems. We can imagine, among other possibilities, how Tarde might have studied imitation with attitudinal data based on a national sample, perhaps refining his ideas about the lag between attitudinal and behavioral changes.

4) Research clarifies theory — in our efforts to observe something (to develop an operational definition), we often clarify our theoretical concepts. We may speculate, about how Parsons might rethink his concepts of pattern-maintenance and integration to produce operational definitions for an intensive comparison of these functions within the American nuclear family and the extended family of pre-Communist China.

In Merton's opinion, *middle-range theory* provides the best vehicle of exchange between theoretical ideas and empirical observations (1948a:165-66) :

> . . . what I have called *theories of the middle range*: theories that lie between the minor but necessary working hypothses that evolve in abundance during day-to-day research and the all-inclusive systematic efforts to develop a unified theory that will explain all the observed uniformities of social behavior, social organization and social change. (1967a:39)

At one extreme, Parsons wrote about the functions of societal community in a social system; at the other, Lundberg studied the sociometric choices of the non-Jewish white majority in two Seattle high schools. In contrast, middle-range theorists merge ideas with observations to consider the wide applications of generalizations built from specific situations. Durkheim combined abstract notions about social facts with concrete data on suicide rates to generate a middle-range theory of anomie. Weber united his concept of social action with the history of seventeenth-century Europe to study the interdependence of social institutions. In other words, these middle-range theorists summarize old information in an explanatory framework that also highlights areas for future research (1967a).

According to Merton, functional analysis provides a comprehensive framework for these middle-range statements and, therefore, the most promising strategy for the study of society.

As Merton defined it, *functionalism* deals with the "observable objective consequences" of social behavior (1949d:78). Parsons, the grand-theorist, had developed a different outlook when he combined social action with functional analysis. In his pattern-variables he considered the subjective orientations held by groups within a social system and the corresponding effects of these orientations on action. Later he examined the survival needs of a system and studied the common values and behavioral patterns people develop to meet these needs. In essence he asked "Why did they act that way?" Merton asks a different question: "What happened because they acted as they did?" To examine these results of social behavior, Merton has suggested that we concentrate on middle-range problems. Instead of speculating about the abstract "needs" of a total social system, needs we can never define empirically, we should list the specific needs in a situation and then compare the ways people plan to meet these needs with the actual results of social activity. Instead of assessing the abstract cultural patterns of motivations within a society, we should examine motives that appear within a specific situation (1948).

As he moved from abstract theorizing about system needs to the examination of action and its results in a specific situation, Merton had to identify empirical phenomena that had not been discussed by Parsons. Parsons did consider how alternative structures could function to solve the same systems problems: religion and societal community could both function to integrate society; open-class and caste structures could both motivate people to perform their social duties. He also suggested that some alternatives were related to each other (at least empirically) and likely to accompany each other in the same society. Investigating different and more explicitly empirical problems, Merton noticed that the objective consequences of an action may differ sharply from the intended plans of the actors. Any investigation of such action must account for consequences that are planned and unplanned, functional and not-so-fuctional. Therefore, when we analyze social life we must consider the intended-*manifest* functions and the unintended-*latent* functions along with *dysfunctions,* non-functions, and alternative functions of social values and related behavior. Consumer behavior provides one example. Buyers will tell us that they purchase more costly goods because expensive items are "better" than cheap ones (a manifest function). But as many observers have noted, expensive goods also serve to bolster the status of their owners (a latent function). Furthermore, such spending habits may eventually lead to fiscal instability, repossession by creditors, and life in the Poor House (a dysfunction) (1949d: 60-82).

In other words, Merton shifted attention from the total system to structural patterns, from functional imperatives to functional structuralism. He explicitly substituted the needs of the people in the system for the needs of the system itself. In effect, he recommended two functional-causal approaches: 1) studies of how structures suit the needs of people in the system; and 2) studies of how personal-social values promote structures which, in turn, have broader consequences. Both of these approaches lie well within Merton's middle range of studies more significant than descriptions of the data-of-the-moment but more limited than Parsonian theory.

RESEARCH — THE PRACTICE

Merton has retained his functional, middle-range framework throughout his substantive work, explaining many specific phenomena with terms that can be reapplied in a wide variety of social situations. Whatever his current interest, he continuously exhibits his basic priorities, stressing theoretical ideas and methodological approaches. In his theory building he often uses material from various research projects — but he highlights the ideas first; then the approaches; and last, the explicit substantive findings. His priority on ideas shows very clearly in the three-stage process he outlined for verifying theoretical ideas in research: 1) the development of logical syllogisms (along the Durkheim-Merton model mentioned earlier); 2) the explicit statement of these in research reports; and 3) the presentation of findings to support or change the theories (1949b:100). Merton himself does not follow this mechanical formula religiously, but its outlines are implicit in his work. He typically formulates middle-range statements (without explicitly tying them to a logical-theory format) and uses empirical data to demonstrate that his propositions describe an existing functional relationship. However, Merton's most memorable contributions occur when he reviews research (his own and the work of others) to formulate new ideas or new elaborations — about reference groups, self-fulfilling prophecies, ritualistic performances, role-sets, anomic responses, cosmopolitian outlooks, and about numerous middle-range explanations of social life. We will review some examples of his work here: first a sample of Merton's middle-range theory testing; then a few of the theoretical ideas he has developed from research.

Merton has not provided us with an example of a research report, complete with statements about his general orientation, middle-range hypothesis, and specific predictions, and followed, of course, by findings to support or refute the logical conclusion. However, his study of social class in the U.S. (written before he proposed the syllogism format) shows how he could use it to predict empirical results. In "Paternal status and the economic adjustment of high school graduates" (1944), Merton and a coauthor (Bryce Ryan) compared the effects of achieved and ascribed status by examining the first-year income of 25,000 Boston high school graduates. After eliminating those who had gone on to college, they compared the mean first-year income with the social class of the graduate's father to delineate a significant difference between class groups. Reformulating Merton's thought in terms of a syllogism, we could suggest:

1) Social class membership implies participation in life-style patterns (including know-how) and influence (including the ability to exchange favors).

2) Life style and influence are part of a family complex (ascribed status) rather than simply the results of individual achievement (achieved status).

3) People from higher-class families have more know-how and influence than lower-class family members.

4) Therefore the children of higher-class families will enter the occupational world in better jobs than the equally educated children of lower-class families.

This work (based on Ryan's dissertation data) is not a typical Merton product. He is more likely to argue: "I believe some relationship exists between two basic structures of society. The elements I am observing are examples of this basic tendency. If the basic relationship does, in fact, exist, then there should be a relationship between the two sample items. . . ." Consider Weber's Protestant Ethic. Weber had first hypothesized, on a rather abstract level, that social institutions are interdependent and then demonstrated, in the concrete, that Puritanism affected economic life (1967a:63n40). Merton examined another relationship implied by Weber's basic hypothesis. Reviewing historical data, Merton documented the ties between Puritanism and the growth of seventeenth-century English science (1938). Puritanism, he argued, favored scientific growth. Assuming God had created an orderly world that could be rationally addressed through empirical procedures, Puritans encouraged physics, the study of God's order. They also stressed education in "useful" subjects — once again fields like physics and its handmaiden, mathematics. The combined belief in rational approaches, empirical studies, and utilitarianism underlay a flowering of "hard" science. If this argument is true, Merton reasoned, then a disproportionate number of Protestants should have pursued physical-science studies and entered scientific groups like the Royal Society. And indeed they did. So Merton concluded that the religious climate in seventeenth-century England created a fertile atmosphere for scientific growth.

However, he did not buttress his argument with a cross-cultural experiment as Weber had done for his related thesis about religious and economic institutions. Aside from the herculean difficulties of amassing data for this comparison, Merton would face the problem of finding a society with all the preconditions of science except the Protestant Ethic. Perhaps such a society has never existed.

Instead of conducting cross-cultural comparative studies to delineate the relationship between religion and the origins of modern science, Merton supported his basic hypothesis about the interrelationship of values and institutions by examining the subsequent growth of science. He noted that Puritanism had created a social value encouraging the rapid spread of scientific ideas. This in turn lead to a stress on scientific priority. Merton reviewed scientific literature, diaries, notes, letters, and other documents to examine the values held by scientists and the effects of these values. He concluded that the emphasis placed on scientific priority (in other terms, the race to publish original findings) produces two results: steady work in the difficult frontier borders of science, along with fraud, plagiarism, and other research piccadilloes practiced by those who would publish first at any cost (1957b).

Even more recently, Merton has used available records and interview data to document other ties between social values and scientific institutions. There is, even within the scientific community, a lingering tendency to accept traditional authority: hence the Matthew effect — those who have, get — famous men get more credit for the same work than their lesser known fellows (1968). Finally, examining another network in the institution of science, Merton (and Harriet Zuckerman) have noticed how age (and the traditions of authority associated with age) affect a scientist's reputation among his peers. In areas with a well-developed theory, the scientific community will quickly recognize and acknowledge the supporting contributions of a newcomer. In contrast, recognition in less codified fields is accorded to the mature judgment of "big-name" scientists (1972a).

These works in the sociology of science exhibit two typical features of Merton's research technique. As a rule, he looks beyond the bare details about a social phenomenon to argue the possible existence of a functional relationship, "This pattern tends to appear along with that one and I suspect one produces the other." Second, although he does use interview and questionnaire data gathered by researchers at Columbia, in his own personal research he prefers to evaluate the documents of intellectual history — to compare the "primare Masse" mentioned by Freud with the primary group discovered by Cooley (1967b:18), to tell us how long young scientists have "stood on the shoulders of giants" in order to see farther than their forebearers (1965), and to use historical data for tracing the functional relationship between Calvinism and science, between scientific priorities as a value and scientific integrity, between one type of thought and its objective consequences (1938; 1957b).

Turning to Merton's theory building, we see a master craftsman constructing concepts and propositions out of common-place material less skillful workers would ignore. In *Mass Persuasion: The Social Psychology of a War Bond Drive* (1946), for example, Merton (and coauthors) examined the Kate Smith bond-selling marathon, reviewing the actual sales messages along with the reactions of people who heard the messages. Using a very personal sales pitch, Smith had sold $39,000,000 worth of war bonds in eighteen hours to a population that did not trust personal messages from pseudo-*Gemeinschaft* salesmen. But how? After reviewing the data. Merton hypothesized that Smith's actions sold more than her words. Her persistence, despite fatigue spoke louder than her stories about the bravery of combat soldiers, the sacrifices of bereaved mothers, or the needs of a war-time government. "Propaganda-of-the-deed," he concluded, may be effective among the very people who distrust "propaganda-of-the-word" (1946:88-96; 1949b:108-11). In similar fashion, Merton used another study (also from the Columbia Bureau of Research) to develop ideas about the process leading to friendship. The Columbia researchers had compared sociometric choices with attitudes toward racial liberalism (among whites) in two biracial communities. They found that people name friends who have attitudes like their own. But how do they find these friends in the first place? Once again, Merton suggested an answer, in this instance a friendship-formation process that allows both sides to reinforce the other's similar attitudes and to discourage all dissimilar attitudes — or dissimilar friends (1954).

In each of these studies, Merton explained the findings by creating a new proposition in a *post factum* analysis. Merton warns us, however, that we can rationalize some *post factum* explanation for any set of facts. We can explain that unemployed men read less than employed ones because they are depressed, or, to suit the other data possibility, they read more because they have extra time (1949c: 93-95). The solution, of course, is to set up a new research project aimed at documenting the existence and effects of unemployment, friendship-formation processes, and propaganda-by-deed in new situations. Merton advocates such theory testing. But he has not specialized in it himself.

Indeed, Merton's main contribution may result from his purely conceptual work, from the new problems he discovered after reviewing the current state of sociological thought. For example, Merton has asked if anomie can predict the rise (and expected fall) of syndicate crime. To analyze such a problem, Merton usually details the history of the underlying ideas — the interplay between thought and evidence, theory and research. In the end he proposes a middle-range hypothesis about the functional relationship between cultural values and social structures.

In his work on *anomie,* Merton hypothesized that the disparity between cultural goals and access to efficient, licit means of achieving these goals encourages deviance. Durkheim had long since documented the relationship between group anomie and suicide rates: when, with a changing situation, the old socially created norms no longer guide society, group rates of deviance increase. Merton refocused the concept and used it to explain the possibilities for individual deviance within groups. He suggested that people can respond to anomie in a variety of ways. They can, for example, ignore the goals and cling to a *ritual* of means, like the bureaucrat who plays by the rules even when the rules no longer suit the purpose of the game. Another adaptation, the one that interests us here, is *innovation*: clever types can create new means to reach old goals (1949e). Assuming that Americans prize financial success, Merton examined the behavior of people who lack family background, education, influence, and other routes to big money. The political "machine" or organization provides one illicit institutional avenue to wealth and power for whichever ethnic group happens to control it (1949d:72-82). During the 1920's and 30's, when Jewish and Irish groups controlled big-city political power, some Italian groups discovered another illicit opportunity for financial rewards, namely syndicate crime (1957a: 192-94). After members of these groups achieved success, their children often found more socially acceptable ways to remain in the comfortable socio-economic positions. Meanwhile, other deprived people are pimping, committing strong-arm robbery, and engaging in other nefarious, but profitable activities.

However, we may ask, how do we explain the behavior of deprived people who do not rob their neighbors or sell their girlfriends or join the syndicate but choose, instead, to do as well as they can within the system? Merton does not attempt to answer this question. Although his anomie describes possible responses to social pressures, it does not predict the rate or direction of personal deviance. Merton documented the existence of cultural goals and means; he outlined some possible relationships between these ideals and social behavior; he provided examples of the behavior involved; but, using his framework, he could not predict whether Al Capone would become a gangster or a longshoreman, or, for that matter, whether a typical boy in the Al's neighborhood would join the mob or the establishment. For this we need a more detailed theory listing the types of situations that encourage different types and rates of deviance.

We have considered three ways Merton used research: to verify specific hypotheses; to develop simple propositions; and to refine theoretical concepts. However, we have not considered a well-rounded functional analysis complete with a definition of system needs in a limited situation, the description of activity filling these needs, a delineation of the processes selecting the functional activity, an assessment of personal motives behind manifest and latent structures, and an account of different subgroups using the structure in different ways.

Merton has not published such a comprehensive analysis, but he has presented interesting segments that suggest the possibilities inherent in the functional approach. For example, he wrote his discriptions of illicit opportunity structures to illustrate unplanned functions (1949d:72-82). He noted that the "machine" — regardless of its origins or the motives of its originators — serves four latent functions. It provides a source of humane assistance — more personal than welfare, less humiliating than charity — for the deprived classes. It possesses the power to settle strikes, restrict competition, and provide other services for the dominant business interests. As we have already seen, its mere existence provides a mobility ladder for oppressed ethnic groups. Finally using different techniques — regulating competition through arrests instead of licenses — it provides the same services for illegitimate enterprises that it provides legitimate business. Since Merton wrote his description of the machine to depict unintended consequences of social structures, we cannot fault him for omitting other aspects of functional analysis. But, as it stands, Merton's commentary lists machine activities and labels them as latent functions serving needs of various groups. We may ask: Doesn't every structure serve some need? Although Merton's description is useful in identifying the needy, it would be more revealing if Merton had also traced the origins of bossism, examined manifest functions, suggested alternative structures that could fill the manifest and latent needs, and considered why bossism prevailed over these alternatives. In other words, Merton has explained what caused bossism to persist: it served the latent needs of subgroups in a growing immigrant city. But he has not explained how the machine, rather than some alternative, came to be built in the first place. Further-more, in spite of his strictures against teleological grand-theory func-tionalism, he has substituted needs-of-the-people for needs-of-the-system as a teleological cause.

In sum, Merton typically used research to document the existence of a relationship, to generate new theoretical propositions, or to elaborate a concept — all valid practices in his system of sociology. He left unfinished the task of outlining the conditions under which his variables would operate. This omission is particularly critical in his functional analysis. He has not analyzed a total functional situa-tion separating the original cause from the function that may cause a structure to continue. Indeed, most of his empirical work has con-sisted in depicting a structure and noting its possible or actual empir-ical consequences. His basic conclusion: this structure or value tends to produce that result; the protestant ethic tends to encourage science; anomie tends to elicit non-conformist responses . . . this cause has that effect.

Merton's basic outlook may explain why his work is in such an "unfinished" state. In contrast to the other sociologists whose work we have reviewed, Merton did not concentrate on a particular sub-ject matter like social action or symbolic responses or societal evolu-tion; nor did he examine problems in a specific substantive area like social norms or urban life; and he did not try to develop a comprehensive theoretical framework or to exhaust a method of analysis. Instead, he used his technique to mine productive problem areas as they occurred to him. In this way, he could begin by de-fining a problem like personal responses to anomie and then explore its implications in a series of statements about innovative criminals, ritualistic drones who inhabit government offices, and others who respond to anomie in their own way. Or he could begin with an idea like W. I. Thomas's "definition of the situation" in order to discuss how we define an "in-group" and "out-group": how we use our definitions to transform the "in-group" virtue into an "out-group" vice, to change our thrift into their shylock tendencies, our easy-going ways into their shiftless irresponsibility — to create a self-fulfilling prophecy which predicts that we will always be right and they will always be wrong (1948b). Later he analyzed the different perspectives that an insider and outsider bring to their evaluation of the same group activity (1972b). Moving in this fashion from topic to topic, Merton often began by observing a pattern — usually a common pattern that most of us would regard as unremarkable. In terms of his categories relating research to theory, he used the empirical patterns as sociological problems that form the basis for reformulating theory — for explaining normal action with fresh concepts and propositions.

CONCLUSION

Merton's middle-range work stands between the operationalism of Lundberg and the generalization of Parsons. In method, Merton lies closer to Lundberg: we can formulate concrete empirical hypotheses directly from some of his statements. But in theory he retains his teacher's outlook and general view: first he looks for the values, the goals cherished by people in some social group; then he tries to observe the functions, or consequences, that occur because people seek these goals.

Like Parsons, he assumes that all social groups do have values, that values define appropriate behavior, and, a very important assumption, that people really act according to their values. Merton tells us that these value-inspired actions produce many results — the intended, or manifest, functions; the hidden, or latent, functions; and the dysfunctions. Because scientists value scientific priority, for example, they rush to publish ahead of other scientists with similar ideas. This practice serves the manifest function of getting the good word into print where others can learn it. The rush to publish also supports a growing number of editors, publishers, and printers. But at the same time it encourages some venal types to cheat a bit in order to publish first.

We may wonder about the details of these functional relationships. Does the value of scientific priority cause a great advance of science along with some minor abuses by scientists? Or does it promote widespread dysfunction with some little good? Under what conditions are scientists most likely to engage in dysfunctional activity? These are the types of questions Merton does not answer. He points up relationships, general tendencies. Using his own research and the work of others, he documents the existence of these tendencies, but he does not estimate their magnitude or specify the conditions that might explain why one pattern is chosen over the others in various types of situations.

Bibliography

Merton, Robert King
  1938 *Science, Technology and Society in Seventeenth Century England.*
      New York: Howard Fertig (1970).
Merton, Robert K., and Ryan, Bryce
  1944 "Paternal status and the economic adjustment of high school grad-
      uates." *Social Forces* 22 (March) : 302-06.
Merton, Robert K., with the assistance of Fiske, Marjorie, and Curtis,
Alberta
  1946 *Mass Persuasion: The Social Psychology of a War Bond Drive.*
      Westport, Conn.: Greenwood Press (1971).
Merton, Robert K.
  1948a "Discussion of Parsons's 'The position of sociological theory.'"
      American Sociological Review 13 (April) : 164-68.
  1948b "The self-fulfilling prophecy." Pp. 421-36 in *Social Theory and
      Social Structure.* 2d ed. rev. Glencoe, Ill.: Free Press, 1957.
  1949a "Acknowledgement." Pp. ix-x in *Social Theory.* . . .
  1949b "The bearing of empirical research on sociological theory."
      Pp. 102-17 in *Social Theory.* . . .
  1949c "The bearing of sociological theory on empirical research."
      Pp. 85-101 in *Social Theory.* . . .
  1949d "Manifest and latent functions." Pp. 19-84 in *Social Theory.* . . .
  1949e "Social structure and anomie." Pp. 131-60 in *Social Theory.* . . .
Lazarsfeld, Paul F., and Merton, Robert K.
  1954 "Friendship as social process: a substantive and methodological
      analysis." Pp. 18-66 in Morroe Berger, Theodore Able, and Charles
      H. Page (eds.), *Freedom and Control in Modern Society.* New
      York: D. Van Nostrand.
Merton, Robert K.
  1957a "Continuities in the theory of social structure and anomie." Pp.
      161-94 in *Social Theory.* . . .
  1957b "Priorities in scientific discovery: a chapter in the sociology of
      science." *American Soicological Review* 22 (December) : 635-59. Also
      Pp. 286-324 in Merton (ed.), *The Sociology of Science: Theoretical
      and Empirical Investigations.* Chicago: University of Chicago Press,
      1973.
  1959 "Notes on problem-finding in sociology." Pp. ix-xxiv in Robert K.
      Merton, Leonard Broom, and Leonard S. Cottrell, Jr. (eds.), *So-
      ciology Today: Problems and Prospects.* New York: Basic Books.

1965 *On the Shoulders of Giants: A Shandean Post Script.* New York: Free Press.

1967a "On sociological theories of the middle range." Pp. 39-72 in *On Theoretical Sociology.* New York: Free Press.

1967b "On the history and systematics of sociological theory." Pp. 1-37 in *On Theoretical Sociology.*

1968 "The Matthew effect in science." *Science* 159 (January): 56-63. Also Pp. 439-59 in *The Sociology of Science. . . .*

Merton, Robert K. with Zuckerman Harriet

1972a "Age, aging, and age structure in science." Pp. 497-95 in *The Sociology of Science. . . .* Merton, Robert K.

1972b "Insiders and outsiders: a chapter in the sociology of knowledge." *American Journal of Sociology* 78 (July): 9-47.

Secondary sources

Davis, Kingsley

1959 "The myth of functional analysis as a special method in sociology and anthropology." Pp. 379-402 in N. J. Demerath, III, and Richard A. Peterson (eds.), *System, Change, and Conflict.* New York: Free Press, 1967.

Deutsch, Morton, and Krauss, Robert M.

1965 "Role theory — Robert K. Merton." Pp. 190-203 in *Theories in Social Psychology.* New York: Basic Books.

Hempel, Carl G.

1959 "The logic of functional analysis." Pp. 271-307 in Llewellyn Gross (ed.), *Symposium on Sociological Theory.* Evanston, Ill.: Row Peterson and Company.

Loomis, Charles P., and Loomis, Zona K.

1965 "Robert K. Merton as a structural analyst." Pp. 246-326 in *Modern Social Theories.* New York: D. Van Nostrand.

Martindale, Don

1960 *The Nature and Types of Sociological Theory.* Boston: Houghton Mifflin.

Turner, Jonathan H.

1974 "Functional structuralism: Robert K. Merton." Pp. 60-76 in *The Structure of Sociological Theory.* Homewood, Ill.: Dorsey Press.

George Caspar Homans

George Homans (1910-   ), has characterized his career as "a life of synthesis" (1968), chiefly a synthesis of work on small-sized groups to develop propositions describing the activity of individual men within these groups. Beginning with Pareto's framework, Homans analyzed the system of social organization in a traditional society. He has retained this basic systems model in later studies of smaller, more temporary groups like the warship crew, the clerical office staff, the street-corner gang, and others he has encountered in his travels or in his reading. Working backward from social interaction to personal motivation, he has concluded that the group or system itself does not explain man's behavior. To answer the question "Why?" we need psychological explanations. And to provide these explanations, Homans has proposed a series of propositions enumerating the personal motives that impel men to action within their groups.

Although Homans explains social phenomenon in terms of psychological predispositions, his reductionism does not simply look at individual motives, label them, and use these labels to define social life. Homans would not tell us, as Pareto did, that we have a conservative society because "lions" dominate the ruling elite. Instead, he examines motives common to all men — the desire to obtain maximum rewards at minimum costs — and uses these to explain how elites (and the rest of us) behave in society.

This emphasis contrasts sharply with the grand-theory approach of Talcott Parsons and anticipates the work of mathematical-model builders like Hubert Blalock. Indeed, using his own studies and the research of others, Homans has summarized many ideas about groups and reworked them into more precise propositions, statements that can be phrased in mathematical terms and tested against our observations of the empirical world. Furthermore, although he has never built such mathematical models himself, he expects others to use his ideas in this way (1968).

255

INTELLECTUAL BACKGROUND

As an unemployed (but solvent) Harvard depression graduate with "nothing else to do," Homans drifted into the Harvard academic community, into the graduate seminar on Pareto, the Society of Fellows, and eventually, the faculty itself. En route, he acquired his ideas about the subject matter and methods of sociology.

Starting in the special seminar, Homans first coauthored a book on Pareto's theory (1934) and then applied the master's framework to a study of medieval English villages. At the time Homans accepted the functional postulates inherent in Pareto's work. However, further reading in Durkheim's work and that of the functional anthropologists made Homans question some aspects of this framework. How, he asked, can we determine the "functional prerequisites of a society?" Even if we could document the existence of such prerequisites, how can we explain why individual men chose to serve these goals? Faced with these problems, Homans shifted his attention from medieval villages to the more simple structure of small groups; from interdependence of institutions in a complex system to social exchange modeled after B. F. Skinner's behavioralism; from a description of society to an account of the basic units of behavior that occur in any group.

With the change in subject focus, came a new perspective on methodology. During his Harvard years, Homans had read Bacon's *Novum Organum* and Bridgeman's *The Logic of Modern Physics,* two works that review the problem of defining elements in the empirical world. Later Homans studied modern philosophy-of-science writers who stressed propositional statements, logical deduction, and other tools that encourage rigorous thinking. His own approach — part reaction, part extention — grew from his effort to move sociology beyond fact-gathering, beyond simple measurement, beyond the establishment of descriptive typologies to the development of a deductive system, perhaps like the one Newton had developed for physics. Science, he concluded, should do more than provide labels for concepts; it should predict relationships and detail the reasons for them (1962:36-49).

DEFINITION OF SOCIOLOGY

For Homans, whose work ranges from historical research on institutions to psychological explanations in theory, the real concern is social science. However, in "Giving a dog a bad name," he defined a special interest, a corner of social science called sociology or "the study of what happens when two or more creatures are in a position to influence one another" (1956:114). Judging from his other work, we may assume he meant "human creatures." Indeed, the bulk of his writing reflects on the way that humans influence each other in small groups, although Homans himself would quickly admit that the study of small group interaction is only one aspect of sociology.

SUBJECT FOCUS

Like Comte and Durkheim, Homans identified group cohesion as the critical theme for social research: "The central problem of social science remains the one posed, in his own language and in his own era, by Hobbes: How does the behavior of individuals create the characteristics of groups?" (1967b:106). But Homans redefined this "central problem." Where Durkheim and Comte had considered how groups command the individual, Homans researched the effects of the individual on the group. He identified *elementary social behavior* — "the face-to-face contact between individuals, in which the reward each gets from the behavior of the others is relatively direct and immediate" (1961:7) — as the cohesive element in groups and, therefore, the definitive subject matter of his sociology.

To explain behavior, he built on four basic descriptive terms (first activities, interaction, and sentiments; then, a later addition, norms) and two variables (value and frequency). *Activities* are a "kind of behavior," what people do; *sentiments* are the special activities that signify attitudes or feelings; *interaction* consists of social activity (or sentiment) that elicits a reward or punishment from someone else; and *norms* provide a guide to appropriate activity for a situation. These qualities exist in any human system. We work to earn a raise; we frown at a naughty child — everyday life features a continuous round of interaction between someone who acts and someone else who rewards or punishes the action. Variations in these exchanges depend, in turn, on the *value* we place on activity — the rewards we seek, the costs we are willing to pay, the punishments we avoid — and the *quantity* of activity, — the frequency with which we will seek a reward, pay a cost, or avoid a punishment (1961: 30-50).

The whole network of such behavior is a social system (1950:87). As Homans conceived them, social systems exist in any cohesive

group, in the society, the warship, the office. . . . It is the task of
sociologists to discover how elementary social behavior binds these
groups together. But, until sociological reasoning becomes much
more sophisticated, Homans advises us to conduct our research in
relatively small groups. First, because small groups are easier to
view, easier to comprehend *in toto* than whole societies: if we care
to outline the structure of relations in a system, we would do well
to begin with a system small enough for one observer to see (1962:
39). Second, not only are these small groups easier to examine, but
they are the understandable locus of everyday life. We may belong
in a society, but we run with a gang or work in an office or join
a club or live with a family. Thus, these groups — the social units
that serve the needs of everyday life — are the proper arenas for
studies of how we influence each other (1950:1-2).

SCIENCE — THE PLAN

Homans, who seems as interested in sociology-the-science as he is
in sociology-the-study-of-human interaction, has written extensively
on the nature of social science, defining it as an activity that must
include both discovery and explanation. In the course of developing
his theoretical view, he drifted from his graduate-student status as an
overt functionalist to his current position as a thorough-going critic
of some aspects of that sociological framework. He has concluded
that functionalist speculation about how roles or institutions serve
to maintain a society in equilibrium simply cannot provide empirical
measures for research or inspire explanatory theory. Here we will
explicate Homans' criticisms by reviewing his key ideas about the
nature of science and the unscientific nature of functionalism.

To begin, Homans defined science as an empirical study that tries
to document the relationships between natural phenomena. As long
as it retains its empirical base — "when nature, however stretched
out on the rack, still has a chance to say 'No'" — our discipline remains a science (1967b:4). To maintain more than the minimal
standing, however, " . . . science has two main jobs to do: discovery
and explanation. By the first we judge whether it is a science, by the
second, how successful a science it is" (1967b:7).

Discovery requires two conceptual tools, the operating definition
and the proposition. The *operating definition* points to something
observable in the empirical world, qualities the researcher actually
uses to make a discovery. We do not observe a role; "role" is a

general concept embodied in a *non-operating definition*. Frequency, specificity, value — these are variables that appear in operating definitions. Instead of looking at a "role," we observe how frequently a role is performed or how specifically it is defined or how highly it is valued. But by themselves these definitions (with or without operations) tell us only that roles exist or that we think roles exist. Even an elaborate set of definitions (like the Parsonian taxonomies) cannot reveal the relationships between the variables defined by such concepts. To compare two or more variables, we need *propositions*, "statements of the relationships between properties of nature." Unfortunately, many good sociological ideas are phrased in *orientating statements*, vague suggestions about fruitful possibilities for research. For example, Marx wrote that the means of production affects other institutions of society — an orientating statement that includes two unspecified clumps of variables. Rephrasing this as a proposition, we might suggest: the sooner a city has predominantly industrial employment, the sooner it will be the target of revolutionary activity carried on by the proletariat. As Homans noted, a scientist must get on with the business of formulating and testing such propositions. As long as we continue to think in the vague terms of non-operating definitions and orientating statements, we can never be proved wrong. And, therefore, we can never further science by testing our ideas empirically (1967b:7-18).

For discovery, in other words, we must observe interaction, state relationships between variables, and test our statements. Then, we can proceed to *explanation*, "the process of showing how empirical findings following from, can be deduced from general propositions under particular given conditions" (1967b:79). We may discover, for example, that the rise and fall of the tide corresponds to phases of the moon. For explanation, we must show how these empirical findings follow logically from some more general principle, like the law stating that the force of gravity causes the tide to respond to the "pull" of the moon (1967a:30-32).

According to Homans, two compelling considerations require us to use psychological explanations for explaining sociological findings. First, human behavior grows from psychological motivation: men seek rewards, weigh costs, and avoid punishments. Second, since we do not, in Homans' opinion, have powerful explanations about group activities per se, we really should not waste time debating about the relative merits of propositions based on group or individual behavior. It is true we are beginning to collect· data about the behavior of such groups as bureaucracies, classes, and societies. But we have not, thus far, formulated many propositions that both hold for all groups in a category and provide us with new information about them. We know that all societies are stratified, at least to a minimal degree. But does this statement do more than name one of the obvious, defining characteristics of society? In the absence of more informative propositions, Homans argues, we would do well to examine the behavior of individuals within the groups — not because the group as a whole is unimportant, but rather because we can observe the individual more easily and would do better by starting our research where the observation problems are relatively simple (1967b:79-87).

These psychological propositions and explanations are not end products in Homans' sociology. They are elements of an *axiomatic-deductive* system of theory. Starting with given abstract statements, *axioms* about the human proclivity to seek maximum rewards at minimum cost, we can deduce numerous propositions to explain why men in a factory-assembly group curtail their daily output to conform with group norms. When we acquire the technical ability to rephrase these propositions as mathematical equations, we will build even better theories because mathematical models require us to spell out all our terms and assumptions, provide us with a system of logical reasoning, and enable us to make deductions in situations too complicated to handle with words (1964b:955-56).

Homans also insisted that the model of functionalism can never produce deductive theory. First, the basic tenets of this framework cannot be phrased with operational definitions. How does one measure a "functional prerequisite" of society? How do we judge, for example, that a society has died — when the political powers lose a war, even though everyday life goes on as before? Most cultures continue in spite of the vicissitudes suffered by one institution. When a whole society does die, it is often because its members have been exterminated by something like measles or superior firepower. Does that make immunity to measles and a well-stocked armory "functional prerequisites" of society (1962:24-26)? Second, the functional approach ignores originating causes. This framework depicts an institutional structure and its present effects without suggesting why these occur in the first place. Men perform the roles that keep society functioning but why do they develop these roles and why do they agree to perpetuate them? In "Bringing men back in," Homans tells us that the functionalists tend to provide description without explanation. However, when they do venture into causal analysis, they often retreat from a consideration of teleological causality exerted by functional prerequisites to an examination of the efficient causality originating in psychological motivations. They start by describing what is good for society and end by admitting that the average citizen performs his social duty for rather personal reasons (1964a).

In sum, Homans expects all science, including sociology, to describe the empirical world and to explain it in a deductive framework. Moreover, the descriptive statements should specifically relate two (or more) variables about the conditions of a relationship. Such statements should tell us that an increase in X accompanies an increase (or decrease) in Y, not simply that the means of production "affects" society. These statements describing empirical relationships can then be used as the conclusion of a deductive explanation. And, in Homans' opinion, any theoretical system like functionalism that does not include these properties is simply not a proper scientific theory.

RESEARCH — THE PRACTICE

As we noted earlier, Homans seems more concerned with science generally than with any particular substantive area. In "A life of synthesis" he explained, "My great interest and pleasure in life is bringing order out of chaos" (1968:2). Consequently he has spent a great deal of time on synthesis — often pulling together the disparate elements in several research projects conducted by other men. Homans tells us, his three main works exhibit three types of synthesis: 1) the synthesis of data into a concept in *English Villagers of the Thirteenth Century;* 2) the synthesis of concepts into propositions in *The Human Group;* and 3) the synthesis of propositions into a theoretical system in *Social Behavior.* For the first book, he searched parish records and other economic-historical documents from medieval, rural England. For the other two, he compared available research reports about small social groups (the Hawthorne studies. Whyte's *Street Corner Society,* his own study of cash posters, and other similar material) to provide the basis for his generalizations. In one other important study, a full-scale attack on certain aspects of functionalism entitled *Marriage, Authority, and Final Causes,* he reviewed available ethnographic data on 250 societies to make cross-cultural comparisons of marriage patterns and authority structures. In this section, we will consider these works of synthesis to discern how closely they reflect Homans' ideal of social science.

Homans researched the *English Villagers* . . . while he was a graduate student in Harvard's Society of Fellows or, in his words, "just another WASP looking for his ancestors" (1968:2). The study stands as an empirical investigation of history as well as an attempt to label types of medieval economic structures and show their relationships to other institutions. For example, Homans documented the effects of land-holding practices. Among other things, open-field and champion agriculture required different inheritance rules. On the other hand, these basic economic differences often persisted in areas where other institutional structures were quite similar (1941). Clearly, economic structures did not determine other structures in any strict sense. Instead, Homans suggested, the total institutional complex in each type of area really depended on centuries of history, especially previous migration from other cultural areas (1957).

In *The Human Group* (1950) and *Social Behavior* (1961; 1974) Homans developed his explanatory theory. He began inductively in *The Human Group* by reviewing studies of five different groups, developing basic propositions, and adjusting them to reflect the additional data from other groups. In *Social Behavior* he explained these empirical propositions in terms of theoretical axioms (very abstract propositions) about rewards, costs, and exchange.

Consider, for example, the relationship between prestige and norms. In *The Human Group,* Homans described the Bank Wiring Room from the Hawthorne study in some detail and then reflected on these observations to formulate a definition of social norms:

> A norm, then, is an idea in the minds of the members of a group, an idea that can be put in the form of a statement specifying what the members or other men should do, ought to do, are expected to do, under given circumstances. A statement of the kind described is a norm only if any departure of real behavior from the norm is followed by some punishment. (1950:123)

Norms, in turn, delimit the rights and duties of a behavioral position, that is, they define status (1950:11). The evaluation of status, the prestige facet, is rank (1950:179).

In order to use these definitions in propositions, Homans reviewed the literature on his groups and suggested:

1) In the bank Wiring Room, "the higher the rank of a person within a group, the more nearly his ·activities conform to the norms of the group" (1950:141).

2) Among the Tikopia, in factory work groups, in Indian society, people who perform "more important" activities are accorded higher rank (1950:265-68).

So far, so good: two relationships first observed on one group and later found true, with some modification, in several others. But how does Homans explain these propositions?

He begins his explanation with the basic problem of obedience to norms. Men do not obey simply because norms exist: "When we say that some people conform to a norm 'for its own sake,' we mean that they are rewarded by the result that the norm itself, if obeyed, will bring" (1961:116). More abstractly, obedience to norms can be explained in terms of a general proposition (an axiom, really) about human exchange:

If in the past the occurrence of a particular stimulus-situation has been the occasion on which a man's activity has been rewarded, then the more similar the present stimulus-situation is to the past one, the more likely he is to emit the activity, or some similar activity, now. (1961:53; reworded in 1974:22-23)

Or:

The more valuable to a person is the result of his action, the more likely he is to perform the action. (1974:25)

In other words, men tend to perform valuable or rewarding activity. Therefore, since obedience to the norms is valuable, or conversely, disobedience is costly, the men in the Bank Wiring Room will respond to group pressure and keep their output in line with the group's definition of a "proper" day's work.

In Homans' research he measures how rewarding any activity is by observing the amount of the activity. Frequency, in other words, is the operational definition of value: the more valuable the reward, the greater the amount of action a person will spend to get it. But since a surfeit reduces this value, the cost a person will pay for any reward varies over time depending on how much he valued it in the first place and how much of it he has obtained in the past (1961: 39-49; 1974:28-30). In terms of norms, people conform because obedience is rewarding. But over time, they may change their minds about the reward and become less obedient. Therefore, when we research a normative situation, we will find that people do or do not obey the norms because conformity is or is not rewarding.

To escape this circle, we must first distinguish a definition from a proposition. Homans measures the value of an activity solely by its frequency. We could supplement this measure, with questionnaires perhaps, but activity alone is Homans' choice. Given this strategy, we know by definition that a rise in frequency indicates a rise in value: when the amount of red paint on a wall increases, the amount of paint with red pigment increases. Defending this circularity, Homans compares his value "proposition" to Newton's definitional equation on force "f=ma" or "force equals mass times acceleration." Like "value," "force" cannot be observed directly, but only through its operational definition. Therefore Newton uses "mass times acceleration" in equations when he really means "force" (1974:33-37). True, however, when Newton records an increase in "force" as an increase in "mass times acceleration," he does not introduce the relationship as new information. The relationship exists by definition. To acquire new information about relationships, we must list the additional variables that correlate with "force" or with "value."

Two overarching questions arise when we try to specify these added variables needed to explain conformity to norms: Through what process does value affect conformity? and What are the values or valuable commodities in a given group?

Homans' first empirical proposition about norms addresses this first question. After reviewing additional evidence, Homans modified the proposition to state that middle-status group members conform most closely to group standards, while upper and lower-status members enjoy license for different varieties of deviance. Homans explained this phenomenon by comparing alternative actions and alternative rewards combined with a balance between the value of that reward and the probability that a given action would secure it. Low-status people may possibly win approval through conformity, although the chances of winning enough to raise their status appreciably are quite small, so small that they may well choose some alternative behavior for a more certain alternative reward. For them, the tangible enjoyment of sin outweighs the faintly possible reward of a small increment in status. High-status people, in contrast, enjoy more social approval than they need. They can afford to risk disapproval, to flout convention by enjoying some illicit activity or exercising some unusual judgment. Conformity to norms, in other words, is most rewarding for those middle-status people who enjoy and depend on group approval (1961:336-58; 1974:319-39). An interesting explanation. . . .

In developing this explanation, Homans first argued from the data of experimental, small-group studies. Since the groups were artificial collections of people assembled for the experiment, they did not develop natural rankings or statuses. Subjects were simply told that other group members had observed their contributions early in the experiment and rated them within the group. Then "non-conformity" was measured by a person's ability to make honest judgments about facts even when he was being told that the rest of the group had judged differently. Those who were assured of middle status agreed most often with the group judgment regardless of the objective facts. With modifications these results were also obtained in a social-work office, a factory work team, and other natural groups. So we can conclude that Homans has identified a relationship — the valuable commodity of status correlates with the valued commodity of conformity to norms — and developed a plausible explanation of this mechanism.

Nevertheless, the explanation seems too simple, indeed simplistic, because at the abstract level it still traces a circle. Once Homans introduced alternative activity and alternative rewards, he could discuss any behavior and explain that it is, somehow, rewarding. Thus he could explain that when lower-status people (who do, after all, conform most of the time) obey norms, they are seeking status, and when they disobey they are seeking alternative rewards.

If we would formulate a more satisfying line of reasoning, we must answer the second question: What are the values or valuable commodities in a given group? Homans acknowledged the importance of these group values when he linked them to status in his proposition assigning high rank to people who perform "more important" activities. Middle-status people trade conformity (which is valued by the group) for the reward of secure membership. Low-status people opt out of the exchange, neither helping the group nor seeking its rewards. Upper-status people, however, provide unusual services for the group and receive high status in return. In other words, leaders provide followers with "rare and valuable rewards in individual exchanges" (1974:270) and these individual exchanges result in a high-status pay-off for the talented members. One leader, Taylor in the Bank Wiring Room, provided critical guidance for the wiremen: through example and direct help to others he defined the group's daily output — guided the group in its most important task — and therefore enjoyed the highest status in the group (1974:274).

But what is a "rare and valuable service" in society? Although Homans admits "followers in some groups find some of the damnest things valuable" (1974:270), he does not consider delineating this value structure as a task in his sociology. He describes conformity and other social processes but warns us:

> . . . although we try to explain the fundamental processes, we do not, for instance, try to explain how they combine in the behavior of men of varying backgrounds, in varying numbers, and in varying environments to produce the particular structures of particular groups (1967a:31).

However, these group differences that Homans excludes from his studies are at the heart of many sociology problems. The "varying backgrounds . . . numbers . . . and environments" combine to produce very different values and structures existing in different groups and in smaller cliques and subcultures within these groups. So to say, for example, that "the more rewarding an activity is, the more men will perform it," does not begin to explain why some groups reward men for their skill on the battlefield while other groups provide gratification for a deft performance in treaty negotiations or wisdom in religious prophecy. Nor does it explain why the same society might reward different classes of men for different types of activity.

Homans often ignored such group variables because he stressed individual motivations that occur in all situations. Nevertheless he certainly acknowledged the importance of group differences in some of his studies. *English Villagers* . . . depicts two clusters of institutions: open-field and champion agriculture, each with a distinct set of inheritance rules and other economic patterns. Later, in his attack on functionalism titled *Marriage, Authority, and Final Causes* (1955), Homans (and coauthor David M. Schneider) argued that the peculiar structure of a particular group affects individual behavior. In an earlier study of kinship, Claude Lévi-Strauss had hypothesized that matrilineal cross-cousin marriage occurred more often than the patrilineal form, because the former produced a higher degree of organic solidarity in societies. Looking at the problem differently, Homans and Schneider noticed a strong relationship between certain types of authority patterns and certain forms of marriage. They concluded that people favor certain marriage patterns because such alliances are "better" for personal-economic reasons, or "better" for the individual's political security, but hardly because they are "better" for society. In other words, they attacked the ideas of teleological causality present in some forms of functionalist thinking and substituted personal motivations as an explanation for individual behavior (1962:22-35).

However, Homans does support the functionalist tenet that group structure encourages varieties of individual behavior. But instead of trying to determine what forms of behavior would be profitable given a specific structure, he examines individual exchanges to determine what activity people within the structure judge to be rewarding. So, instead of reporting, as Merton did, that the stress on priority in scientific discovery encourages plagiarism, Homans might observe a plagiarist and then look for the rewards that could motivate this deviance. Merton's approach enables us to predict that some unknown percentage of scientists will plagiarize and that this unfortunate practice will increase as the value placed on scientific priority increases. Homans can tell us that plagiarism exists and therefore, for some people, its rewards must outweigh its costs.

Of course, Homans did not analyze problems like the relationship between a specific cultural value and institutional patterns of interaction. However, he hopes that eventually such problems can be reduced to the terms of elementary social behavior. Consider, for example, how a national leader (a king like Henry II of England) might effect a major judicial reform. Homans suggests that Henry II must have borrowed heavily from his "social capital" when he deployed his own circuit judges to outlying baronial courts. Why else would the nobles allow the king to assume their power? Henry must have traded his social capital with individual nobles in exchange for conformity to his newly established norms (1974:365-66). This may well be true. However, whatever the personal exchange Henry may have effected between himself and each individual noble, he drew his basic capital from one source: he had won the war and he clearly had the ability to impose his peace on the country. In short, Henry could make non-conformity prohibitively expensive. If we wish to explore why each individual noble decided to obey him, we could resurrect local chronicles, court orders, and other records to examine the exchange between Leicester and Henry. However, if we wish to explore the perquisites of power or the prerequisites of judicial reform, we might find it more efficient to count how often and under what circumstances a man like Henry gets his way.

In conclusion, Homans uses research to demonstrate his ideas of social science. He has defined basic units of social behavior and linked them together in psychological propositions and axioms about balance in interaction exchanges. As they stand, however, his propositions can apply to a wide variety of human exchange systems. Generally his axioms are so abstractly worded that they will always appear true. Specifying the conditions under which they apply is the next step for those who would elaborate from the outlines of Homans' theory.   CONCLUSION

In his theory Homans attempts to order the chaos of sociological explanation by constructing deductive explanatory systems of psychological axioms defining universal motivations and derived propositions describing the operation of these motives in group life. Group interaction, he reasoned, exhibits psychological-economic elements — people seek rewarding experience and pay for it with activity. This is the basis for rewards and costs in an economic exchange. His axioms state, in a very abstract way, the relationships between rewards and activity. The propositions state that a reward like status elicits an activity like conformity or deviance.

In his explanations, Homans describes interaction processes within an undefined group. Like a psychologist he accepts group peculiarities as given. In effect he argues that just as an insecure man displays his symptoms on the job, with his friends, and in his home, so the low-status person enjoys the license to sin whether he is a member of the Tikopia tribe, the factory wiremen's crew, or the unemployment-office bureaucracy. On the other hand, Homans also accepts psychological and cultural background as given. Many sociologists examine the person-group interaction that occurs regardless of the background of the person. For example, Simmel has suggested how the structure of a triad limits the possibilities for interaction among three allied nations as effectively as it limits possible interaction among three thieves. Another sociologist, Cooley, has outlined universal aspects of child development that occur in the small tribe and the urban metropolis. Homans, however, examines two key variables — frequency and value — abstracted from both psychological-cultural background and group structure.

Using this double abstraction Homans has eliminated most elements of social life and therefore must define his variables in terms of each other. The variable of value is measured by the variable frequency: the more frequent an activity, the more valuable its elicited reward. Naturally, if the frequency with which people seek a reward measures the value of the reward, we will find that frequency and value correlate highly. If the degree of conformity to group norms measures the degree of middle-class desire for acceptance, we can expect to find middle-status people obeying the party line more consistently than upper-status leaders (who have more acceptance than they need) or lower-status dropouts (who have no hope of being accepted). Thus, although Homans developed empirical propositions in *The Human Group* that stand as adequate statements about the relationships between two concrete variables, his explanations in *Social Behavior* turn these propositions into a set of definitions. If our measures do not reveal the predicted results, then by definition we have selected the wrong measures.

Perhaps the most fruitful way to utilize Homans' ideas is to make his abstractions more concrete by bringing the group back in — either by defining the reward-value structure of a given group and then using his explanation to predict when, where, and how often men will pay for particular rewards with specified activity or by examining interaction exchanges to describe how a group develops a reward structure in the first place. Either strategy would complicate Homans' theory by introducing causal sequences, chains of causality to supplement the more simple two-variable relationships characteristic in axiomatic theory. In the next chapter we will consider this possibility by reviewing the work of Hubert M. Blalock.

Bibliography

Curtis, Charles P., and Homans, George C.

1934 *An Introduction to Pareto.* New York: H. Fertig (1970).

Homans, George Caspar

1941 *English Villagers of the Thirteenth Century.* New York: Russell and Russell (1960).

1950 *The Human Group.* New York: Harcourt, Brace and World.

Homans, George Caspar, and Schneider, David M.

1955 *Marriage, Authority, and Final Causes.* Glencoe, Ill.: Free Press. Also Pp. 202-56 in *Sentiments and Activities.* New York: Free Press, 1962. Homans, George Caspar

1956 "Giving a dog a bad name." Pp. 113-19 in *Sentiments.* . . .

1957 "The Frisians in East Anglia." Pp. 158-82 in *Sentiments.* . . .

1961 *Social Behavior: Its Elementary Forms.* New York: Harcourt, Brace and World.

1962 "Autobiographical introduction." Pp. 1-49 in *Sentiments.* . . .

1964a "Bringing men back in." *American Sociological Review* 29 (December): 809-18.

1964b "Contemporary theory in sociology." Pp. 951-77 in Robert E. L. Faris (ed.), *Handbook of Modern Sociology.* Chicago: Rand McNally and Co.

1967a "Fundamental social processes." Pp. 30-78 in Neil J. Smelser (ed.), *Sociology: An Introduction.* New York: John Wiley and Sons.

1967b *The Nature of Social Science.* New York: Harcourt, Brace and World.

1968 "A life of synthesis." *American Behavioral Scientist* 12 (September-October): 2-8.

1974 *Social Behavior: Its Elementary Forms.* Rev. ed. New York: Harcourt Brace Jovanich.

Secondary sources

Abramsson, Bengt

1970 "Homans on exchange: hedonism revived." *American Journal of Sociology* 76 (September): 273-85.

Buckley, Walter

1967 *Sociology and Modern Systems Theory.* Englewood Cliffs, N.J.: Prentice-Hall.

Deutsch, Morton

1964 "Homans in the Skinner Box." *Sociological Inquiry.* 34 (Spring): 156-65.

Loomis, Charles P., and Loomis Zona K.

1965 "George C. Homans — interaction theorist." Pp. 171-245 in *Modern Social Theories.* New York: D. Van Nostrand.

Maris, Ronald

1970 "The logical adequacy of Homans' social theory." *American Sociological Review* 35 (August): 1069-81.

Hubert M. Blalock, Jr.

by Elizabeth A. Freidheim
and Daryl Chubin

More than the other men we have considered here, Hubert Blalock (1926-   ) has concerned himself with the methodology of theory testing. He seems as interested in how he obtains a result as he is in the result itself; as concerned with constructing and testing theoretical models as with making discoveries in some particular substantive field. Without adequate research methodology, he argues, sociologists can never have any real faith in the validity of their substantive discoveries. Therefore, Blalock has chosen to specialize in the construction of research designs, specifically, mathematical-causal models.

In these models, Blalock posits a causal framework and considers the complex problems of tracing causality in situations that preclude experimentation. We may wonder about the causes of lynching, for example, but who would dare provoke a series of lynchings just to test our ideas? Since we must observe such events as they occur in nature, often with hundreds of variables, we must also assume the burdens of hypothesizing about a few major causal variables and assessing their relative importance within a natural situation. It is the technical problems of analyzing complex social situations, of describing them in theoretical, operational, and mathematical language, that interests Blalock. For solving these problems, he urges us to articulate our theoretical ideas, single out a limited number of crucial variables, predict their operation in the empirical world, observe empirical reality, and reformulate our ideas to reflect these observations. This approach differs sharply from the deductive logic advocated by Homans. Instead of conceptualizing from induction to a deductive schema, Blalock urges us to make a direct tie between the induction and theory testing. According to Blalock, our immediate problem is not the need to construct an encompassing explanatory system, but rather the need to develop a research technique that enables us to judge whether empirical reality is being explained by limited theories.

We must proceed cautiously in our examination of Blalock's ideas, however; the man is still young, productive, and capable of choosing a new emphasis for his work. Even so, we should consider his contributions to date and his impact on the discipline — helping make empirical research more precise.

INTELLECTUAL BACKGROUND

Blalock's undergraduate training in mathematics and physics probably stimulated his interests in such technical concerns as measurement error, operational definitions, linear models, equations of change over time, and path analysis. After his conversion to social science, Blalock discovered that econometricians had already been grappling with these problems in their field. Almost single handedly Blalock introduced econometric causal-modeling techniques to sociology. Adapting the tools to the needs of his discipline, he has written extensively on those technical details all too frequently ignored by researchers who are so anxious to get on with the "real" work of sociology that they neglect to concern themselves with the adequacy of their evidence. In sum, Blalock came to sociology with a special interest in the problems that confront sociologists who would examine the validity of their insights by testing their theories with the tools of mathematics.

DEFINITION OF SOCIOLOGY

Blalock has not defined sociology: rather he has defined the conduct of sociological research. In his writing he uses examples (power in minority-group relations, Homans's interaction propositions, rationality in bureaucracy) that most sociologists would recognize as falling within the compass of their discipline. But he usually concentrates on the technical aspects of empirical work, using substantive concerns as a working ground for research techniques.

Specifically, he appears to be interested in the peculiar difficulties that accompany *nonexperimental* research work in complex systems. In his *Causal Inferences in Nonexperimental Research* (1961), he outlined the technical problems inherent in any quantitative causal study: problems of sampling, manipulation of variables, randomization and identification of measurement error, estimation of parameters, and the ordering of variables according to causal priorities. Then he noted that typical social science data — extracted from complex situations that develop over time — present additional challenges. In social science we cannot create an experimental vacuum to uncover a pure variable like velocity or weight without the effects of unmeasured friction, humidity, and pressure. We cannot separate racial tensions and lynching from economic depression, hot weather, local custom, family history, and a thousand other variables with incalculable effects on the activities of one evening. So Blalock stressed the need to "explore the problem of making causal inferences on the basis of data from nonexperimental studies," to develop research models that explore the causality of complex social interaction in its natural setting (1961:3-4).

SUBJECT FOCUS

Blalock's causal models affect his ideas about the appropriate subject matter for sociology. His research approach requires him to do several things: state assumptions explicitly, link all theoretical ideas precisely, and avoid or compensate for technical pitfalls that can invalidate his findings or inferences. To achieve these goals, Blalock (and others of his persuasion among social scientists) emphasize two practices: the careful definition of the variables with their relationships and the actual measurement of these defined elements. As Blalock noted, our studies must be designed to handle measurement error (1970a:111); the problem lies not only in what we study but in how well we study it.

For example, research exploring racial tension as a cause of lynching could define "tension" as a product of cultural values or a correlate of economic competition. Each of these definitions requires its own data. Perhaps, literature or newspaper editorials could indicate the interracial tension that forms part of a cultural milieu. On the other hand, ethnocentric-cultural values may simply name the scapegoat when citizens are really agitated for other reasons like unemployment or crop failure. Blalock proposes methods for effectively probing whatever it is we really want to study, methods that will isolate the effects of cultural-racial tension from the effects of economic hardship.

In other words, Blalock concentrates on the methodological problems of defining and measuring the elements in a theory, rather than the substantive problems of acquiring new knowledge. Although he has no quarrel with those who explore various subject areas in sociology, he believes that we should consider fewer subjects more thoroughly, conduct the replication studies essential to a maturing science, design research to measure and compare the same variables in several situations:

> There is now a "sociology of X" for just about every social phenomenon X that exists, even a "sociology of pets"! . . . It seems to me that such diversification is one reason why there has not been sufficient attention given to the careful measurement and conceptualization of variables and to the need for replication studies of the kind that are commonly found in the physical sciences. (1970b:114-15)

In the research section we will review an example of how Blalock has used the subject matter and substantive ideas of other sociologists to illustrate the research problems that should be carefully considered in empirical work.

SCIENCE — THE PLAN

Testing causal theories is Blalock's research goal: he develops models that can be verified — or more likely falsified — by observation in the empirical world. Since we tend to think in terms of causality (economic production affects family life; Calvinism affects capitalism), our theoretical models state *causal relationships*. But we never observe Calvinism constructing an economic system. Instead we see empirical relationships or *covariances*. We observe that the farming economy in rural Ireland encourages landless younger sons to emigrate from their rural villages and seek city jobs, or that the incidence of Calvinism was high among seventeenth-century entrepreneurs. Blalock has developed a system for using causal theory to predict these empirical covariances before they are verified by observation. If predictions hold in our later investigations of the empirical world, we can be somewhat more confident of our causal models. If the predictions prove false, we must reject or modify our models (or indirectly support the plausibility of alternate ones). Perhaps the most important point is this: to design research that will test our ideas in the empirical world, we must define a finite set of variables, assert how these interrelate causally and make a series of predictions — in short, we must spell out the implications of each item in our theory. As Blalock has noted, "My basic message is 'be explicit' . . . " (1971b).

Blalock has refined his theoretical system building to deal with the mathematical implications of problems like continuous time change, interaction effects between variables, causal feedback, one-way *vs.* reciprocal causation, and correlation of errors and independent variables. However, we will not consider these sophisticated techniques here. Rather we will concentrate on four basic steps he has suggested for quantitative causal research: 1) the construction of causal statements based on some theoretical ideas; 2) the translation of theoretical variables into research operations; 3) the measurement of variables at the interval (or at least ordinal) level; and 4) the use of mathematical operations to test predictions.

In step one, a scientist must define explanatory causal models that outline the relationships among a few crucial variables, while ignoring the numerous contributing causal forces in a complex situation. He must "select models that are at the same time simple enough to permit him to think with the aid of the model but also sufficiently realistic that the simplifications required do not lead to predictions that are highly inaccurate." His basic problem in developing an understandable explanation is determining "how much to over-simplify reality" (1961:8). For example, when we discuss how gravitation causes bodies to fall, we are actually describing bodies that fall in a vacuum at sea level. In discussions about gravity, we normally eliminate two important variables (resistance and atmospheric pressure) and assume, theoretically, that they have no effect in the gravitation model. Fortunately for our empirical verifications, the effects of these intervening variables, though real, are small enough to permit reasonably accurate predictions based on calculations of gravity alone. Using a similar strategy, we can build a model of delinquency to argue that socialization, peer influence, and neighborhood "cause" delinquency — ignoring the effects of economic opportunity, psychological balance and other variables. In sum, the causal model is a theoretical statement about relationships among a limited number of variables operating in a type of situation.

Blalock often sketches a diagram that depicts the causal relationships (1960:337-43; 1961:61-94; 1969:27-47), and thereby provides a visual aid for translating verbal theory into symbolic language. Returning to the juvenile-delinquency example, we find three hypothetical causes of delinquency (Y): family socialization (X_1), peer influence (X_2), and neighborhood (X_3). Graphically, the theoretical model (without error terms) would look like this:

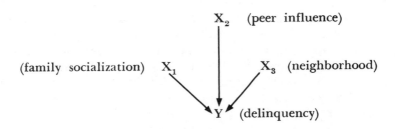

We are hypothesizing that three factors (along with numerous other less important variables) cause delinquency, but these causes have no effect on each other. Although we usually intend more sophisticated reasoning, our verbal models are often so loosely stated that we do not say what we "really" mean. With a diagram that forces us to outline our reasoning visually we are also encouraged to delineate our ideas more carefully. We may reason that socialization (X_1) and neighborhood (X_3) both operate on a child's willingness to accept peer influence (X_2), which in turn causes delinquency. In diagram form:

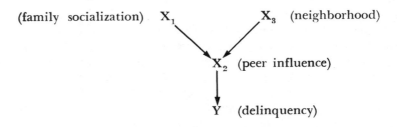

After deciding on such a hypothetical causal sequence, we should proceed to step two of the causal-model process and connect the theoretical ideas with empirical operations. An explicit consideration of this step is necessary because we think of "causes" between theoretical variables, but observe correlations between empirical events. Both our explanations and our theoretical variables almost inevitably suffer a change between the world of theory and the world of research. So, once again Blalock advocates that we make explicit statements linking theoretical ideas to corresponding operations: that we develop two sets of theories, a main theory containing abstract concepts and an auxiliary theory with research operations (1968a; 1969:151-54). We do not observe delinquency. Instead, we survey police intake records, court findings, and other evidence that the official world has adjudged someone delinquent. Police records do not count all boys who have committed delinquent acts, only those who are officially booked. A careful consideration of this problem should inform any research project. When we measure the relationship between peer influence and police statistics, we should be aware that we are only approximating our theoretical notion of delinquency — unless, of course, we define delinquency only in terms of those who get caught!

In his third causal-modeling step, Blalock raises an important statistical question. What levels of measurement do we need for testing causal models? Since Blalock tests his theories by rephrasing the propositions in regression equations and then observing if the equations describe empirical reality, he assumes interval measurement. He measures data so that it can be represented in a (more or less) precise position on some sort of scale, rather than simply placed in discrete categories or ranked in order. For example, he would prefer to measure the precise amount of delinquency exhibited in an area (ten percent of all boys are delinquent) than to simply label the area as "delinquent" (has "many delinquents") or to state that one area has "more delinquency" than another. While recognizing the usefulness of discrete-attribute data, he chooses to work with interval measures (or at least very discriminating ordinal ones) for two main reasons: he can apply more rigorous statistical tests to such continuous data and he can use interval data in the traditional types of asymmetric causal models (1961:32-35; 1974). To appreciate Blalock's fourth step, we should reconsider the diagram:

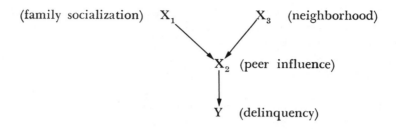

While forcing us to define the relationships between our variables in detail, the diagram also shows us whether or not we have a testable model (1961:61-126; 1969:48-75). If we translate these relationships into regression equations and if the model reflects empirical reality, then the partial correlation and regression coefficients linking socialization (X_1) directly to delinquency (Y) and linking neighborhood (X_3) directly to delinquency (Y) should equal zero; except of course, for the effects of sampling error.

Translation: if socialization and neighborhood are important only because they operate through peer influence, if peer influence is the critical variable deflecting the other two, then boys with certain kinds of peer influence will tend to be either delinquents or nondelinquents regardless of socialization and neighborhood. If this is true, then there is no direct link between socialization and delinquency or between neighborhood and delinquency. In regression false and others statements we can predict:

$$r_{yx_1x_2}=0; \; r_{yx_3x_2}=0; b_{yx_1x_2}=0; \; b_{yx_3x_2}=0.$$

Here we have a model with predictions that can be tested in the empirical world. If the predictions prove false, we can alter the model by introducing new variables to account for the "error," by rearranging the sequence or causal paths of the variables, by removing some variables, or by making other adjustments until we construct one that produces some relatively accurate predictions. But we can never prove that empirical-mathematical correlations equal theoretical causes. We can only show that some models are obviously false and others somewhat plausible. Even these plausible models will have unexplained residual and "error" variations, so it is not likely that our partials and regression coefficients will ever really equal zero.

Blalock formulates more sophisticated causal theories than our four-variable model and hopes ultimately to include large numbers of interrelated factors in his designs. This goal depends on more precise and reliable data — perhaps from data banks assembled by many sociologists using the same operations to measure the same variables in many different settings. Such reliable data would enable a few sociologists (with finite research budgets) to test complex theories instead of confining themselves to theories with information about a few variables collected in one research project (1973).

RESEARCH — THE PRACTICE

As we have noted, Blalock's focus is methodological, given the conditions of a substantive problem. He defines the two key methodology problems in sociology as poor data and poor conceptualization (1971b). In his work, he dwells on the latter concern — building theoretical models and translating them into mathematical equations, a process that often involves "formalizing" previously formulated theories. Blalock has also contributed to substantive knowledge. He has, for example, used census figures to analyze discrimination against blacks (1956), distributed questionnaires (among University of Michigan students) to inquire about status consciousness (1959), and reviewed previous findings about minority-group relations to codify ninety-seven strategic, testable propositions (1967b). But more typically, he builds causal models and devises ways to solve the measurement problems occurring when we attempt to validate them in empirical research.

Here we will review examples of his work that illustrate three stages in causal modeling: first, an article on defining relationships in a complex theory; then, a discussion about formulating adequate operational definitions; finally, a consideration of measurement levels as they affect theory testing. There is, however, no fourth article demonstrating these steps and bringing them to completion in an original research project. That fourth step must be taken by others; Blalock himself concentrates on the first three.

In his article on "Status inconsistency, social mobility, status integration and structural effects" (1967a), Blalock presented current theories describing the effects of social status and mobility on prejudice. Here he explicitly considered the difficulties of work with certain types of complex theories, ones in which the dependent variable is caused by interaction between two or more independent variables. Available research suggests that prejudice varies with occupational status, often with blue-collar workers and their children exhibiting more prejudice than higher-status workers and their families. Further, the occupationally mobile children may become more prejudiced as they join blue-collar ranks or less prejudiced as they enter white-collar work. Finally, the difference between the old and the new status, multiplied by some magnitude of change effect, may produce a level of prejudice in addition to the level produced by present status plus childhood status. Using Blalock's diagram format, we can suggest:

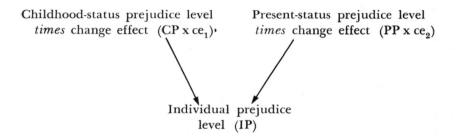

Childhood-status prejudice level *times* change effect $(CP \times ce_1)$,

Present-status prejudice level *times* change effect $(PP \times ce_2)$

Individual prejudice level (IP)

The research problem is this: How can we separate — empirically — the effects of childhood socialization in a previous status, life style in the present status, and change between statuses — particularly if the change sometimes produces more prejudice and sometimes less depending on its direction? We can measure old status, present status, and the prejudice level associated with each. We can also verify whether downwardly workers display more prejudice than stable ones and upwardly mobile workers display less. However, isolating the degree of "change effect" is another matter, particularly if we suspect there is *also* a change in attitude associated with maturation. Often in research situations there is no way to measure such a factor independently of other variables. In these instances we are left with the choice of reconceptualizing the theory into one we can test or, at least, recognizing the untestable provisions in very complex theories.

In his second model-building stage, Blalock specifies how we should travel that distance between the theoretical world and the empirical one. Here we will consider one aspect of this process, the problem of finding measurement error introduced by our operational definitions. Of course, all measures suffer the effects of random error caused by a series of undetermined — and we hope unrelated — minor variables. We assume that the overall effects of random error cancel each other out. Non-random error, however, presents quite a different problem. Non-random, systematic bias distorts our measures in one direction, and renders them invalid. How can we identify and reduce these non-random measurement distortions? In "Estimating measurement error using multiple indicators and several points in time," Blalock combined the ideas of other methodologists to suggest a two-pronged attack on the problem, the use of multiple indicators (two or more measures for each variable) and data collection at two or more points in time (1970a).

Assuming we have operationalized our concepts at the interval level. Blalock has developed equations for estimating if our actual measures approximated the values we were trying to tap. I will not outline the technical details here but concentrate, instead, on the reasoning behind these procedures. For example, if we want to measure childhood prejudice levels (X), we might distribute an attitudinal questionnaire to school children with enough questions so that two or more sets can be considered separately. With two separate operational definitions of childhood prejudice $(x_1$ and $x_2)$, we can estimate if systematic error has been introduced by leading questions, interviewer effect, and a number of other forces we may not have anticipated. Then, if we use the same questionnaire at a later time with the same children, we can discover if these measures are stable over time or subject to some non-random bias introduced by changes in the environment: Although these operational definitions are just part of a larger project, they too can be conceptualized in a causal model: the theoretical variable (along with random error) "causes" the behavior measured by the operational definition. Using Blalock's causal diagram, we can visualize this relationship between concept, operational definition, and random error:

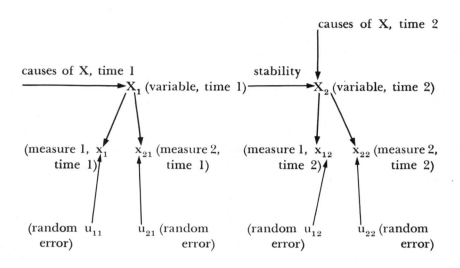

If this diagram depicts the true relationships between the concept, measurements, and *all* error, then we should be able to solve certain equations describing the causal paths between known (measured) and unknown elements. If the equations Blalock suggests cannot be solved satisfactorily, then we must search for the systematic error — an additional causal force probably signified by additional arrows pointing to one of the measures during both time periods or to both measures during one time period — that invalidates our research. In other words, the diagram helps us to conceptualize the problem of measurement error.

In the two articles we have just considered, Blalock discussed important research problems; in the first theoretical conceptualization, in the second valid measurement of concepts. Both discussions presuppose data will be collected to yield interval level scales. However, for various reasons we do not always analyze interval data. When we compare forms of "democracy" in one hundred countries, we may not have the time, money, and energy to construct and apply a sophisticated operational definition to each of these cases, even if we could argue, theoretically speaking, that one country may be "twice" as democratic as another. In such projects we may have to settle for "Australia is more democratic than Zanzibar" without counting the units of distance between them. Alternately we may conceptualize democracy as a set of discrete types of government. All may share certain "democratic" characteristics, but differ so much in other ways that they could not possibly be conceived as cases on a continuum even if some are "more democratic" than others. In both situations, we must conduct analysis with nominal (discrete) or ordinal (ranked) data. How can we apply Blalock's testing procedures to such information? Sometimes we cannot. If, according to our theory, types of democracy really are quite distinct from each other, then we should not hope to use statistical tests requiring interval-level data. However, if our theory presupposes there really is a continuum of democratic forms, even though we have not managed to measure it with our operational definition, then we may be justified in pretending our ordered scales are actually crude interval ones. In "Beyond ordinal measurement: weak tests of stronger theories" (1974), Blalock suggests when and how we can apply interval procedures to such ordinal data. However, this is a make-do expedient. The third step in model building should not consist of devising ways to compensate for inadequate data. If we would use Blalock's procedures, we should collect interval-level data whenever possible. In other words, we should build a theoretical model, consider the problems of measurement error, and then use operational definitions that will yield the data appropriate for the technical problems we need to solve.

In sum, Blalock generally uses data to illustrate some point about theory testing. With the exception of his early work — written before he developed his causal models for theory testing — he has not designed and executed his own empirical projects. He concentrates on showing us the types of information we must collect and how to use the data once we have gathered it. And, indeed, others are beginning to complete his causal-modeling process by applying his techniques in research projects, for example, Peter M. Blau and Otis Dudley Duncan in *The American Occupational Structure*. A recent book edited by Blalock, *Causal Models in the Social Sciences* (1971a), also reveals some of his impact on social science: articles in the book report on research testing theoretical ideas with real populations, using Blalock's designs.

CONCLUSION

Blalock, like Comte, has pioneered social research and suggested new methods for the study of society. Unlike Comte, however, Blalock has benefited from more than a century of success and failure in social science research. He has also benefited from his own rigorous training in mathematics and physical science. So rather than vaguely recommending a "positive" approach, he presents detailed instructions on how to build causal models, limit measurement error, and handle other methodological problems. These instructions often presuppose technical expertise, including knowledge of statistics (the assumptions as well as the formulas) and ability to use the computer. But Blalock's potential contribution extends well beyond the circle of math-model enthusiasts. His basic message — define all important variables, state the hypothesized relationships between them explicitly, examine the assumptions underlying these hypotheses — should guide all researchers to clarify their thinking.

Whether we will ever build the elegant mathematical theories advocated by Blalock is another issue. Perhaps there is no set of formulas that describe empirical reality. Perhaps we will never be able to gather the relevant information needed to test sophisticated, mathematically phrased hypotheses. Since Blalock concentrates on developing the mathematical statements and pointing out the areas that others must research, he himself has not provided examples of research using his ideas on concrete empirical problems. In effect, he has suggested the form that our theories could take. Now we must determine how closely this form of theory reflects the substance of social life.

Even if causal modeling proves to be a sociological fad or the enduring interest of an esoteric cult, Blalock's example will still hold one more value for researchers. He presents a technical solution to a perennial problem in sociology, the problem of validity. He does not explicitly examine the problems of researching a subjective, human topic with objective observations; clearly he prefers objective measures. He works to refine these measures, fitting them as closely to the "real" topic as possible. Like Lundberg, he stresses reliability and replication studies. However, Blalock does not assume that reliability will insure validity. Rather, he places measurement within the context of causal reasoning: if reasoning is valid and measures are both valid and reliable, then a causal model will predict empirical outcomes. In other words, Blalock does not search for the truth about an object, but for the truth about a relationship. If we discover, as Lundberg did, that our "majority" group does not behave like a homogeneous group, then we must reexamine both our operational definition of "majority" and our reasoning about dominant-subordinant relationships among ethnic groups. As Blalock argues, it is much easier to locate such a problem in a well-articulated set of causal hypotheses than to find "something wrong" in a muddled conception of how "lots of factors" influence "many others." Blalock's work provides a procedure for finding errors in our theory, for assessing the validity of our research.

In one sense Blalock can be evaluated as a technical counterpart to theorists like Merton and Homans. Using different approaches, both developed a set of strategic middle-range propositions. Blalock fits these kinds of propositions into his causal theories. Causes of delinquency, changes in prejudice, a variety of substantive propositions form the hypothetical relationships he would like to test with his models. So the ultimate criteria for assessing Blalock's work is whether he can provide the tools for valid tests of middle-range theories.

Bibliography

Blalock, Hubert M., Jr.

1956 "Economic discrimination and Negro increase." *American Sociological Review* 21 (October) : 584-88.

1959 "Status consciousness: a dimensional analysis." *Social Forces* 37 (March) : 243-48.

1960 *Social Statistics.* New York: McGraw-Hill.

1961 *Causal Inferences in Nonexperimental Research.* Chapel Hill, N.C.: University of North Carolina Press.

1967a "Status inconsistency, social mobility, status integration and structural effects." *American Sociological Review* 32 (October) : 790-801.

1967b *Toward a Theory of Minority-Group Relations.* New York: John Wiley and Sons.

1968a "The measurement problem: a gap between the language of theory and research." Pp. 5-27 in Hubert M. Blalock and Ann B. Blalock (eds.) , *Methodology in Social Research.* New York: McGraw-Hill.

1968b "Theory building and causal inferences." Pp. 155-98 in *Methodology.* . . .

1969 *Theory Construction: From Verbal to Mathematical Formulations.* Englewood Cliffs, N.J.: Prentice-Hall.

1970a "Estimating measurement error using multiple indicators and several points in time." *American Sociological Review* 35 (February) : 101-11.

1970b *An Introduction to Social Research.* Englewood Cliffs, N.J.: Prentice-Hall.

Blalock, Hubert M., Jd., (ed.)

1971a *Causal Models in the Social Sciences.* Chicago: Aldine-Atherton.

Blalock, Hubert M., Jr.

1971b "Lectures on social-science causal models." Chicago: Loyola University Methodology Institute, July-August.

1972 *Social Statistics.* 2d ed. New York: McGraw-Hill. (Material on pp. 61-94 in the 1st ed. is on pp. 442-50 in this edition.)

1973 "Open forum: thoughts on the development of sociology." *ASA Footnotes* 1 (March) : 2.

1974 "Beyond ordinal measurement: weak tests of stronger theories." Pp. 424-55 in Blalock (ed.) , *Measurement in the Social Sciences: Theories and Strategies.* Chicago: Aldine.

Some Contemporary Viewpoints

As we know, sociology was born of the nineteenth-century marriage between scientific planning and social progress. Sociologists recognized the evils of their day and many of them hoped, either by direct intervention or by discrete non-interference, to effect social improvement. Even the most pessimistic expected sociology to further the understanding of societal stability, and of mechanisms that encouraged social order and regularity. It is understandable that, in an age of failing utopian rationalism, these reform-minded thinkers stressed a positivistic approach, a concern for the empirically observable realities of social life. Indeed, reading this book, one may infer that sociology has been progressing — with occasional regression — toward a clear-viewed analysis of concrete, objective reality. One may also infer that the major task of sociology is to examine the basic institutional patterns of society — the structural forms of political power, the present functions of stratification, and of course, the unending struggles with anti-institutional deviance — often depicted as facets of a functional system.

These inferences would not be entirely correct. Although their major methodological emphasis has been on the natural-science "outsider's" approach, sociologists have not forgotten the subjective insight that can distinguish the study of social patterns from the study of molecular interaction. And, although sociology's dominant emphasis has been on mechanisms of stability — often reified (or deified) in the systems analogy — sociologists have not ignored social change and its frequent companion, social conflict.

Indeed, the breakdown of the functional-systems model may be signaling a new direction for sociology. As sociology progressed in the nineteenth and early twentieth centuries, its practitioners turned to the natural sciences for a conceptual framework. Many come to describe social life as a natural system with interrelated parts. From

287

the beginning, however, there have been major attacks on this phys-
ical-biological analogy from several sources including: sociologists
who emphasize conflict, disharmony, and other system-changing
mechanisms; sociologists who focus on the technical frontiers of
social research; and sociologists who analyze the "system" as man's
own creation, a creation he may choose to reshape or redirect. For
the first group, the biological analogy denies the reality of data —
civil war, revolution, and other upheavals are not accounted for by
the model of an orderly system-in-equilibrium. For many methodological technicians, the biological analogy is irrelevant. When Blalock
discusses how to refine data gathering and analysis in order to reduce measurement error, he need not account for distant functions
of the system. Further, his causal models are an explicit alternative
to functional analysis — a search for the origins of an activity, not
its manifest and latent functions. The subjective-interpretive sociologists have undermined the functional-systems analogy by depicting
man as the source of social life. Exploring subjective motivation,
Weber detailed how different mental states can revolutionize a system. Rationalization, for example, transformed the magical-garden
world into a universe controlled by intelligible laws. Moreover, as
many intrepretive sociologists have noted, man personally creates his
complex of subjective meetings. Whatever the reasons, whatever the
lures or pressures in the surrounding social world, each of us plays
our roles with a personalized script. Thus, the system is not only
our own creation, but a fragile and precarious one. Indeed, some
interpretive sociologists have recently begun to further examine the
fragile-subjective nature of this creation by exploring the possibility
that the social system may not even exist beyond our mental pictures
of it.

    In the remaining sections of this concluding chapter, we will briefly
consider some contemporary aspects of these contrasting viewpoints
that inform present-day sociology: certain technical advances in conceptualization and theory building made by modern "positivists,"
the epistemological questions raised by ethnomethodologists and other
"subjective" sociologists, and the renewed emphasis on the disorderly
side of social order that is stressed by both theoretical camps. The
section on positivism will first review the nature of this orientation
and the interests of positivistic sociologists studied so far; then it
will introduce two current technical interests, typology construction

and the use of linear graphs. The section on subjective interpretations will begin by reviewing the main concern of sociologists who use this approach, that is, the focus on either social interaction or cultural meanings. Then it will outline the modern extensions of these concerns, symbolic interaction and phenomenology. The final section will discuss the radical critique of contemporary society and contemporary sociology.

POSITIVE SOCIOLOGY: THE SEARCH FOR OBJECTIVE REALITY

When Auguste Comte defined sociology as a "positive" science, he meant that sociologists should proceed with a "steady subordination of imagination to observation." He thus attacked the negative-critical commentary of those who "knew" what society ought to be and who judged the world against their preconceived model. We should not, Comte cautioned, try to shape society to our moral expectations, but rather discover what society is and thereby learn what natural route leads to moral good. Sometimes positivism has been interpreted as a call for pure induction, a blessing on atheoretical research. This interpretation is incorrect. Comte himself had very definite ideas about causation, laws, and types as these exist in society. More often, positivism has been an "outsider's" approach to social reality, a stress on the observable empirical realities. Clearly, this approach eliminates the interpretive sociologies as practiced by Weber, Cooley, and others who designated the meaning of social behavior as its defining characteristic. However, all of the sociologists who are not explicitly interpretive could be included in the positivistic group.

This large group includes most of the men we have studied so far. Spencer, of course, claimed to be totally inductive. Few scientists have taken sociological "objectivity" quite so far as he did. Nevertheless most sociologists have shared certain positivistic assumptions and practices, especially the stress on observable behavior and the search for an external mechanism that either accounts for some degree of determinism or "causality" in this behavior or, at least, sets limits on its patterns. Some sociologists, focusing on the nature of social life, worked to identify its determining mechanisms. Durkheim, for example, examined how structures maintain society by providing the pressure that enforces normative rules. Parsons, and later Merton, extended this vision to include the values that shape both structures and norms. Park and Sumner considered the external environment, focusing on the background of man's struggle for existence. Marx analyzed this struggle in terms of wealth and the power that comes from wealth. In very different ways, Tarde and Pareto explained how psychological predispositions affect social activity. Simmel outlined the types of social situations as they limited the possibilities for action. Other sociologists have focused on the nature of social science. Homans advocated reductionism, reducing the group to its component individual parts, as a tenet of his explanatory strategy. Lundberg questioned the epistemological base of sociology. Symbols are what we study, he said, not reality. And Blalock developed statistical techniques for sorting out the important variables in complex, "non-experimental" social situations.

All of these sociologists worked within the positive tradition by trying to detail how one or more aspects of the external social world affect or relate to others. It is technical considerations, however, that form the pioneering aspects of positive or objective sociology today. Scientists like Blalock are arguing for better sociology through better research techniques. As many researchers continue to explore human ecology, to trace the effects of normative structures, to advance the substantive inquiries that have long interested sociologists, the technical pioneers are searching for new apparatus to describe the shape of social life or to realign the shape of social theory. Their models are more sophisticated than those of early theorists. Instead of simply describing functional relations in a system, these sociologists may use mathematical forms like Markov chains to depict social process as a series of probable events or they may employ game theory to predict outcomes in a rationally determined social situation with a limited number of possible choices (Bartos: Beauchamp). Instead of searching for a key theoretical principle like gravity, these sociologists debate the merits of using classical statistics to judge a sample in terms of unknown parameter values or of employing Bayesian strategy to predict the unknown parameter from information about the sample (Iversen).

Here we will consider two examples of these technical-sociological concerns: first, some problems in typology construction; second, the use of linear graphs to depict relationships.

Types and typologies

Social thinkers have long defined types within a concept —

types of suicide based on social causes; types of authority based on social meanings; types of elites based on motivating residues. In each instance, types were distinguished on the basis of key variables that affect the problem or reality being considered. Beyond this attempt to isolate key variables, there are a variety of approaches to constructing types. Some types do not exist in empirical reality. Weber created "bureaucracy" by listing a theoretical-ideal set of variables and compared real-world administrations to this type. At the opposite extreme, there are atheoretical types pulled directly from data. We can, for example, measure one-hundred variables that affect delinquency, feed the results into a computer, observe which variables relate to each other, and define types of delinquency based on these observed relationships.

Whatever their origin, types have proved useful in sociological analysis. Distinguishing between rational, traditional, and charismatic legitimacy, for example, enables us to understand different kinds of behavior among people who exercise authority. Further, the types help us to investigate the link between patterns of legitimacy and other social features like religious perspectives or levels of economic development. It would be impossible to adequately understand patterns of authority if we either examined authority as a unitary concept or looked at each authority figure individually. In the first instance, authority could relate to all other group variables indiscriminately, since some kind of authority exists in all stable groups. In the second situation, it is likely that authority figures would each display a unique set of concomitant variables. Clearly we need typologies to dispel the conceptual confusion.

Understandably a great deal has been written about the construction of such useful tools, for example, techniques of cluster analysis and procedures for developing exclusive-exhaustive categories. The *mini-max* dilemma is one of the current concerns in typology construction: in order to be truly useful, a concept should have a minimum number of types and each type should have a maximum amount of homogeneity (Bailey). Perhaps 8192 types of delinquency exist in "reality" or on a computer printout. But, it is easier for us to understand two or three. On the other hand, two types based on a single variable — for example, gang delinquency and non-gang delinquency — may prove so broad, so inclusive, so heterogeneous that they do not really tell us anything. If it were true that gang

TABLE 1. Number of Delinquent Acts by Kinds of Participants and Kinds of Criminality

Participants		Felonies				Misdemeanors			
		Violence		No violence		Violence		No violence	
		Theft	No theft	Theft	No theft	Theft	No theft	Theft	No theft
Gang members	Adult participants					20		10	
	No adult participants		200	200		50		25	25
Non gang members	Adult participants							50	
	No adult participants			200				50	

members and non-gang delinquents commit the same acts, would we learn anything by classifying delinquents into these two types?

Finding the middle way requires both artistry and technical expertise. Consider the hypothetical example in Table 1. This table records delinquent acts according to the following criteria: felony and misdemeanor; violent and non-violent action; theft and crime without theft. It also notes whether the act was part of gang activity or not, and whether adults (fences, old gang members, *etc.*) were involved as instigators or active participants. Examining delinquency in terms of these variables, we have produced a table of thirty-two cells — representing thirty-two possible types. In this example, however, many types are logically possible but empirically non-existent. Therefore we can reduce the number by eliminating the empty cells. By this procedure we have already collapsed our hypothetical typology from thirty-two types to ten (something much more difficult to accomplish in real research where a few odd cases would, no doubt, settle in the "vacant" cells). In the remaining cells, we can find certain relationships: for example, non-gang, non-violent theft seems to be part of a pattern, although it is evenly divided between crimes with and without adult participation. In later analysis, we might redefine our types according to these patterns.

But if we were examining thirteen variables instead of five (not an unreasonable possibility in research on a complex phenomenon like delinquency), we would have 8,192 possible types instead of 32. In such a contingency, we could not simply inspect the table to detect types; instead we would have to use the computer. Computer analysis can sort the acts into clusters with related variables or variable values. The adjacent clusters can then be combined until we have a typology small enough to understand but large enough to explain divisions that we might not grasp intuitively. Although the specific procedures for such analyses are technical and complicated, the underlying rationale remains simple: search for a small number of relatively homogeneous types.

Scaling is another method of type construction. To construct a scale based on some theory (instead of building directly from data) we might list theoretically important variables, and then define the types according to how many of the important variables they display or according to both the number and specific content of the key variables. Naturally, these two approaches yield different results in terms of "mini-max." Looking at sociological theories, for example, we might rate them according to the degree of concern they display for subjective elements — ranging from theories that do not even allude to the existence of norms, values, and other social-mental constructs, to theories that explicitly consider these constructs as cause and effect in social life, but still remain "positive" only because they preceed interpretive analysis with some description of objective behavior. A typology with such a scale based on increasing concern with "subjective" elements could prove very homogeneous, assuming that each new concern adds to the sum of all the others; for example, that a theory incorporating values also considers norms, that a theory including socialization also includes norms and values, that each incorporation includes all previous ones. Often, however, reality does not arrange itself so neatly. A theory might include a number of subjective elements without respect to order. Simply counting the number of variables might produce a scale of increasing subjectivity that groups Parsons and Marx in one category because both observed a relationship between values and structures.

Thus, whether we use the computer as a fishnet to catch related variables, or whether we erect an abstract edifice without reference to empirical data, we face a critical unsolved problem — the choice and ordering of important variables. Although computer programs are available for reducing the number of variable clusters and sensible guidelines exist for combining types, there are no rules for making that initial choice about the variables to be analyzed. Consider our loosely defined typology of "objective" and "interpretive" theories. I chose these types because they highlight problems that have informed sociology from the beginning (Wagner, 1963). However, additional variables could sharpen the typology considerably by increasing homogeneity at the cost of a slight increase in the number of types. Walter Wallace began to build his theory typology with a slight modification of this basic objective-subjective idea. All sociological theories, he notes, explain behavioral reactions. But some, the subjective theories, stress dispositional behavior — motives, aspirations, sentiments, meanings. Others, the objective theories, stress motor behavior — writing, speaking, fighting, eating. This distinction separates Parsons, who pointed to economic values as one of the defining features of a society, from Marx, who identified class consciousness as an observable effect of economic conditions and a prelude to action. To this distinction, Wallace added the difference between sociological subject matter (as defined above) and the variables that theorists use to account for this subject. The added dimension distinguishes Marx, who argued that economic situations affect behavior, from Cooley, who argued that symbolic-meaningful exchange with others shapes a "looking-glass self" which later serves as a social conscience for the individual in action.

Expanding these simple ideas, Wallace developed a much more sophisticated typology than the one I originally outlined. However, the point is not which typology is more satisfactory, but rather that the choice of variables one makes can transform a simple exercise in cataloging into a sharp analytical tool. Even computer analysis — despite its deceptive appearance of straight-foreward mechanical procedure — requires true creativity by a typologist selecting his variables. If, for example, variables are intrinsically related to each other, they produce clusters that do not tell us anything. If we measure "membership in a gang" and "association with delinquent peers," we are comparing two overlapping variables which, naturally, will correlate highly. Beyond avoiding such tautologies, if we want to develop a useful analytic tool, we must also select variables that will enhance analysis. When Weber defined rational-legal meanings, he wanted to study the development of such meanings in the normative structures of Western civilization. Mere descriptive identification would not serve his purpose. In studying juvenile delinquency, we might follow his lead by choosing structural variables to trace the etiology of delinquency or by focusing on symbolic processes to determine how learning takes place in criminal subcultures.

In sum, the selection of variables is a complex and critical aspect of typology construction for which the technical pioneers have not formulated any rules. Perhaps this is an artistic activity, not reducible to a formula. But, if there is to be a significant advance in typology construction, the problem of variable selection must be examined more closely.

Linear graphs

Linear graphs depict binary relationships between elements. Given a set of elements — people, groups, variables — we can define and illustrate relationships — friendship, alliance, causality — between

the elements, two at a time. For example, the hypothetical sociogram below (similar to those Lundberg used) could describe friendship between members of a work group:

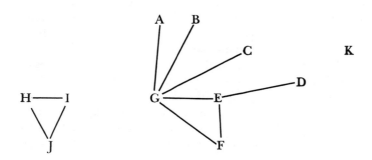

Graphs like this sociogram are intuitively appealing because they
easily illustrate complex relationships. Whereas the verbal description of these relationships would occupy a long, dull page, a glance
at the sociogram above quickly reveals several groupings — a sociometric star, a minor clique, a subgroup, and an isolate — and iden-
tifies the members.

Since sociology is a study of relationships between elements, an
abstract tool for depicting, measuring, and tracing these relationships
can prove intriguing. Expanding on the simple sociogram, theorists
have elaborated graphs to signify the direction and quality of relationships. Directed graphs specify who acts toward whom: Aldebert
likes Bertha:

$$A\longrightarrow B$$

Signed graphs distinguish positive from negative relations: Aldebert
likes Bertha (who reciprocates) but detests Dirk (who also reciprocates); Bertha and Dirk detest each other.

Looking for numerical expressions of these relationships, theorists have used linear algebra, ratios, matrices, and other mathematical forms to evaluate group properties depicted by the graph. For example, the relationships described in a signed graph are defined as stable if the product of each cycle is positive. With the ordinary rules of multiplication for signs, we can determine that the one-cycle signed graph above is positive and, therefore, stable:

$$(+1) \quad (-1) \quad (-1) \ = \ (+1). \text{ * See below.}$$

The graphs we have just considered describe relationships between people or between subgroups in a group. Looking at the graph of relationships between variables, we find other possibilities. Blalock, for example, uses graphs to portray causal sequences and, through this procedure, forces us to think clearly about them. Instead of referring loosely to a multitude of causes, Blalock is compelled to specify distinct causal paths like:

(causes) +   (causes) +

neighborhood ————————▶peer influence ————————▶delinquency

Once he has specified the one-way causal paths, he can measure the correlations between variables two at a time or measure two variables controlling for the influence of intervening causes (as we have seen in the last chapter). Through the use of regression equations and the algebra of linear operations, Blalock and others have also analyzed the sum causal force encouraging a given dependent variable (Land; Heise).

Arthur Stinchcombe expands the graphs to include "loops" or two-way relationships common in functional situations:

————————————

* For more concrete suggestions about ways to measure group structure, consult Beauchamp and Harary *et al*: Beauchamp for the novice's overview, Harary for detailed discussions of digraph (directed graph) theory.

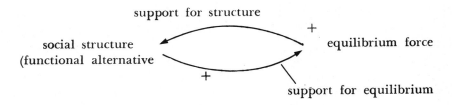

We frequently theorize that a structure contributes to stability in a total social system and that the total system, in turn, reinforces the structure. Magic reduces anxiety; the need for reassurance in the face of anxiety-provoking situations evokes magic. Elites train their sons to run a political system; the rewards of being elite reinforce commitment and encourage future fathers to train their sons. Other factors — particularly the originating cause that first enabled certain groups to acquire elite positions and current tensions, like class conflicts, that threaten the present equilibrium — expand the loop into a more realistic causal-functional chain. The graph portraying this more complex explanation looks like this:

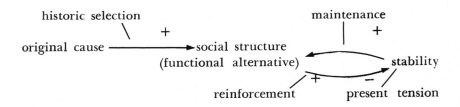

Applying the algebra of linear operators, we could put the present action into an equation showing how a given level of tension necessitates certain levels of other activity to maintain stability in the system. As lower-class unrest occurs, the elites may need to issue pro-establishment propaganda, purge malcontents, send out the Army, or co-opt the rebel leadership.

Although Stinchcombe used graph theory for outlining this action, he did not fill in the outline with empirical research. As Stinchcombe demonstrates, once we have assigned values to each path we can manipulate the numbers algebraically to estimate the relationship between tension and compensating mechanisms. However, he has not yet suggested how we find such values. To do this, he would need to go beyond Blalock's regression techniques. Correlations estimate the simultaneous existence of two variables, but do not distinguish between Blalock's one-way causality and Stinchcombe's reciprocal causal-functional loops. Theoretically, Blalock assumes that causation goes in one direction and then examines the empirical world to see if the correlations there correspond to his theoretical predictions. But to estimate reciprocal causation as Stinchcombe recommends, we would need experiments or longitudinal studies that trace the sequence of events and measure each side of the loop independently.

Stinchcombe's main concern here, however, is theory-building, not theory testing. For his immediate purposes, he need not discover these numerical coefficients. Although he uses graphs as Blalock did — to force clear thinking about the relationships between variables — Stinchcombe did not devise a testing program and, therefore, he is not bound by such restrictions as one-way causation. On the contrary, Stinchcombe' specifically advocates the use of graphs to carry analysis beyond Blalock's one-way sequences into the less testable but more realistic theories with feedback, spiral effects, and other complex causal relationships.

Perhaps this is the ultimate usefulness of graphs — as tools for thinking through the causal sequences of complex situations. Although they have long been used to describe group structure, these tools obviously work best with small groups (where any one member could, in theory, have a relationship with any other member). Given this limitation, we may prefer to expend energy describing a small group of variables instead of a small group of friends.

SUBJECTIVE SOCIOLOGY: THE SEARCH
FOR INTERPRETIVE UNDERSTANDING

The positivists have demonstrated that sociology can be a science. It is the interpretive sociologists, however, who have explored the peculiar properties of a social science. They met the nineteenth-century challenge of trying to interpret unique subjective states and describe them as abstract concepts. Of course, all sociologists acknowledge man's subjective nature and its effects on social life Even an extreme positivist like Lundberg who insisted that we can only know the objective, sensible outer appearance of the social world, used his objective indicators to detect "ethnocentrism," "friendship," and other social-mental meanings. But interpretive sociologists explore what lies beyond what we can see, hear, or touch. Lundberg defined the concept of ethnocentrism, decided how ethnocentric people would act, and looked for people exhibiting this behavior. Interpretive sociologists more commonly look at a situation and then judge what motivates the important characters. Instead of defining certain actions as symptoms of a specific internal state, they survey a variety of activities to detect the common (or uncommon) motives that occur across situations.

With the shift in subject focus comes a corresponding shift in methodology. Lundberg defined "ethnocentrism" as sociometric choices in favor of leaders, co-workers, friends, and others who were members of one's own group. Lundberg began by using creative judgment to devise an operational definition that would provide high reliability in field investigations. Once a concept has been defined in such empirical terms, however, measuring the empirical reality is a mechanical task, easily performed by any researcher who can follow instructions. In contrast, when Weber investigated the cultural ideal of "inner-worldly asceticism," he examined Calvinist sermons — shifting through references to hell, God's nature, and the idolatry of the flesh — looking for signs of a Calvinist vocation that compelled these religionists to work in the world as the elect-instruments of God. Clearly Weber's personal judgment affected his vision as he read old sermons. The problem of the investigator's own judgment becomes even more acute for interpretive sociologists who use literary records to trace the changing self-perceptions of mental patients or participant observation to document the development of a child's self image. In other words, these researchers sacrifice some reliability for the chance to explore their data with on-the-spot insight.

Two interpretive sociologists we have considered so far — Cooley and Weber — represent opposite approaches to the study of subjective meanings. Defining sociology as the science of "personal intercourse" or "mental communication" that comprises the mental-social network called "society," Cooley detailed the common interaction processes that establish and maintain this network. Defining sociology as the study of subjectively meaningful action, Weber analyzed the meanings as they informed an individual's action in various objective situations. Cooley traced the development of common human nature through interaction in the primary group. Weber examined the growth and consequences of rationality, a powerful cultural idea. Both explored the wider effects of mental-social constructs — how primary-group moral ideals spread to the social structure, how charisma can break the rational-legal tyranny of government. Cooley's approach reappears in the work of George Herbert Mead and his disciples, the *symbolic interactionists*. First, Mead transformed the "looking-glass self" into the concept of the *"social self"* that we construct by interpreting symbolic messages sent from significant people who interact with us. Mead's work has subsequently inspired studies of the symbolic interaction process through which we shape and are shaped by social groups. The Weberian approach reappears in the work of Talcott Parsons as he examines the social meanings and common values that inform "volunteeristic social action," and in the work of the *phenomenologists* as they explore the ways each of us mentally construct a social world that may or may not exist in empirical "reality."

In the next few pages we will review the modern subjective approach as it appears in studies of interaction and of individual social meanings. First, we will consider the social process that shapes self-perceptions, specifically, the techniques that staff members use when teaching mental patients and convent novices how to "act right." Then, in a section on phenomenology (a more recent addition to subjective sociology), we will discuss the construction of our social-mental images, for example, how we decide to think of a returning veteran as if he were a John Wayne hero. In each section, we will be reviewing an alternative to technical positivism. The symbolic interactionists use *emergent theory,* concepts and propositions both built and refined with the researcher's subjective judgment on his data. Phenomenology attacks positivism directly by questioning the importance of "real" interaction, indeed, by asking if such exchanges even exist.

Symbolic interaction

Symbolic interaction (SI) combines positive interaction theory with the insights of George Herbert Mead. Like Simmel, SI theorists appreciate how a situation sets limits on possible actions for its members. But they add a dimension that Simmel deliberately omitted. SI considers the motives and perceptions of these inter-actors. Where Simmel analyzed the possible coalitions in a triad, SI researchers might detail the process of changing self-perceptions within such a group. They might describe how each member inter-prets the symbolic signals sent by the others, and comes to view him-self as a beleagured outsider, a victorious plotter or a staunch ally. In other words, Simmel defined society as a number of individuals connected by interaction. SI theorists, in contrast, define society as a pattern of activity dependent on our mental-social vision of ap-propriate interaction. For Mead and the SI theorists, the central question of sociology is: How do we collectively create society's normative agreement and, further, how do we discover the rules that apply to us in particular?

Erving Goffman addressed the second half of this question in his study of self redevelopment among asylum inmates. Since inmates spend all their time inside total institutions, they cannot avoid con-stant contacts with staff-superiors and with each other. Since they are physically separated from "outside" contact, they cannot assess their situation by discussing it with people from their old everyday world. Consequently, they are peculiarly vulnerable to pressures exerted by the institution; these pressures include persuasive reso-cialization techniques. For example, when inmates enter the institu-tion — the mental hospital, POW, camp, monastery, prison, or boarding school — they are stripped of their old identity. Typically they are required to trade old clothes for a standard uniform; to exchange old names for a prison number, hospital nickname, or re-ligious title, to drop the symbols of an old social self. In prison in-terviews, therapy sessions, or other confessional forms, they are re-quired to reveal intimate details about past and/or present behavior. Additional interaction pressures — regimented activity, constant surveillance, absence of "free" time — combine to produce a lowly self-image among inmates and correspondingly obedient behavior. In his second *Asylums* essay, Goffman developed this theme further by focusing on the "moral career" of inmates, particularly mental patients. Here he described the "self" as a property that "dwells . . . in the pattern of social control that is exerted in connection with the person by himself and those around him" (1961:168). As his "career" progresses, the patient must adjust his self-image to job or marital problems, betrayal by the people (often relatives) who "turned him in," association with "sick" fellow inmates, negative "sick" definitions of himself that are projected by the staff, new moral standards acceptable in the ward, and — finally — reentry into a society that now labels him as a "former mental patient."

In both essays Goffman depicted the individual as shaped by events beyond his control: both his self-image and the resulting behavior are determined by the group which labels him as a patient, prisoner, or other deviant. This labeling perspective — only one among the SI possibilities, although presently a popular one — portrays the powerful group forcing a label on a helpless individual over a period of time. However, one-way determinism is a departure from both the example of exhaustive analysis set by Simmel and the theory of dialectical self-group development posited by Cooley and Mead. The general SI perspective includes the dialectical process and there is no theoretical reason why it could not also include group-to-group interaction. This broader view could improve labeling theory by incorporating the conflict between an established power and the group that fights back. We already know what happens to the individual who challenges something as powerful as a total institution — he looses. On the other hand, a deviant group can often obtain enough leverage to apply some of its own labels to the dominant members of the interaction situation.

However, even this broader SI vision leaves some problems. When Goffman discussed the "underlife of a public institution" — the inmate's revenge on the system — he fleshed out one presentation of this broadened view. As a whole, *Asylums* describes reciprocal influence, a causal spiral: the institution influences the individual, who, in turn, bands with other inmates to influence the staff, who react by exerting pressure on some inmate individuals . . . symbolic interaction affects the self which changes behavior and influences other people's perceptions of the social structure and then the newly perceived structure affects the self. . . .

This causal spiral, found in many SI studies, describes an ongoing process detached from its place in the social structure. Like Simmel and Mead, SI researchers explore possible actions but generally ignore historical circumstances. Like Cooley, they seem to assume that human nature is uniform, that differences in behavior grow primarily from differences in interaction situations and not from cultural or personal predispositions. SI methodology facilitates this detachment from structure. It frequently documents interaction process through participant observation, perusal of literary records, and other techniques that permit the researcher to define his concepts while gathering his data. The resulting emergent theory necessarily builds on data that appears during the course of fieldwork, and is not designed to anticipate what factors, outside of those immediately impinging on interaction, might affect a situation. In *Asylums,* for example, we are left wondering what differences might separate the mental hospital from the prison or the monastery. People join a monastery motivated by high self-commitment to the institutional ideals; people are forced to enter a prison or a mental hospital or a POW camp because their selves are unacceptable to powerful elements in outside society. We may suspect that self-development among inmates would differ with these circumstances. Specifying such historical and social background features would enrich SI theory. It would also provide a conceptual link between this branch of subjective sociology and the positivistic studies that so often ignore the human meaning of social life.

Phenomenological sociology

SI considers how we interact and, in the process, make rules to determine our future social behavior. Phenomenology probes more deeply into the individual-human facets of social life, by challenging the fundamental positivistic assumption that truth lies in developing conceptions to correspond with the empirical reality "out there." Phenomenologists *bracket* the "real" world, that is, they suspend judgment about its ontological status and the uniqueness of our encounters with it. For these sociologists the important issues are not whether a social hierarchy, integrating religion, primary-group realignment, or other interaction pattern exists within a given society, but *how* members come to *perceive the existence* of these patterns. For them the "real" world is studied simply as an object of our immediate conscious perception, something we deliberately see and comprehend. This perception requires that phenomenologists account both for the process of experience — the way we come to "know" what we do — and for the object of our experience — what it is that we "know." Naturally this "knowing" and experiencing occur in everyday life, so the world of everyday experience forms the arena for phenomenological studies.

Combining these ideas with the insights of Max Weber, Alfred Schutz identified a critical sociological question: How do one's private perceptions become common, standard social meanings? Schutz expanded and embellished the methodology of the ideal type to include *personal types,* that is, types of people acting with predictable behavior and motives. We construct these types both in sociological investigations and in the course of our daily life. We notice the appearance of a person's behavior; we connect this apparent activity with the "appropriate" motive and, in the end, we assume that typical behavior and typical motives tend to link together regardless of the idiosyncratic preferences of a particular actor. In our own minds these personal ideal types become *puppets,* creatures who possess the qualities we have defined and who can be activated (at least in our imaginations) to perform a "typical" scenario. Thus, using these puppets, we can experiment with meanings in different situations. If we endow the puppet types with cultural qualities, if we bid them to perform in a culturally standardized pattern, we can use them to study cultural-personal meanings.

The homecomer — home from World War II — was such a "puppet type," (Schutz). His prolonged absence had broken the intimate, personalized sharing that normally occurs in primary groups. Both the soldier and his loved ones had continued to live, but in a life apart and very different one from the other. The soldier had forgotten some of his civilian concerns and dismissed others as no longer relevant. Furthermore, his civilian family and friends could not even know, much less evaluate, the important concerns of life on Anzio Beach. Consequently, each side had lost its intimate knowledge of the other. In place of knowledge, they substituted pseudo-types. The waiting family read about John Wayne heroics and Parisian bordellos. The soldier could not imagine his sister filling his old job at the cigar store. The family waited for a "hero" to rejoin local life. Instead, the soldier often returned to school on the GI bill or drifted into alcoholism. Each side misunderstood the other by relying on its pseudo-types rather than on personalized, intimate knowledge. In other words, the soldier and the other members of his old primary group had created their own disjointed mental world and decided to live in it.

Ethnomethodologists advance one step further into the subjective realm by bracketing the very existence of common ideas. They investigate how, during the adventures of everyday life, people decide that they must act in special ways and, even more, how other members of a group seem to share these perceptions about appropriate behavior. These perceptions — conscious recognitions of a phenomenon that may or may not exist outside the individual mind — are the objects of ethnomethodological investigation. Moving beyond Schutz who asked how we come to share social meanings, ethnomethodologists ask: How do we acquire a *sense* of shared social meanings, a sense of group culture? Beyond that: What are the rules we follow in constructing this appearance of shared meanings?

Two interview studies by Harold Garfinkel — one on jurors explaining their decision-making rules and another about an "intersexed" person accounting for her "normal, natural femininity — illustrate this approach. In sharp contrast to Goffman's research, both studies describe actors who negotiate a continuous mental set. For Goffman, the individual's basic concern it to acquire an acceptable social self and to present this front to the public. People living in total institutions have a peculiar problem because the process of acquiring the self necessarily involves allowing others to know many damaging facts about one's personal sin, insanity, and other social gaffes — facts that one would normally not advertise. For Garfinkel, the individual's basic problem is to acquire an inner sense that all is well, that one "fits" in his social situation. This perception depends, of course, on one's conviction that others also recognize the "fit," — hence the need to negotiate an agreement with others, or at least the sense of agreement.

Jury duty illustrates this need for self-negotiated agreements. Jurors often make problematic decisions that require the use of everyday rules for discerning truth — "what we can see" — modified by legal procedures. However, everyday truth and legal truth do not always coincide. Thus, ambiguity, not decision making, becomes the jurors' real problem: somehow they must justify the ambiguous process that produced their judgment. Typically — after the fact — each juror manages to rationalize the rules for his decision-making process until he achieves an inner conviction that he proceeded properly and that others would approve his conclusion. In the study, this inner conviction persisted despite aggressive questioning by the researchers: " . . . Are you certain that point was discussed before the vote? According to the other jurors . . . Is that the way it was decided? In your first interview you said. . . . " Such remarks destroyed rapport but did not alter the juror's new, erroneous conviction that he had methodically followed the rules to a correct decision, correct both logically and legally.

The story of Agnas, the "intersexed" female who spent her first seventeen years as a male, demonstrates the continuous nature of inner convictions. Agnas consistently argued that she was truly female even though, thanks to nature's cruelty, she had male primary sex characteristics and female secondary ones. Not only did she ask for a sex-change operation, but she also developed a complete set of female behavior traits. Furthermore, no matter how persistently and clearly she was questioned, she recounted her history by stressing episodes that revealed her constant feminine nature: she had always preferred girls' games; she always "lined up" with the girls at school; she had always been "delicate." But no, she had not collaborated with relatives to establish a female identity; she had never experienced any sexual pleasure from her unwanted organ; she had no sexual feelings for "other girls." It was only much later, when the operation and Garfinkel's research were both safely over, that Agnas mentioned she had been taking female hormones since she was twelve. In effect, she used her female behavior to show others what she "really" was, to obtain social recognition of the "true" facts produced by chemical magic. She wanted to sense that others were as convinced of her femininity as she was herself.

This sense of inner conviction resides in a person's mental state, not in the empirical world of interaction. Ethnomethodologists study personal convictions, not interaction fronts. Once they have suspended the question of whether a "real" empirical world exists, ethnomethodologists obviate the need for operational definitions, and other tools designed to compare our perceptions with empirical "truth." Indeed, they insist, scientific canons of investigation, as perceived by the scientist, are part of the subject matter we investigate. Like the jurors, we shape our findings by the rules we follow while observing social life, and we may readjust the rules if necessary to "fit" our findings. Like the jurors, ethnomethodologists rely heavily on commonsense "folk" interpretations of the data presented by their subjects.

Comte would have disputed this conception of science. However, modern sociologists who seriously examine ontological and epistemological issues discern a difference between empirical reality and their observation of it. The sheer complexity of social life is not the only facet that confounds our studies. More critical is the discontinuity between the theoretical world of understanding and the empirical world of data. There are ontological gaps between our idea of "cause" and actual causal mechanisms, between our ability to observe causes and the empirical existence of a force compelling someone to commit suicide, elect a President, or file for divorce.

Ethnomethodologists and phenomenologists highlight this discrepancy between perceptions and reality. But whether their efforts will produce a major breakthrough in sociology is questionable. Ethnomethodology taken at its extreme cannot analyze our social world. Since, by definition, each person possesses a unique vision that may or may not relate to anyone else's unique vision, the researcher using this approach can only describe his findings as his own interpretations of what he thinks is someone else's interpretation of a possible situation. Although it is one thing to acknowledge the possibility that we may live in a world created entirely by our own conscious minds, it is quite another to act as if ours are the only minds that matter. Even if the more positivistic approaches to sociological analysis reveal a mechanistic dream, they are none-the-less fairly efficient about predicting or describing events that appear to be happening in this "dream" world and, just as important, they seem to be describing a common "dream." Phenomenology itself need not require such an extreme subjective stance. Indeed, Schutz and others insist that *the* sociological problem is revealing the operations of intersubjectivity and interaction based on the common understandings that grow from intersubjective activity. However, as frequently practiced, phenomenology avoids verifying the extent to which its conclusions are in contact with the "real" world. Schutz built ideal types like the homecomer and discussed them in terms of possibilities, illustrated with examples selected from personal experience, magazine articles, news reports, and other available evidence. From this illustrative data, he developed plausible arguments to support his conclusions. Garfinkel, on the other hand, interviewed jury members, worked with Agnas, constructed his findings from systematically collected data. A combination of these approaches could avoid the dangers of solipsism inherent in pure ethnomethodology and analysis-by-plausibility often practiced by phenomenologists. A return to intersubjectivity would rescue the ethnomethodologists, and additional data systematically collected would give phenomen-- ological plausibility a firmer empirical base. Perhaps it is this com- bination that will provide sociology with a counterbalance to ex- treme positivism.

OBJECTIVE REALITY AND SUBJECTIVE MEANING — IN RETROSPECT

The nineteenth-century debates about "natural" and social science recur in somewhat altered form in the twentieth-century distinction between "positive" and "interpretive" sociology. We are not con- tending with an either-or quarrel on this issue, but rather with two trends of sociological theory and research. The positive or objective theorists stress knowledge that can be acquired through purely em- pirical techniques. In their efforts to improve the empirical accuracy and truthfulness of sociology, some have specialized in the technical problems of data collection and theory testing. The subjective or interpretive sociologists use empirical data to unveil the hidden subjective meanings that inform social life. Although many of these researchers employ (and even develop) sophisticated objective tools, there are fewer technicians among the subjective sociologists; indeed, some subjective sociologists even criticize such methodology for mis- sing the subject matter of sociology altogether.

Each position carries substantive implications. At one extreme, the positivists can envision a world determined by functional or causal forces. The group creates these forces and man simply re- sponds, perhaps by committing anomic suicide or by choosing an ethnocentric circle of friends. In this perspective, the identification of subjective states often becomes an exercise in tautological reason- ing. We may be told that marginal man "feels" marginal. Subjective sociologists reverse this conceptualization to highlight personal in- put, existential drift, the process of experience. They often ignore group structure — revealing a subject's reaction toward a half-seen social world. They tell us that people learn to adjust to total insti- tutions without carefully distinguishing between those inmates who enter by choice and those who enter at gunpoint. The extreme sub- jectivists ignore the "outside" world altogether and describe society as the product of an individual mind. In contrast, some objective technical experts avoid the subject-focus problem by specializing in methodology. Their causal models, typologies, linear graphs, and other tools are sometimes constructed and refined without explicit reference to the data they are designed to describe or explain. In effect, the tool can become the subject.

Besides affecting the choice of substantive problems and viewpoints, objective and subjective stances also foster certain methodological tendencies. Positive sociologists usually favor deductive theory (based on earlier inductions), rigorous verification and, very often, quantitative measures. These preferences, in turn, encourage the study of data that can be measured at interval or ordinal levels — census counts, attitudinal responses, or homocide occurrences; not judicial decision making, the stock panic of 1837, or interaction in a symphony orchestra. Since the technical pioneers sometimes avoid the choice-of-problem by choosing no problem, they may contribute more to statistics, graph theory, and other modes of formal thought than they do to sociology itself. On the other hand, subjective sociologists (who never forget their subject matter) often use inductive research guided only by sensitizing concepts. This is a methodology that allows them to center on interaction and ignore group structure, to discuss the development of a deviant self-image without considering why, in American society, the marijuana smoker seems to feel more deviant than the stock manipulator. At the subjective extreme, ethnomethodologists can retreat into solipsism and preclude the possibility of any verification. Although few of us would follow them in their retreat from the objective world, we must all acknowledge at least one of their basic tenets: every research study, no matter how objective or subjective, reflects the personal mental world of the researcher.

In sum, the nineteenth-century tension between "natural" and "social" science remains today. Few modern scientists deny the possibility of social science. However, virtually all who work in the field recognize its peculiar difficulty: social science carries the double burden of being scientific and being human. Whichever side we choose to emphasize, we must be wary of the particular biases imposed by our choice.

RADICAL-CRITICAL SOCIOLOGY: THE SEARCH FOR A MORAL IMPERATIVE

Radical-critical sociology does not question the epistemological basis of social science or plead for more rigorous methodology.

Rather its perspective preceeds these issues by confronting the moral nature of sociology. For radical-critical thinkers, the primary question is not "How do we study a topic?" but "Why do we want to study it?" The primary concern is with morals, not methodology. Further, this concern begins with the problems of power and order in society. Instead of perceiving society's basic institutions as the necessary tools of social order, radicals view these patterns as policing mechanisms designed by the powerful to control the powerless. Certainly neither the moral imperative nor the concern for power and order are new in sociology. Most of the nineteenth-century theorists, both American and European, were explicitly concerned with broad social issues. And several contributed to the radical perspective on these concerns. Marx explained that, historically, the major institutions of society have usually served the dominant economic groups and exploited the minorities. Others, like Weber and Tarde, detailed how the dominant ideas that shape the institutions of an era are often associated with small, creative groups within the society. Overall, however, sociologists either have accepted the definitions of social normalcy and deviance promulgated as the cultural ideals of the majority or have simply not examined this issue. Radical sociologists, in contrast, ask "Who ordains a given social order and why must we accept it?" Why, they ask, must we judge prostitution and purse snatching to be more deleterious than militarism or political misfeasance? How did we come to define the value behind these judgments?

The moral imperative of radical sociology implies that the social order can be changed. In fact, radical-critical sociology has been defined as "the study of root relationships of the historically conditioned — and therefore changeable — social order" (Horowitz:12:1971). It contains an "open avowal of a critical intention with respect to society" and begins "with the adumbration of our historical secularities" (Birnbaum:1971). Such a sociology does not reveal ahistorical "laws," universal relationships, or abstract propositions. It concentrates instead on tracing relationships within a specific situation. The important radical issues in the study of authority, for example, are not the forms of address we use to acknowledge our superiors (a la Goffman) or the chains of command that rationalize bureaucratic structures (a la Weber). Critical research probes beyond these problems to expose the conditions that enable dominant groups to acquire authority in the first place. In understanding these conditions we grasp the roots of change.

Once we recognize the social order as something molded by a dominant group, unequal access to knowledge, economic goods, and other concomitants of life style can be seen as consequences of this dominance, not inalterable elements of an absolute Master Plan. Like other scarce and valuable commodities, the knowledge produced by sociology becomes a possession of the more powerful groups. Therefore, the radicals insist, sociologists must consider what class interests they serve. Are we providing clues about how to motivate the fighting infantryman or analyses of why there is a war for the infantryman to fight? Both studies may be needed. Radical sociologists criticize the discipline for concentrating on the first kind of knowledge while generally ignoring the necessity for the second. We investigate ways to maintain order without first examining whether a particular order ought to be maintained. In other words, radical sociologists argue that sociology cannot be a morally neutral pursuit. Since sociological knowledge becomes part of the stratification structure, we are responsible for supporting or undermining that structure.

If we accept this argument, choosing sides becomes an urgent moral problem. Some sociologists even assume that any power structure is, *ipso facto,* a moral evil and part of the "wrong" side. Alvin Gouldner, for example, suggests that sociology could free itself from servitude to the powerful only by focusing on man himself. "Reflexive" sociology should integrate man's current existence as he executes a constant process of reform. But, since Gouldner defines all powers-that-be and, by implication, all temporary values as "inimical" to "reflexive" sociology, it is very unclear where his reform can lead.

According to critical thinkers, social science (along with religion, philosophy, and other thought structures) presents special moral challenges, because it is more than a simple commodity unequally distributed in society. Scientific knowledge is not only possessed by dominant groups; it also grows in response to their needs. Gouldner argues that a functional-systems framework developed to provide the rationale for a stable political state, while Marxist analysis developed to support changing regimes. He predicts that the growing American welfare state is creating a "crisis" for "academic" functionalism, a "crisis" that can only be met when academic sociologists incorporate

Marxist ideals about change into their stable-systems theories. Meanwhile the Marxist-orientated sociology-of-political-change prominent in Eastern Europe will experience a similar "crisis" as non-revolutionary governments require a new ideology of stability.

Gouldner's thesis — that sociology functions as an ideology for the existing regime — may be an overstatement of the problem; its validity is certainly very difficult to demonstrate. However, approaching the problem indirectly, critical sociologists have demonstrated a relationship between social theory and power structures. Norman Birnbaum (1959), for example, reexamined the Marx-Weber debate about religion and economic institutions by tracing the origins of Zwinglianism in Zurich. Weber had claimed that existing Calvinism encouraged capitalistic practices. Birnbaum looked at the beginning of such a relationship. By outlining the temporal development of economic crisis and theological response in Zurich, Birnbaum could show that the moral questions raised by capitalism not only defined theological problems but also shaped the solutions. Zwingli had written his theology in a debate with members of the economic community. Here Birnbaum analyzed the origins of theological doctrine growing in a relatively isolated environment. Gouldner, on the other hand, overviewed all of sociology as it exists in the Western world today, using Talcott Parsons as a "representative" example of its dominant mode of thought. The U.S. is a technically developed nation with sharply defined distinctions between political and religious power, therefore, Gouldner argued, Parsons had written about the importance of independence between the goal-attaining and integrating institutions. Although we may doubt that the entire corpus of "academic" sociology represents political interests (with, one supposes, contradictory theories representing antithetical interests), we cannot ignore a crucial radical hypothesis: knowledge structures do, somehow, reflect and support social conditions. Therefore, as sociologists we must consider what sort of conditions we care to promote (Swanson, *et al.*).

A pervading interest in "life as it could be" instead of "life as it is" has lead the radicals to certain methodological stances: they criticize interpretive sociologists for stressing individual reactions without revealing the structural conditions that provoke such reaction. They castigate the systems analysts for providing ahistorical descriptions of current functions, functions that appear to be universal necessities. They condemn the methodological pioneers for specializing in irrelevance, for contributing more to our knowledge of formal thought than to our knowledge of the social problems we should think about. They have not, however, provided a methodological tradition of their own. T. R. Young suggests that a "conflict theory" requires a "conflict methodology," that is, a politically informed sociology must discover more than respondents are willing to tell. People often reveal their true position only when threatened or tricked by an aggressive interview (like the one's in Garfinkel's jury study), or by a devious maneuver, torture, legal action, or some other device that strips away usual excuses. He is quite correct: being nice to respondents does not always elicit the full truth. On the other hand, there is no reason why any efficient methodology (including this one) cannot be used by both radical and non-radical sociologists. In fact, some of the "conflict" techniques that Young suggests have long served as standard procedures for various established governments. As Becker and Horowitz note, the same information can serve several ends. A good marketing survey on the effects of advertising can tell the marketing expert how to sell his product and the consumer-affairs advocate how to promote sales resistance. For radicals, then, the real problem is not how we get information, but how we use it. Their basic criticism of conventional methodology is that it fails to uncover the whole truth, that it often centers on trivia and ignores vital power issues.

In considering radical-critical sociology, it would be wrong to see it as a unified body of substantive thought. Radical sociology is a perspective shared by scholars and activists. Its pronouncements range from a sharp critique of established, pro-establishment sociology, to thoughtless rhetoric on behalf of miscellaneous underdogs; from serious analyses of power structures to simplistic remarks damning all establishments (except its own!). Within this range, we find two serious concerns: praxis (which is more strongly emphasized by the radicals) and the study of historically conditioned relationships (which has always been the key concern of the critical sociologists). Praxis provides the moral force: if theory must include practice in order to be fruitful, then we must be always alert to the practical implications of our science. The concern for historically conditioned relationships provides the substantive focus compelling sociologists to probe for the origins of societal structures, instead of delimiting the *status quo* and accepting it as an eternal good.

To date, the radical-critical perspective has encouraged a wider sociological range of study — particularly by urging us to examine the taken-for-granted dominance structure — but is has not produced landmark research. Perhaps, however, the radical concerns for praxis and root relationships will become part of the discipline's tradition. Instead of becoming the focal point of a school, radical sociology may become the moral force to correct the conservative bias that has typified much of twentieth-century sociology, particularly as this science has become academically respectable, has thrived on government research grants, and has in other ways become more and more indebted to the existing social order. A truly perceptive social scientist needs both the radical and conservative perspectives on the all-important problems of order, dominance, stratification, and other power issues. At the very least, radical sociology serves to remind us, once again, of the moral-social issues that inspired nineteenth-century scholars to develop a discipline called sociology.

Bibliography

Friedrichs, Robert W.
  1970 *A Sociology of Sociology.* New York: Free Press.
Sherman, Lawrence W.
  1974 "Uses of the masters." *American Sociologist* 9 (November) : 176-81.
Positive Sociology: The Search for Objective Reality
Bailey, Kenneth D.
  1972 "Polythetic reduction of monothetic property space." Pp. 83-111 in Herbert L. Costner (ed.), *Sociological Methodology* 1972. San Francisco: Jossey-Bass.
  1973a "Constructing monothetic and polythetic typologies by the heuristic method." *Sociological Quarterly* 14 (Summer) : 291-308.
  1973b "Monothetic and polythetic typologies and their relation to conceptualization, measurement, and scaling." *American Sociological Review* 38 (February) : 18-33.
  1974 "Cluster analysis." Pp. 59-128 in David R. Heise (ed.), *Sociological Methodology* 1975. San Francisco: Jossey Bass.
Bartos, Otomar J.
  1967 *Simple Models of Group Behavior.* New York: Columbia University Press.
Beauchamp, Murray A.
  1970 *Elements of Mathematical Sociology.* New York: Random House.

Harary, Frank, Norman, Robert Z., and Cartwright, Dorwin
1965 *Structural Models: An Introduction to the Theory of Directed Graphs.* New York: John Wiley and Sons.
Heise, David R.
1969 "Problems in path analysis and causal inference." Pp. 38-73 in Edgar F. Borgatta (ed.), *Sociological Methodology* 1969. San Francisco: Jossey-Bass.
Hill, Richard J.
1969 "On the relevance of methodology." Pp. 12-19 in Norman K. Denzin (ed.), *Sociological Methods: A Sourcebook.* Chicago: Aldine, 1970.
Iversen, Gudmund R.
1970 "Statistics according to Bayes." Pp. 185-99 in Edgar F. Borgatta (ed.), *Sociological Methodology* 1970. San Francisco: Jossey-Bass.
Land, Kenneth C.
1969 "Principles of path analysis." Pp. 3-37 in Edgar F. Borgatta (ed.), *Sociological Methodology* 1969.
Stinchcombe, Arthur L.
1968 *Constructing Social Theories.* New York: Harcourt Brace and World.
Wagner, Helmut R.
1963 "Types of sociological theory." *American Sociological Review* 28 (October): 735-42. Also Pp. 41-52 in R. Serge Denisoff *et al.* (eds.), *Theories and Paradigms in Contemporary Sociology.* Itasca, Ill.: F. E. Peacock, 1974.
Wallace, David L.
1968 "Clustering." in David L. Sills (ed.), *International Encyclopedia of the Social Sciences.* New York: Macmillan and Free Press.
Wallace, Walter L.
1969 "Overview of contemporary sociological theories." Pp. 1-59 in Wallace (ed.), *Sociological Theory.* Chicago: Aldine.
Subjective Sociology: The Search for Interpretive Understanding
Blumer, Herbert
1969 *Symbolic Interactionism: Perspective and Method.* Englewood Cliffs, N.J.: Prentice-Hall.
Garfinkel, Harold
1967 *Studies in Ethnomethodology.* Englewood Cliffs, N.J.: Prentice-Hall.
Goffman, Erving
1961 *Asylums.* Garden City, N.Y.: Anchor Books.
Heap, James L., and Roth, Phillip A.
1973 "On phenomenological sociology." *American Sociological Review* 38 (June): 354-67.

Huber, Joan
  1973 "Symbolic interaction as a pragmatic perspective: the bias of emergent theory." *American Sociological Review* 38 (April): 274-84.
Lemert, Edwin M.
  1974 "Beyond Mead: the societal reaction to deviance." *Social Problems* 21 (April): 457-68.
Manning, Peter K.
  1973 "Existential sociology." *Sociological Quarterly* 14 (Spring): 200-25.
McHugh, Peter
  1970 "On the failure of positivism." Pp. 320-35 in Jack D. Douglas (ed.), *Understanding Everyday Life*. Chicago: Aldine.
Schervish, Paul G.
  1973 "The labeling perspective: its bias and potential in the study of political deviance." *American Sociologist* 8 (May): 47-57.
Schutz, Alfred
  1945 "The homecomer." *American Journal of Sociology* 50 (March): 369-76. Also Pp. 294-308 in Helmut R. Wagner (ed.), *Alfred Schutz on Phenomenology and Social Relations*. Chicago: University of Chicago Press, 1970.
Strauss, Anselm
  1964 "Introduction." Pp. vii-xxv in Strauss (ed.), *George Herbert Mead on Social Psychology: Selected Papers*. Chicago: University of Chicago Press.
Turner, Jonathan H.
  1974a "Ethnomethodology: an alternative theoretical paradigm?" Pp. 321-31 in *The Structure of Sociological Theory*. Homewood, Ill.: Dorsey Press.
  1974b "Symbolic interactionism." Pp. 177-92 in *The Structure. . . .*
Wagner, Helmut R.
  1970 "Introduction." Pp. 1-50 in *Alfred Schutz. . . .*
  1974 "The influence of German phenomenology upon American sociology." Paper presented at the Eighth World Congress of sociology. Montreal.
Zimmerman, Don H., and Power, Melvin
  1970 "The everyday world as a phenomenon." Pp. 80-103 in *Understanding. . . .*
Zimmerman, Don H., and Wieder, D. Lawrence
  1970 "Ethnomethodology and the problem of order: comment on Denzin." Pp. 285-98 in *Understanding. . . .*
Radical-Critical Sociology: The Search for a Moral Imperative

Becker, Howard S., and Horowitz, Irving Louis
   1972 "Radical politics and sociological research: observations on method-
        ology and ideology." *American Journal of Sociology* 78 (July) : 48-
        65.
Birnbaum, Norman
   1959 "The Zwinglian reformation in Zurich." Pp. 133-61 in *Toward a
        Critical Sociology*. New York: Oxford University Press.
   1971 "Preface." Pp. vii-xii in *Toward a Critical Sociology*.
        Oxford University Press.
Colfax, David J., and Roach, Jack L. (eds.)
   1971 *Radical Sociology*. New York: Basic Books.
Gamberg, Herbert
   1969 "Science and scientism: the state of sociology." *American Sociologist*
        4 (May) : 111-16.
Gouldner, Alvin W.
   1970 *The Coming Crisis of Western Sociology*. New York: Basic Books.
Horowitz, David
   1971 "General introduction." Pp. 1-12 in Horowitz (ed.), *Radical Socio-
        logy: An Introduction*. San Francisco: Canfield Press.
Lenski, Gerhard
   1966 *Power and Privilege*. New York: McGraw-Hill.
Mullins, Nicholas C.
   1973 "Radical-critical theory." Pp. 267-93 in *Theories and Theory Groups
        in Contemporary American Sociology*. New York: Harper and Row.
Swanson, Guy E., Deutsch, Steven E., and Peterson, Richard A.
   1971 "Review symposium: The Coming Crisis of Western Sociology."
        American Sociological Review 36 (April) : 317-28.
Thio, Alex
   1973 "Class bias in the sociology of deviance." *American Sociologist*
        8 (February) : 1-12.
   1974 "The phenomenological perspective of deviance: another case of
        class bias." *American Sociologist* 9 (August) : 146-49.
Young, T. R.
   1971 "The politics of sociology: Gouldner, Goffman, and Garfinkel."
        American Sociologist 6 (November) : 276-81.

SUBJECT INDEX

Abstraction, and type building, 21, 85-86, 135; used by theorists, 33-35, 60, 156-57, 239, (Homans) 265-66, 268-70.
Action frame of reference, 214-16, 218-31
Activities, Homan's definition, 257
Adaption in a system, 225-30
Adaptative capacity, 227-28
Affectivity orientation, 223-24
Affectual action, 136
AGIL scheme, 220, 226-31
Alienation, 46, 48
Anomie, types of, 235, 247-49
Axioms, definition of, 260-62
Axiomatic system, 260, 270
Behavioralism, 256
Biological analogies, 17-18, 288; and specific theorists, 151, 169, (Comte) 29, 35, 39, (Durkheim) 100, 107, (Small) 125-27, 130
Biology as a model, 7, 10-11; and specific theorists, 70, 83, 213, (Park) 183, 194-95, (Spencer) 56-57, 61, 64-65
Biotic level, 184, 192, 194. See also Human ecology
Bracketing, 304-305
Bureaucracy, 133, 138; used in analysis 13, 18, 21, 291
Causality, and correlations, 16, 274, 278-79; and specific theorists, 31, 46, 77, 86, 157-58, 202, (Homans) 260-61, 269-70; in interpretive sociology, 303-304, 308; in positivistic sociology, 243, 288-89, 309; in type analysis, 97-107, 133-34, 140-46
Causal models, 275. See also Blalock
Change analyzed 100, 103, 106-107, 193. See also Dialectical change; Natural history; Social change
Circulation of the elite, 149-50, 159-61
Cluster analysis, 291-93
Cohesion, 93-94, 169. See also Solidarity
Collective consciousness, 102-104
Combinations residues, 153, 159, 162

Common value integration, 214, 216. See also Parsons
Comparative studies, 36, 56, 99, 139, 141-46
Concentric zones, 188-90
Concepts, 7-14, 23-24, 139, 246-48, 256
Content analysis, 81-91
Covariance, 274
Cultural level, 184, 192, 194. See also Human ecology
Cultural meanings. See Interpretive sociology; Weber
Cultural system, 220, 224
Cultural values, 111, 119, 190, 237-51. See also Merton
Cybernetic system, 217
Data, 20; measurement problems in, 304, 310. See also Research section in theorists' chapters
Data bank, 56
Deduction, 15-20; and specific theorists, 57, 62, 155, 171, (Homans) 256, 259-61, 268-70
Derivations, 151, 153
Determinism, 96, 97-101, 303
Dialectical change, 42, 70, 76-77
Discrete-attribute data, 277
Division of labor, 45, 94, 97, 101-105
Dysfunctions, 229, 243, 251
Economic institutions, 89-90, 113, 126, 244-45, in Homans, 267, 268; in Parsons, 217, 226-28; in Weber 141-46. See also Interests; Marx
Economic zones, 188-90
Elementary social behavior, 257-58
Elites, 149-50, 159-61
Emergent properties, 216
Emergent theory, 301, 304
Equilibrium systems, 150, 153, 155
Ethnocentrism, 117-18, 205-207, 300, 309
Ethnomethodology, 305-309
Evolution, 70-72, 123. See also Comte; Spencer; Sumner
Exchange theory, See Homans

319

AUTHOR AND TITLE INDEX